DATE DUE

MR 2 9 '99			

DEMCO 38-296

Women's
Studies
A Guide to Information Sources

Sarah Carter and Maureen Ritchie

McFARLAND

MANSELL

First published 1990 by Mansell Publishing Limited
A Cassell imprint
Villiers House, 41–47 Strand, London WC2N 5JE

Published in the United States of America by
McFarland & Company, Inc., Publishers
Box 611, Jefferson, NC 28640

Reprinted 1991

British Library Cataloguing in Publication Data
Carter, Sarah.
  Women's studies: a guide to information sources.
  1. Women's studies. Information sources – Bibliographies
  I. Title   II. Ritchie, Maureen
  016.3054′07

  ISBN 0–7201–2058–6

Library of Congress Cataloging-in-Publication Data
Carter, Sarah.
  Women's studies: a guide to information sources / Sarah Carter
  and Maureen Ritchie.
     p.   cm.
  Includes bibliographical references.
  ISBN 0–89950–534–1
  1. Women—Bibliography.   I. Ritchie, Maureen.   II. Title.
Z7961.C37   1990
[HQ1206]
016.3054—dc20

Printed and bound in Great Britain by
Biddles Ltd, Guildford and King's Lynn

Contents

CONTENTS

For
Ellie, Isobel, Lily, Natty and Oliver

Acknowledgements

All bibliographical work builds on the work of countless other people. In compiling this book we have been struck with admiration for the energy and determination of the women whose works we have listed, and to them, therefore, goes our primary acknowledgement.

It would not have been possible for us to do the work without the resources of the University of Kent Library, and we especially wish to thank Will Simpson, the Librarian, for his support and encouragement, and in particular for allowing us extensive use of the interlibrary loan service and a room to work in. We thank also the staff of the Social Sciences Division in the Library for their forbearance in coping with a colleague whose mind was seriously distracted from her normal work, and who was absent from her post for long periods. In particular we would like to single out Ann Murphy, who was forced to acquire an unwarranted expertise in law librarianship, and Fay Cooke, who was thrown in at the deep end and managed never to seem out of her depth. Also Margaret Smyth, Jane Lovelock and Helen Buhler who had to bear with the frequent absence of a colleague. Enid Dixon's knowledge of the interlibrary loan system was especially valuable and her and Olive Lindstrand's patience and helpfulness in dealing with our unprecedented number of interlibrary loan requests is much appreciated. Thanks also to Roger Cooley whose unfailing willingness to solve data processing problems made all kinds of technological magic possible. Finally our families, who will be glad to have us back again.

Introduction

Women's studies is a vital and expanding activity existing in a diffuse interdisciplinary area. This book is an attempt to describe the reference sources available within women's studies, and to tease out some of the patterns of bibliographic control. It is not a bibliography itself, but a guide to the sources of information available on the subject, which have proliferated in the last fifteen years or so. We were frequently surprised to find material in what seemed to us obscure areas, and yet none for apparently more important subjects. Consequently there often appears to be an imbalance between the amount of material described for different areas.

When we started work four years ago, we had no idea how complex the task would be. The reason for this complexity is partly the broad cross-disciplinary scope, and partly that women's studies as an academic subject, in the UK at least, consists largely of collections of courses put on by interested people rather than programmes organized under a departmental structure within universities and colleges. Moreover, much teaching and research goes on at a more diffuse level still, in continuing and adult education classes and workshops. In addition, there is a good deal of activity at a grassroots level. We hope that this book may be able to identify sources of information for all those people engaged in teaching and research, and all those students who choose to write essays and dissertations on the subject of women in one aspect or another.

SCOPE OF THE WORK

The material included covers broadly the decade from 1978 to 1988. We have included as much material from 1989 as we possibly could, some of it pre-publication, and in these cases any information we have provided comes from publicity material rather than the books themselves. Earlier material is included where it is the only source, or where a subject warrants it.

Our starting point is inevitably British, but our aim has been to provide a worldwide coverage. In many ways this is an admission of failure, since the material included is still overwhelmingly American. It is with some feelings of despair that we have time and again come up against the inadequacies of resources in Britain, the main collections being evicted from temporary premises, the lack of funding causing organizations to rely entirely on voluntary labour – an endless story of cuts in finance and staffing. Our extensive use of the admirable British interlibrary loan system has given us some insight into the scatter of material in libraries throughout the country; the inability in some cases to obtain quite important works, especially publications from other European countries, illustrates the inevitable patchiness of such uncoordinated acquisition. The energy of the American women's movement and its academic offshoots, and above all the availability of funding, have meant that the rest of the anglophone world has had to rely heavily on American resources. We do not wish to seem churlish about this – time and again we pay tribute to the excellence of the work done in North America. However, we hope that this book may help to redress the balance somewhat towards the rest of the world. It has proved easier to trace material in the Third World than in Europe, somewhat to our surprise, and it is clear to us that an adequate study of European information sources would require extensive research and travel, and undoubtedly justify separate study.

We have tried to include all major woman-centred English-language reference works, monographic and serial. For other sources, e.g. journals and organizations, we have been more selective, hoping to provide information about the most important, and to give starting points to the interested enquirer. With one or two exceptions, we have included only works specific to women. General reference sources have a valuable place in women's studies research, but they are well described elsewhere (e.g. Searing, no. 14). We have not included material on children's literature, nor have we listed bibliographic work on individual women writers.

ARRANGEMENT

The arrangement of this book has been dictated partly by the material available, and partly by the characteristically holistic approach to women's lives. However, there is basically no real way round the linear nature of a book, or for that matter a library shelf; we have used cross-references fairly freely to link areas which are not as separate as they look.

THE INFORMATION EXPLOSION

Women's studies has been the success story in publishing over the last decade. An enormous market has been uncovered for both fiction by women, including the rediscovery of forgotten or under-valued authors, and works on women's studies. Publishers have jumped on the bandwagon by setting up women's studies series and imprints. The major reference publishers in particular have been producing bibliographic and other reference works at an astonishing rate over the past ten years.

These vary in usefulness. Any bibliographer will appreciate the hard work and attention to detail that go into the compilation of these reference sources, many of which are possible only because of computerized production methods. Unfortunately publishers are often in our view too ready to present them in a raw state, thereby reducing their accessibility. When consulting a complex reference work, the quality of the typesetting can make all the difference to its usability. This applies especially to the index, in most cases the entry point for the use of such works, and in our experience too many publishers are content to accept an index with long lists of numerical references under subject headings (many of which are of marginal use anyway, because they are too broad). The fact is that these publishers know they have a captive market. These books will rarely sell to individuals, but libraries will feel constrained to buy them, although as cost-cutting becomes more stringent this may be less and less the case, particularly in Britain.

The collection of material for this book has been a matter of painstaking delving into likely and unlikely sources, and also partly serendipitous. Paradoxically the vitality and variety of women's studies writing was both the most encouraging aspect of the work, and also the factor most likely to engender despair, as we stumbled blindly and almost too late on yet another major source, of which we had been incomprehensibly unaware, yet couldn't possibly leave out. We relied a good deal on second-hand references and clues, especially in the admirable publications such as *Feminist Collections*, *Resources for Feminist Research* and other journals which we scanned for current information. We realized in doing this what an advantage it is for compilers of such information if they have ready access to a broad collection of periodicals and reference literature. There is no such collection in the UK which serves women's studies: no library has the funds to acquire systematically in the field.

PART I

GENERAL MATERIAL

CHAPTER 1

Reference sources

The bibliographic control of women's studies literature presents particular problems for a variety of reasons. First, its intrinsically interdisciplinary character means that the indexing net has to be flung wide to provide a useful coverage. Secondly, the rapid growth of literature, particularly in the last fifteen years, means any abstracting service has constantly to expand, and any bibliography goes out of date very quickly. This can be discouraging. Thirdly, as feminism, or rather, women's studies, becomes accepted if not respectable in the academic environment, more articles about women's issues appear in 'regular' journals. This means that the number of serial titles to be scanned is constantly increasing, and is no longer easily identifiable. Fourthly, much work and publishing in women's studies is underfinanced, without resources for adequate publicity or dissemination; this means many periodicals and organizations have a more transient existence than they would like.

In the light of all this it is a quite remarkable achievement that since 1972 when *Women Studies Abstracts* (no. 4) and *RFR/DRF* (no. 8) began, there has been continuous and increasing bibliographic control of a very disparate literature. The welcome arrival of a pilot issue of *Women in BHI* (no. 3) in 1989 will increase the coverage of general British literature substantially. We hope it is an encouraging sign that a major general index sees a market for a service specifically about women.

BIBLIOGRAPHIC SOURCES

Abstracting and indexing publications

1. *New Literature on Women/Ny Litteratur om Kvinnor*, 4/yr, Göteborgs Universitet, Universitetsbibliotek, Centralbiblioteket, Box 5096, S-402 22 Göteborg, Sweden, 1980–.

Bibliographic journal indexing mainly the holdings of Göteborg University Library, and including papers and reports as well as periodicals. The list of references on women are divided into twenty-six broad subject groups, with author and subject indexes. The coverage is international, and needless to say includes a good deal of Scandinavian material (which is untraceable elsewhere). The journals indexed are predominantly standard academic periodicals. A valuable additional bibliographic resource, which ought to be more widely available than it is.

2.   *Studies on Women Abstracts*, 6/yr, Carfax, Abingdon, Oxon, 1983–.

An impressive list of journals 'regularly scanned' is not reflected in the quantity of material abstracted, which is sparse compared with *Women Studies Abstracts* (no. 4). There has been less emphasis on coverage of feminist journals and a broader range of mainstream academic journals and magazines is scanned, including British news-stand magazines. Lack of subject organization makes the user totally dependent on the index. A considerable part of each issue is taken up with abstracts of books which usually appear well after the book has been publicized and reviewed, and which in any case are such a small (and odd) selection of books published in the field that it is hard to see how the editorial decision to include them can be justified. The abstracts are described as 'non-evaluative'. Not so thorough, reliable or useful as *WSA*.

3.   *Women in BHI*, British Humanities Index, Library Association Publishing Ltd, London, 1989–.

This interesting new venture looks likely to become a standard source for the retrieval of articles on women. An extract of the material relevant to women in the British Humanities Index, it provides access to articles in not only an eclectic selection of general and scholarly journals, but also (and this is its most valuable aspect) all the general British 'serious' daily and Sunday newspapers and weekly magazines. Using the BHI's subject headings, it has its parent journal's admirable clarity and ease of use, while gathering together the material on women which is not always so easy to find in BHI proper.

4.   *Women Studies Abstracts*, 4/yr, Rush Pub. Co., PO Box 1, Rush, NY 14543, 1972–.

This service has steadily coped with the rising tide of feminist and women's studies journals, and the spread of articles about women into traditional academic journals. The arrangement is in broad subject groups which makes browsing a possibility, and the cross-referencing is thorough. Not all the entries have abstracts – really it is a joint abstracting and indexing journal. Each issue also contains a list of book reviews, and a list of special issues of periodicals on women. It is a wonderfully eclectic publication and absolutely essential for any library supporting women's studies teaching and research.

Current awareness publications

The following publications are essentially for keeping up to date, not only with publications, but also news, events, research in progress, conferences and so on. *RFR/DRF* (no. 8) has a wider relevance as well as a strong current awareness role.

5. *Feminist Collections: A Quarterly of Women's Studies Resources*, 4/yr, University of Wisconsin System, 112A Memorial Library, 728 State Street, Madison, WI 53706, 1980–.

An excellent current awareness publication with really useful reviews of resources, new reference works, new periodicals, special issues, news and information. It includes material from abroad, although most is inevitably American. Subscription includes *Feminist Periodicals* (no. 6) and *New Books on Women & Feminism* (no. 7). Indispensable to librarians.

6. *Feminist Periodicals: A Current Listing of Contents*, 4/yr, University of Wisconsin System, 112A Memorial Library, 728 State St, Madison, WI 53706.

A current awareness journal, reproducing the contents pages of 'all English-language feminist periodicals with a substantial national or regional readership, with an emphasis on scholarly journals and small press offerings'. The coverage is predominantly American. A valuable feature is the detailed listing of all periodicals covered by the journal, giving bibliographic information and a description.

7. *New Books on Women & Feminism*, 2/yr, University of Wisconsin System, 112A Memorial Library, 727 State St, Madison, WI 53706.

A listing of new books, selected primarily from reviews and publishers' catalogues, arranged by subject, and followed by a list of new periodicals. These are described, but the books are not.

8. *RFR/DRF: Resources for Feminist Research/Documentation sur la Recherche Féministe*, 4/yr, OISE, Toronto, 1972–. (Formerly *Canadian Newsletter of Research on Women*.)

An unparallelled reference source in women's studies, this journal should be the first choice as a resource in the field. It contains a great deal of information on events worldwide, research in progress, new publications, conferences, organizations, etc., as well as substantial articles, often of a bibliographical nature, and book reviews. Issues are frequently devoted to a particular topic, and provide an authoritative overview of resources on it. While *RFR/DRF* has a Canadian bias, this does not prevent its world coverage from being superior to most of the other sources available (particularly in Britain).

9.   *Women's Collections Newsletter*, 2/yr, Special Collections Dept, North-western University, Evanston, IL 60208.

A current awareness bulletin which reviews new journals, special issues, reference books, research in progress as well as giving information about collections in women's studies all over the United States. An extremely useful resource.

Bulletin du CRIF (no. 401) and *Lover* (no. 435) are good sources for European publications. Both *Signs* (no. 62) and *Women's Studies International Forum* (no. 67) have news sections in each issue. These are worth scanning for information about new publications, conferences, calls for papers, etc.

Book reviews

10.   *Belles Lettres: A Review of Books by Women*, 6/yr, PO Box 987, Arlington, VA 22216, 1985–.

A book review journal including scholarly and popular works of 'fiction, nonfiction, essays, biography and criticism. Our purpose is to promote and celebrate writing by women'. Smaller than the *Women's Review of Books* (no. 11), but often covers different ground.

11.   *Women's Review of Books*, 11/yr, Wellesley College Center for Research on Women, Wellesley, MA 02181, 1983–.

'Feminist, but not restricted to any one conception of feminism'; seeks to represent 'the widest possible range of feminist perspectives both in the books reviewed and in the content of the reviews'. A substantial, valuable and readable publication. Includes a useful list of books received each month.

Apart from these two newspaper-format journals, which contain exclusively book reviews and advertisements, most journals include some book reviews. Particularly worth checking are *Signs* (no. 62) and *RFR/DRF* (no. 8), both of which have substantial sections of reviews. *Signs* also carries many publishers' announcements; *RFR/DRF* sometimes has an entire issue devoted to reviews. *Feminist Collections* (no. 5) has detailed reviews of new reference publications. *Feminist Bookstore News* (no. 122) and *WLW Journal* (no. 1066) are also good sources for new books.

Resource guides

12.   ARIEL, Joan, *Building Women's Studies Collections: A Resource Guide*, 48 p., Choice, Middletown, CT, 1987.

Anyone in the position of developing a collection in women's studies should get hold of this book. Primarily intended for librarians, it is a model of organization and clarity, whose mere 48 pages bely its comprehensiveness. Although it is American in focus this should not put off the British user. It is about the only source gathering together lists of feminist publishers, publishers' series, publishers with women's studies lists, working papers and reports, distributors, bookstores, databases and many other resources in women's studies. All the entries are succinctly and helpfully annotated. An indispensable book.

13. LEHMANN, Stephen and Eva SARTORI, *Women's Studies in Western Europe: A Resource Guide*, 127 p., Association of College & Research Libraries, American Library Association, Chicago, IL, 1986.

Conceived as an aid to American librarians in the selection and acquisition of Western European feminist material. In three sections: the first by Virginia Clark is an overview of women's publishing in Western Europe, with an extensive bibliography, country by country, covering bookshops, organizations, etc. The second by Beth Stafford is a survey of women's studies activity in Western Europe, and the third by Rita Pankhurst is an account of the Fawcett Library in London.

RICHTER, Werner, Liisa HUSU and Arnaud MARKS, *The Changing Role of Women in Society: A Documentation of Current Research: Research Projects in Progress 1984–1987*. (no. 361a)

An inventory of research on women in twenty-two European countries.

14. SEARING, Susan E., *Introduction to Library Research in Women's Studies*, 257 p., Westview, Boulder, CO, 1985.

The author's goals are 'guiding students in choosing topics and formulating search strategies for term paper assignments, and . . . recommending reference books that can yield up information about women in a number of disciplines'. Part 1 is a guide to using a library, with particular reference to women's studies topics, including information on using a catalogue and appendices on the Dewey Decimal and Library of Congress classification schemes. Part 2 is called 'The Tools of Research', and is a description of reference works both specific to women's studies and general multidisciplinary bibliographies and indexes. These are usefully discussed from the point of view of searching for women-oriented material. Continuing bibliographies and guides to research for specific subjects are included, and there are chapters on access to other types of material and information, e.g. libraries, microforms, organizations, databases. An unusual feature is a list of the review essays which appear in each issue of *Signs* (no. 62), covering volumes 1–9. As a basic guide to using a library for women's studies teaching and research this is an invaluable work, well organized and informative.

Bibliographies of bibliographies

15. BALLOU, Patricia K., *Women: A Bibliography of Bibliographies*, 268 p., G.K. Hall, Boston, 2nd ed., 1987.

This is the most comprehensive bibliography of bibliographies with 906 entries, each carefully annotated. The arrangement is detailed, with most of the material appearing under geographical subjects or topical subjects, both of which are subdivided. There are name, title and subject indexes. It is less easy to use than it should be because of the undifferentiated type which makes it hard to see the many subject divisions.

16.   EICHLER, Margrit, *An Annotated Selected Bibliography of Bibliographies on Women*, 33 p., Know Inc., Pittsburgh, PA, 1976.

The first bibliography of bibliographies in women's studies, this attempts 'to include all major recent bibliographies'. Contains ninety entries, many on specific subjects. Compared with the bibliographies of the 1980s, it provides a neat illustration of the growth of publishing and writing in the area.

17.   RITCHIE, Maureen, *Women's Studies: A Checklist of Bibliographies*, 128 p., Mansell, London, 1980.

Nearly five hundred references to books, articles and pamphlets published mainly in the late 1960s and 1970s. No annotations.

18.   WILLIAMSON, Jane, *New Feminist Scholarship: A Guide to Bibliographies*, 139 p., Feminist Press, Old Westbury, NY, 1979.

Nearly four hundred entries, about half of which (mostly the books) are annotated. Limited to the English language and very largely (only four exceptions) to US or Canadian publications.

Bibliographies

Ten years ago this section of general bibliographies would have been much longer. That it is not so today is partly due to the greater selectivity of this work, but also to a large extent due to the increasing specialization of workers in fields of interest within women's studies. There are now many more specialist subject bibliographies; in fact there is a steady flow of major works each year, reflecting of course the enormous growth in monograph, periodical and report literature. This means that the task of the general bibliographer has reached almost unmanageable proportions. The size of the Stineman/Loeb compilation (nos 26 and 27) is an indication of this, and probably means there will be fewer general women's studies bibliographies of anything but local interest in future years, as sheer quantity of material forces selectivity and specialization on even the most instinctive polymath amongst us.

19.   CARDINALE, Susan and Jay CASEY, *Anthologies by and about Women: An Analytical Index*, 822 p., Greenwood, Westport, CT, 1982.

This work indexes 375 anthologies published (or republished) since 1960. The bulk of the work consists of a keyword index to the words in the titles of the individual chapters/articles, referring the user to the main listing of the collections themselves. There is also an author index and a subject guide to the collections themselves. This is a particularly valuable work because is makes accessible much writing otherwise bibliographically buried. It is a kind of paradigm of feminism in itself.

20. ROSENBERG, Marie Barovic and Len V. BERGSTROM, *Women and Society: A Critical Review of the Literature with a Selected Annotated Bibliography*, 354 p., Sage, Beverly Hills, CA, 1975.

21. EEN, JoAnn Delores and Marie B. ROSENBERG-DISHMAN, *Women and Society, Citations 3601 to 6000: An Annotated Bibliography*, 277 p., Sage, Beverly Hills, CA, 1978.

These two volumes together form a compendious and pioneering general bibliography on women. Six thousand entries, most of them very briefly annotated, are divided by broad subject (e.g. Women in Sociology/Political Science/History, etc.), with the larger subjects subdivided further. The subject arrangement obscures some categories, e.g. all studies of women in particular countries are subsumed within the subjects, and while it is possible to pick these up via the subject index, this is a cumbersome procedure. There are indexes to authors/organizations, 'persons not cited as authors' and 'places, subjects & topics'.

22. EVANS, Mary and David MORGAN, *Work on Women: A Guide to the Literature*, 82 p., Tavistock, London, 1979.

A brief guide to literature on women, intended as a resource for women's studies programmes. The entries are unannotated, but are chosen to illustrate each subject perspective upon which there is a short exegesis. Useful for seventies publications.

23. HABER, Barbara, *Women in America: A Guide to Books, 1963–1975: With An Appendix on Books Published 1976–1979*, 262 p., University of Illinois Press, Urbana, IL, 1981. (Updated edition of the work originally published by G.K. Hall, Boston, 1978.)

Extensive annotations to a very wide range of books about women, arranged by subject. The appendix, for reasons of space, is organized as a series of review articles, with titles listed at the end. The title of the book rather belies its content, as non-American authors, albeit published in the US, are included. Really a bibliography of major women's studies books of the 1960s and 1970s.

24. HUMM, Maggie, *An Annotated Critical Bibliography of Feminist Criticism*, 240 p., Harvester, Brighton, 1987. (Published in the US by G.K. Hall, Boston.)

The aim is to provide a 'core collection of women-centred materials' by listing feminist writings which have informed debates in the major areas of women's studies. The work is divided into Theory & sexual politics,

Literary criticism, Sociology, politics & economics, Arts . . ., Psychology, History, Anthropology & myth, Education & women's studies. There are brief annotations. The entries are arranged chronologically within each section in order to show the development of debates. There is an index of subjects and an index of 'contributors' (actually of authors). This is in effect another core curriculum bibliography, this time with a British focus.

25. KRICHMAR, Albert, *The Women's Movement in the Seventies: An International English-Language Bibliography*, 875 p., Scarecrow, Metuchen, NJ, 1977.

An enormous bibliography of 8637 references, partially annotated. The title is somewhat misleading – the references cover a wide range of publications in the field of women's studies, including reprints of earlier works. The arrangement is by region and then country, subdivided by subject (e.g. Economic studies, Sociological studies, etc.). Sixty-five per cent of the entries concern the US, only 6 per cent the UK (the country with the next highest total). Though nominally a continuation of his *Women's Rights Movement in the United States* (no. 700) this is far broader in scope.

26. STINEMAN, Esther, *Women's Studies: A Recommended Core Bibliography*, 670 p., Libraries Unlimited, Littleton, CO, 1979.

27. LOEB, Catherine, Susan SEARING and Esther STINEMAN, *Women's Studies: A Recommended Core Bibliography 1980–85*, 538 p., Libraries Unlimited, Littleton, CO, 1987. (2nd volume of Stineman above.)

Together these two volumes provide an unsurpassed presentation of English-language work in women's studies. The later volume selects more stringently material with a feminist perspective and includes a good list of periodicals. The annotations are excellent.

28. OAKES, Elizabeth H. and Kathleen E. SHELDON, *Guide to Social Science Resources in Women's Studies*, 162 p., ABC-Clio, Santa Barbara, CA, 1978.

Although now largely overtaken by other works, this was an important publication in its time, and still provides a valuable resource for material on women's studies in the social sciences; it has a strong anthropological bias. It is divided into broad sections: Anthropology, Economics, History, Psychology, Sociology, Contemporary feminist thought, with separate lists of bibliographies, journals and other resources. All entries are succinctly annotated.

29. STAFFORD, Beth, 'Women's studies: a reference collection for public libraries', *Reference Services Review*, vol. 10, no. 4 pp. 11–15, Winter 1982.

A guide to reference works in women's studies. Now out of date, but useful lengthy descriptions of the thirty-two items. A valuable critical overview of the standard reference works.

30. TERRIS, Virginia R., *Woman in America: A Guide to Information Sources*, 520 p., Gale, Detroit, MI, 1980.

Quite an interesting sourcebook covering general reference works as well as specifically women-centred ones, and listing lots of monographs. This fact makes it more dated as much primary material has been published since 1980. Specifically designed as an aid to American Studies, the reference material is better presented in Haber (no. 23), to which this might be useful as a supplement.

Theses

31. GILBERT, V.F.and D.S. TATLA, *Women's Studies: A Bibliography of Dissertations 1870–1982*, 496 p., Blackwell, Oxford, 1985.

A useful work which attempts a comprehensive listing of theses and dissertations on women's studies in the US, Canada, Britain and Ireland. North American theses are limited to PhDs, British and Irish include MAs. Dissertations dealing with individual women (e.g. writers) are included. The division is by broad subject, with detailed subdivisions. There is a useful subject guide (i.e. list of contents) as well as a subject index. The lack of an author index is a limitation.

See also:

KNASTER, Meri, *Women in Spanish America: An Annotated Bibliography from Pre-Conquest to Contemporary Times*. (no. 457)
Includes lists of master's and doctoral dissertations.

PARKER, Franklin and Betty June PARKER, *Women's Education: A World View*. (no. 655)
Volume 1 of this work is an annotated bibliography of doctoral dissertations.

BENEDICT, Marjorie A., 'U.S. doctoral research on women in French literature'. (no. 819)

SIMS-WOOD, Janet, 'African-American women writers: a selected listing of master's theses and doctoral dissertations'. (no. 832)

PERIODICAL INFORMATION

Here we include bibliographies and lists of periodical titles, bibliographies of special issues of periodicals, and individual journals, magazines and newsletters where they are general in content.

Titles with special regional or subject relevance will be found in Parts II and III. Specialized subject bibliographies frequently include lists of serials. Sometimes journals include notes on new titles, or adverts. Current awareness publications such as *Feminist Collections* (no. 5) and *RFR/DRF* (no. 8) are particularly good for up-to-date information about new and deceased titles, and name changes. Some newsletters, such as *Lesbian Information Service Newsletter* (no. 779), contain a regular list of periodicals. This is particularly likely with publications of networking organizations, and such information is included in the annotations.

The articles in women's studies serials are often abstracted or indexed in the publications described earlier in this chapter. Particularly useful, and covering a wider range of titles than those listed here, is *Women Studies Abstracts* (no. 4), which should also be consulted for current special issues of periodicals. *Feminist Periodicals* (no. 6), which lists the contents of many titles, issue by issue, is also extremely useful, though mainly for American and other English-language titles. European journals are better served by *Lover* (no. 435), *Bulletin du CRIF* (no. 401) and *New Literature on Women* (no. 1).

The list of individual serials is designed to be a selection of the major and most representative titles, at least some of which should be available in major libraries or even, for magazines, on big city news-stands. It is beyond the scope of this book to provide a comprehensive list, and keeping it up to date is a heavy task in such a volatile area. Perhaps the best ongoing list is available annually in the *Directory of Women's Media* (no. 611), and the following guides provide further information.

Guides to periodicals

32. *Annotated Guide to Women's Periodicals in the United States and Canada*, 2/yr, Women's Program Office, Earlham College, Richmond, IN, 1982–1985.

Unfortunately stopped publication, but gives useful descriptions of 'serious' women's periodicals of the early 1980s.

33. CLARDY, Andrea Fleck, *Words to the Wise: A Writer's Guide to Feminist and Lesbian Periodicals and Publishers*, 48 p., Firebrand Books, Ithaca, NY, 1987.

Useful lists of North American presses and periodicals with tables summarizing their policies and practices. Aimed at helping women get their writing published.

34. DANKY, James, *Women's Periodicals and Newspapers from the 18th Century to 1981: A Union List of the Holdings of Madison, Wisconsin Libraries*, 376 p., G.K. Hall, Boston, 1982.

A guide to the holdings of nearly five hundred titles in the libraries of greater Madison. The arrangement is A–Z with 'catchword and subtitle index', and chronological index.

35. DOUGHAN, David and Denise SANCHEZ, *Feminist Periodicals 1855–1984: An Annotated Bibliography of British, Irish, Commonwealth and International Titles*, 316 p., Harvester, Brighton, 1987.

Nearly 1000 feminist periodicals are listed in this compendious work. The authors interpret the word 'feminist' extremely broadly for material up to about 1960. After that date they exclude most periodicals 'which do not define themselves at the minimum as committed to improving the social, legal and economic position of women in relation to men'. The arrangement is chronological, with the post-1960 periodicals accounting for about three-quarters of the total. There is a name and title index, a subject index and a chronological index (giving references by date of starting and ceasing publication). The work includes British, Irish, Commonwealth and international titles, although the coverage of non-British titles is mainly confined to those available in British libraries and is therefore not in the least comprehensive. Its main value is obviously as a resource for the study of the British Women's movement, something which the authors, based as they are at the Fawcett Library, are ideally qualified to do. The entries are rather cryptic in style, making the book somewhat hard to use, which is a pity, since the annotations are interesting, and the arrangement makes the book a historical as well as a reference work.

36. HUMPHREYS, Nancy K., *American Women's Magazines: An Annotated Historical Guide*, c. 150 p., Garland, New York, 1989.

'Covering magazines from colonial times to the present, this book is a chronicle of American women's history and the feminist movement'. (From publisher's announcement.)

37. WOMEN'S STUDIES INFORMATION NETWORK, *A Union List of Women's Studies Periodicals Held in Selected Libraries in the UK*, 31 p., Women's Studies Information Network, c/o Equal Opportunities Commission, Manchester, 1988.

A list of holdings of women's studies periodicals at fourteen libraries in England. The bibliographic information provided is of the most basic, making many of the titles difficult to identify.

For an excellent guide to lesbian periodicals see:

MALINOWSKY, H. Robert, *International Directory of Gay and Lesbian Periodicals*. (no. 771)

The *Directory of Women's Media* (no. 611), an excellent annual publication, includes a long list of serial publications with worldwide coverage.

Special issues of periodicals

38. CARDINALE, Susan, *Special Issues of Serials about Women, 1965–1975*, 41 p., Council of Planning Librarians, Monticello, IL, 1976.

A listing of special issues of periodicals in one alphabetical sequence by periodical. Most, but not all, of the entries are annotated. It would have been useful to have some subject divisions, or a subject index. It contains some different material from Newton (no. 40).

39. EICHLER, Margrit, John MARECKI and Jennifer NEWTON, *Women: A Bibliography of Special Periodical Issues (1960–1975)*, 76 p., Canadian Newsletter of Research on Women, August 1976, Special Publication 3, Toronto, 1976.

See no. 40.

40. NEWTON, Jennifer and Carol ZAVITZ, *Women: A Bibliography of Special Issues, Volume II*, 280 p., 1978. (Canadian Newsletter of Research on Women, Jan. 1978, Special Publication 4.)

The work in two volumes aims to bring together the many special issues on women of periodicals not normally concerned with women's issues. Volume II updates the first through 1977. The contents of special issues are listed and the entries are arranged in broad subject order. There is an index to the journals. Useful for retrospective searching. It overlaps, but also complements Cardinale (no. 38), containing (inevitably) more Canadian material, and listing individual articles in the journals which Cardinale does not.

41. INTERNATIONAL WOMEN'S TRIBUNE CENTER, *Special Issues of Periodicals: Decade for Women* (Decade for Women Information Resources for 1985, no. 3), 34 p., IWTC, New York, 1984.

A list of special issues of periodicals arranged by country of origin, prepared for the Decade for Women Nairobi Conference in 1985.

Subject bibliographies and guides also often include lists of special issues. The following are good examples.

ARNUP, Katherine and Amy GOTTLIEB, 'Annotated bibliography'. (no. 756)

BUVINIC, Mayra *et al.*, *Women and World Development: An Annotated Bibliography*. (no. 242)

CANTOR, Aviva and Ora HAMELSDORF, *The Jewish Woman 1900–1985: A Bibliography*. (no. 1006)

WILKINS, Kay S., *Women's Education in the United States: A Guide to Information Sources*. (no. 657)

Periodicals

JOURNALS

42. *Atlantis*, 2/yr, Mount Saint Vincent University, 166 Bedford Highway, Halifax, Nova Scotia B3M 2J6, Canada, 1975-.

Good looking bilingual periodical, 'an interdisciplinary journal devoted to critical and creative writing on the topic of women'. Articles, book reviews, poetry, photography and art work. Special issues (e.g. one containing the papers for the 9th meeting of the Canadian Society for Women in Philosophy). An attractive journal, aimed at a wide readership.

43. *Australian Feminist Studies*, 2/yr, Research Centre for Women's Studies, University of Adelaide, GPO Box 498, Adelaide, S. Australia 5001, 1985-.

Articles, discussion, reviews, sometimes on a special theme, in 'the fields of feminist research and woman's studies courses'.

44. *Canadian Woman Studies/Les Cahiers de la Femme*, 4/yr, York University, 212 Founders College, York University, 4700 Keele St, Downsview, Ontario M3J 1P3, Canada, 1978-.

Has a 'goal of making current writing and research on a wide variety of feminist topics accessible to the largest possible community of women'. Articles, book, art and film reviews, creative writing, with a special theme for each issue. Bilingual.

45. *CRIAW Papers*, CRIAW/ICREF, 151 Slater St, Suite 408, Ottawa, Ontario K1P 5H3, Canada.

'Series of scholarly papers making a significant contribution to feminist research.'

46. *Critical Matrix: Princeton Working Papers in Women's Studies*, 6/yr, Program in Women's Studies, 218 Palmer Hall, Princeton University, Princeton, NJ 18549, 1985-.

Three issues are produced twice a year, each containing one or two scholarly papers in women's studies.

47. *Differences: A Journal of Feminist Cultural Studies*, 3/yr, Indiana University Press, Bloomington, IN, 1988-.

'Focuses on how concepts and categories of difference - notably but not exclusively gender - operate within culture. Situated at the intersection of cultural studies and feminism.'

48. *Feminisms*, 4/yr, Center for Women's Studies, Ohio State University, 207 Dulles Hall, 230 W 17th Ave., Columbus, OH 43210, 1988-.

Replaces *Women's Studies Review*. Its goal is 'to celebrate the varieties of feminist expression'. Contains articles, essays, creative writing.

49. *Feminist Perspectives Féministes, CRIAW/ICREF*, 151 Slater St, Suite 408, Ottawa, Ontario K1P 5H3, Canada.

Series of topic-oriented papers and essays.

50. *Feminist Review*, 3/yr, Routledge, London, 1979–.

The major British academic feminist journal, the articles in which are more politically oriented than in most of the other academic journals. Some of the issues address a particular theme, such as abortion or sexuality. The general emphasis is radical/socialist. It includes some creative writing as well as articles and reviews.

51. *Feminist Studies*, 3/yr, c/o Women's Studies Program, University of Maryland, College Park, MD 20742, 1972–.

An eclectic mixture of scholarly articles on a range of women-related subjects, and creative writing.

52. *Fireweed*, 4/yr, PO Box 279, Station B, Toronto, Ontario M5T 2W2, Canada, 1978–.

A forum for feminist thought and discussion. Includes fiction, essays, poetry, reviews.

53. *Frontiers*, 3/yr, Women's Studies, Campus Box 246, University of Colorado, Boulder, CO 80309–0325, 1975–.

Aims 'to find a balance between academic and popular views on issues common to women'. Many issues focus on a special theme. Includes articles, reviews, creative writing.

54. *Gender and Society*, 4/yr, Sage, Newbury Park, CA, 1987–.

Official publication of Sociologists for Women in Society. A scholarly sociological journal, whose 'focus is the social aspect of gender'.

55. *Hecate: A Women's Interdisciplinary Journal*, 2/yr, PO Box 99, St Lucia, Brisbane, Queensland 4067, Australia, 1975–.

Articles and creative writing, much on Australia/New Zealand, but not exclusively. Aims at 'feminist, Marxist or other radical methodology to focus on the situation of women. . .'.

56. *Hypatia: A Journal of Feminist Philosophy*, 3/yr, Indiana University Press, Bloomington, IN, 1986–.

A scholarly journal devoted to feminist research in philosophy. As well as long articles, there is a Forum section publishing short papers to further continuing dialogue. Also book reviews. Some special issues, e.g. Feminism and science, Feminist medical ethics.

57. *M/F*, 2/yr, London, 1978–86. (Ceased publication)

Theoretical journal, influential during its time of publication.

58. *NWSA Journal*, 4/yr, Ablex Pub. Corp., Norwood, NJ, 1989–.

'Reflecting two decades of feminist scholarship emerging from and supporting the women's movement.' Publishes 'scholarship which continues to link feminist scholarship with teaching and activism'.

59. *NZ Women's Studies Journal*, 2/yr, Women's Studies Association (NZ), PO Box 5067, Auckland, New Zealand.

Independent, non-university based to reflect broader appeal of New Zealand women's studies activities and programmes.

60. *Recherches Féministes*, GREMF, Pavillon Charles-De Koninck, Bureau 2463, Université Laval, Cité Universitaire, Quebec G1K 7P4, Canada.

Interdisciplinary journal publishing original research, mainly empirical but also theoretical and methodological.

RFR/DRF: Resources for Feminist Research/Documentation sur la Recherche Féministe. (no. 8)

Excellent Canadian current awareness journal, with frequent special issues and resource guides.

61. *Sex Roles: A Journal of Research*, 12/yr, Plenum Press, New York, 1975–.

An academic journal concerned with 'the basic processes underlying gender-role socialization in children and its consequences'. A cross-disciplinary coverage, with a psychological/sociological emphasis. It is published in two volumes a year, the twelve issues in each volume appearing as monthly double issues.

62. *Signs: Journal of Women in Culture and Society*, 4/yr, University of Chicago Press, Chicago, 1975–.

An academic journal, containing scholarly articles and reports, many book reviews, and announcements and notes of events, new publications, organizations, conferences, etc. Usually every issue has an extensive bibliographic review article on a particular theme. A list of these up to summer 1984 is contained in Searing (no. 14). There are also pages of publisher's advertisements, in themselves a useful resource for new publications in women's studies.

63. *Spirals/Spirales: University of Ottawa Papers in Feminist Research*, University of Ottawa Women's Studies Program, 143 Seraphin-Marion, Ottawa, Ontario K1N 6N5, Canada.

A series of working papers, appearing irregularly, published in French or English, each examining a particular topic related to feminist research or the women's movement.

64. *Trivia: A Journal of Ideas*, 3/yr, PO Box 606, North Amherst, MA 01059, 1982-.

Articles, reviews. A regular feature called 'Trivial Lives' – a biographical article or interview.

65. *Trouble and Strife: A Radical Feminist Magazine*, 3/yr, c/o Women's Centre, 34 Exchange St, Norwich, Norfolk NR2 1AX, 1983-.

Articles, news, announcements on a great variety of topics. Lively debate in the correspondence columns. Extensively illustrated.

66. *Women's Studies: An Interdisciplinary Journal*, 3/yr, Gordon & Breach, London, 1972-.

'A forum for the presentation of scholarship and criticism about women in the fields of literature, history, art, sociology, law, political science, economics, anthropology and the sciences.'

67. *Women's Studies International Forum*, 6/yr, Pergamon Press, New York, 1978-.

An international academic journal, with articles and reviews by contributors from all over the world, although the largest proportion not surprisingly are American. The latter part of the journal is a section called Feminist Forum containing notes and announcements. This tends to be more British-oriented, as the editor is in England, but aims to cut across national boundaries, and includes much invaluable information on goings on throughout the world. It includes a section on international solidarity with women's campaigns.

68. *Women's Studies Quarterly*, 4/yr, Feminist Press, New York, 1973-.

Double issues focusing on special subjects (e.g. Feminist pedagogy). Includes a regular international feature. From 1988 publishes selected articles from *Samya Shakti* (New Delhi) (no. 313). Annual list of women's studies programmes in the US.

69. *Women's Studies Review*, Annual, 113 Fortfield Rd, Terenure, Dublin 6, Ireland.

Review produced by the Women's Studies Association of Ireland.

MAGAZINES AND NEWSLETTERS

70. *Breaking the Silence*, 4/yr, Station E, Ottawa, Ontario K1S 5J1, Canada, 1982-.

'A feminist alternative to the mainstream press . . . covers a wide range of social, political and cultural topics'.

71. *Communiqu'elles*, 6/yr, 3595 St Urbain St, Montreal, Quebec H2X 2N6, Canada, 1981-.

General news and resources magazine.

72. *Creative Woman*, 4/yr, Governors State University, University Park, IL 60466, 1977–.

A magazine which devotes each issue to a special topic (e.g. Women of Israel, Women in management, Women and photography).

73. *Everywoman*, 12/yr, 34a Islington Green, London N1 8DU, 1985–.

A serious-minded women's magazine, addressing itself to international issues as well as the general range of women's concerns.

74. *Hysteria: A Magazine on Feminist Issues*, 4/yr, PO Box 2481, Station B, Kitchener, Ontario N2H 6M3, Canada, 1980–86.

A magazine with articles, interviews, poems, news, announcements, etc., now ceased publication.

75. *Ms*, 12/yr, PO Box 57131, Boulder, CO 80322–7131, 1972–.

An old-established American feminist news-stand magazine.

76. *New Directions for Women*, 6/yr, Jossey Bass, San Francisco, 1972–.

Newspaper format feminist magazine with wide circulation.

77. *Newsletter on Feminism and Philosophy*, 3/yr, American Philosophical Association, University of Delaware, Newark, DE 19716.

Previously called *Feminism and Philosophy Newsletter*; from 1988 published as part of a combined APA publication containing newsletters of all the APA committees.

78. *Off Our Backs*, 11/yr, 2423 18th St NW, Washington, DC 20009, 1970–.

An old-established newspaper for women, full of information and news of feminism and activities of women, much from across the world.

79. *Outwrite*, 12/yr, Oxford House, Derbyshire St, London E2 6HG, 1982–88.

A feminist newspaper with an international, multiracial focus, which has ceased publication.

80. *Sojourner: The Women's Forum*, 12/yr, 380 Green St, Cambridge, MA 02139, 1975–.

A magazine with feature articles, arts reviews, creative writing and news (mainly of activities in the Boston area).

81 *Spare Rib*, 12/yr, 27 Clerkenwell Close, London EC1R 0AT, 1972– .

The great survivor – a lively news-stand magazine which is the major source for all feminist activities in Britain. Obligatory reading if you want to find out what's going on.

82. *WEA Women's Studies Newsletter*, ?2/yr, Workers' Educational Association, 9 Upper Berkeley St, London W1H 8BY.

Useful for British women in adult education, as learners and teachers.

83. *Women Live*, 4/yr, Middlehill Rd, Colehill, Wimborne, Dorset BH21 2SA, 1987–89 (Ceased publication).

'A collection of writing and illustrations by women about their lives'. Includes articles on women's issues written through the medium of autobiography, poems, drawings, etc.

84. *Women's Research Network News*, 4/yr, National Council for Research on Women, Sara Delano Roosevelt Memorial House, 47–49 E. 65th St, New York, NY 10021, 1988–.

Useful and interesting newsletter describing the work of this and member organizations in the United States.

DICTIONARIES AND ENCYCLOPAEDIAS

Works of broad general interest are listed here, followed by dictionaries of quotations. More specialized collections are included elsewhere, for instance dictionaries of biography in Chapter 2, of artists in Chapter 12, and of mythology in chapter 22. Wordbooks and thesauri are included later in this chapter (nos 117–120).

85. KRAMARAE, Cheris and Paula TREICHLER, *A Feminist Dictionary*, 587 p., Pandora, London, 1985.

The authors describe this book as 'a wordbook . . . to document words, definitions and conceptualisations that illustrate women's linguistic contributions; between women and language . . . and to stimulate research.' It uses women's own words as much as possible, and there is an extensive bibliography for these references.

86. TUTTLE, Lisa, *Encyclopedia of Feminism*, 399 p., Facts on File Publications, New York, 1986.

An A–Z encyclopaedic survey of the feminist movement mainly in the UK and US. Covers central figures, events and organizations and includes some tangential ones, e.g. Freud. Useful first brief information. An unclassified bibliography is appended. The Fawcett Library gets a mention, but not the Schlesinger or Smith College. Erratic.

87. WARREN, Mary Anne, *The Nature of Women: An Encyclopaedia and Guide to the Literature*, Edgepress, Inverness, CA, 1980.

A single alphabetical list of authors and topics, under each of which is a one to two page discussion of the ideas about the nature of women: 'Introduction to the arguments and conclusions about this topic in a wide range of western thinkers from Plato . . . to the feminists of the 1970s.' Includes bibliographical references. A list of the authors and topics at the beginning provides access.

Dictionaries of quotations

88. BROWN, Michèle and Ann O'CONNOR, *Woman Talk: A Woman's Book of Quotes*, 2 vols, Futura Pubs, London, 1985.

Quotations by and about women arranged in various categories. Alas, no index, so more for dipping into than reference.

89. McPHEE, Carol and Ann FITZGERALD, *Feminist Quotations: Voices of Rebels, Reformers and Visionaries*, 271 p., Thomas Crowell, New York, 1976.

Arranged in two sections, The Feminist as Critic and The Feminist as Rebel and Visionary, and then subdivided into smaller chapters by subject. The quotations are arranged chronologically within each subsection, and there are name and subject indexes.

90. PARTNOW, Elaine, *The Quotable Woman: From Eve to 1799*, 533 p., Facts on File, New York, 1985.

Quotations from 804 women listed chronologically with biographical and subject indexes. Quotations from the Bible are in a separate section because of the difficulty of dating the women exactly.

91. PARTNOW, Elaine, *The Quotable Woman 1800–1981*, 608 p., Facts on File, New York, 1982.

Originally published in 1977 and now reissued with supplementary material current to 1981. Arranged chronologically with biographical and subject indexes to the 1471 women included. The introduction has a fascinating table of gender ratios of 'contributors' to various standard dictionaries of quotations, e.g. women represent 7½ per cent of the entries in Bartlett, 8½ per cent in the *Oxford Book of Quotations*, and at most only 16 per cent in *Contemporary Quotations*.

LIBRARIES AND THE BOOK TRADE

This section starts with a group of books and articles which describe and list collections of relevance to or wholly concerned with women's studies. Obviously the big national and university libraries contain masses of vital material, and work is progressing to make this more accessible. For the national libraries this is reported in Pritchard (no. 97) and Gaur and Tuson (no. 93). There are two university libraries in the US, the University of Wisconsin and Northwestern University, which need mentioning for the excellence of their collections, and more especially for the bibliographic work they do to maintain and promote them. This gives their publications a far wider relevance than that of a local library guide. They are listed under Current awareness publications at the beginning of this chapter. In particular see *Feminist Collections* (no. 5) and *Women's Collections Newsletter* (no. 9).

Guides to collections

92.   DARTER, Pat, 'Small is beautiful – but is it feasible?: small special collections in the UK', In Gaur and Tuson (no. 93), British Library, London, 1989.

Brief descriptions of the main individual feminist collections, which are unhappily all small and struggling financially.

93.   GAUR, Albertine and Penelope TUSON, *Women's Studies* (British Library Occasional Papers no. 12), British Library, London, 1989.

Papers produced for a Colloquium of Resources for Women's Studies held on 4 April 1989. 'The aim of the Colloquium was to present an account of the wide range of material available in the Humanities and Social Sciences division of the Library, and to consider the role of the British Library in supporting research in the field of Women's Studies in the United Kingdom and elsewhere.' Papers are included on major UK collections on women outside the BL, and the final session includes suggestions for action.

94.   HILDENBRAND, Suzanne, 'Women's collections: libraries, archives, and consciousness', *Special Collections*, vol. 3, no. 3/4, 194 p., 1985.

In two sections: the first describes the major US collections, and seven smaller 'but noteworthy' collections. The major libraries are Library of Congress, New York Public Library, Bethune Museum Archives, Smith College, the Schlesinger Library, Texas Woman's University Library, University of Waterloo Library. The second section is called Access, and contains an article about feminist library services at the University of Wisconsin, an article on issues of access (mainly about computerization and the general difficulties of searching in many tools), and an article on reference works for minority and Third World women. Several of these articles are annotated separately in this guide. See Collier-Thomas (no. 632), Pritchard (no. 97), Murdock (no. 110), King (no. 108) and Stafford (no. 513).

95.   JACKSON-BROWN, Grace, *Libraries and Information Centers within Women's Studies Research Centers* (SLA Research Series, no. 3), 34 p., Special Libraries Association, Washington, 1988.

An analysis based on a questionnaire to forty-five women's studies research centres in the US, yielding twenty libraries or information services which are described in detail, noting kinds of users, staffing, types of activities and materials collected. An appendix contains a selected bibliography and a directory of research centres.

96. *Library and Information Sources on Women: A Guide to Collections in the Greater New York Area, Compiled by the Women's Resources Group of the Greater New York Metropolitan Area Chapter of the Association of College and Research Libraries and the Center for the Study of Women and Society of the City University of New York*, 254 p., Feminist Press, New York, 1988.

A nicely produced directory of 171 collections on women in the five boroughs of New York City, Long Island, Westchester County and Eastern New Jersey. They include special libraries, historical societies, government agencies, public and academic libraries and other organizations holding resources on women. The entries include a description, sometimes lengthy and detailed, of the women's materials, collections by format (e.g. books, audiovisuals, MSS), services, contact persons, opening hours, objectives of the institution. The index enables the user to locate materials on a particular subject. An excellent guide.

97. PRITCHARD, Sarah, 'Library of Congress resources for the study of women', *Special Collections*, vol. 3, no. 3/4, pp. 13–36, 1986.

A detailed description of the types of material in the Library of Congress, including special collections, events and services.

98. 'Special focus: women', *Assignation: Aslib Social Sciences Information Group Newsletter*, vol. 2, no. 3, April 1985.

This issue includes brief notes on three UK libraries – the Fawcett, the EOC Library and the Feminist Library. This is followed by a section of study and research; six information agencies are briefly described. Finally the work of four professional associations is described. A useful overview.

99. TURNER, Maryann, *Biblioteca Femina: A Herstory of Book Collections Concerning Women*, 117 p., Tower Press, New York, 1978.

Although now out of date, this book is valuable for its historical approach to the development of library collections for women's studies. After a token chapter on Europe, only US collections are considered; many sources are listed for further detail, and the section on the Women's History Research Center library is particularly interesting. The last quarter of the book outlines plans for setting up a women's studies collection *ab initio*. Sadly no index is provided.

There are other books describing collections from a more specialized point of view in several other chapters. Some of the major entries are as follows:

BARROW, Margaret, *Women, 1870–1928: A Select Guide to Printed and Archival Sources in the United Kingdom*. (no. 671)

DANIELS, Kay, Mary MURNANE and Anne PICOT, *Women in Australia: An Annotated Guide to Records*. (no. 354)

Describes archival sources state by state.

HINDING, Andrea, *Women's History Sources: A Guide to Archives and Manuscript Collections in the United States*. (no. 672)

KENNEY, Anne R., *Archival Sources for Women's History: An Annotated Bibliography of Guides, Inventories, and Catalogs to Archives and Manuscript Collections in the United States*. (no. 673)

NAVARETTA, Cynthia, *Guide to Women's Art Organizations and Directory for the Arts: Multi-arts Centers, Organizations, Galleries, Groups, Activities, Networks, Publications, Archives, Slide Registries* . . . (no. 524)

REED, Janet and Kathleen OAKES, *Women in Australian Society, 1901–1945: A Guide to the Holdings of Australian Archives Relating to Women, 1901–1945*. (no. 355)

SAKALA, Carol, *Women of South Asia: A Guide to Resources*. (no. 330) Part 2 describes libraries in India, Pakistan, Bangladesh and the UK.

SCHNEIDER, Susan Weidman, *Jewish and Female: Choices and Changes in Our Lives Today*. (no. 1011)
Networking directory in last section includes lists of libraries and archives.

THOMAS, Evangeline, *Women's Religious History Sources: A Guide to Repositories in the United States*. (no. 1017)

LIBRARIES AND ARCHIVES

Here we include only libraries or special collections within libraries that are explicitly concerned with women. Libraries are listed alphabetically, followed immediately by any publication describing them. Published catalogues are listed in the following section (nos 112–116). Collections are included for their wide coverage and general relevance. More specific subject-oriented libraries are cross-referenced to the main entry in the relevant chapter in Part II or III.

100. EQUAL OPPORTUNITIES COMMISSION INFOR-MATION CENTRE, Overseas House, Quay St, Manchester M3 3HN.

This small but well-organized library contains an eclectic collection of books and periodical runs, as well as a good deal of information in the form of leaflets, etc. The emphasis is on equal opportunities and sex discrimination in the workplace, but the collection is nevertheless eclectic. In contrast to the other UK women's libraries it is properly staffed and funded.

101. FAWCETT LIBRARY, City of London Polytechnic, Calcutta House, Old Castle St, London E1 7NT.

'Britain's main historical research library on all aspects of women in society.' It also contains much current material. Stock includes about 40,000 books, pamphlets and leaflets, 700 periodical titles and 500 boxes of archives including the papers of many eminent nineteenth-and early twentieth-century feminists. Suffers from cramped surroundings and lack of funds for new acquisitions, but remains an incomparable collection.

102. WOMEN'S STUDIES INTERNATIONAL FORUM, 'The Fawcett Library: Britain's major research resource on women past and present', *Women's Studies International Forum*, vol. 10, no. 3, pp. 221–332, 1987.

A special issue of this journal devoted to the Fawcett Library and including articles on special collections, periodicals, ephemera, and an overview of the Fawcett's place in the context of library materials on women in Britain.

103. FEMINIST ARCHIVE, Trinity Road Library, St Philips, Bristol BS2 0WN.

With a central concern in women's lives in the twentieth century, 'the archive holds a huge collection of pamphlets, MSS, conference papers, leaflets, books, posters and periodicals, documenting every aspect of the Women's Movement from the 1960s onwards'. The collection includes more than 600 periodical titles from all over the world, but concentrating on the British women's movement, and several donations of personal papers of feminist writers and activists. It is also a source of feminist material specifically from and about the West of England. Plans, when resources permit, to start a newsletter and accessions list. Dependent on voluntary labour.

104. FEMINIST LIBRARY, 5 and 5a, Westminster Bridge Road, London SE1.

Started in 1975 by a group of feminist teachers and students as the Women's Research and Resources Centre (WRRC), this library has always had to struggle for funds, and has latterly been badly affected by various changes in policy in London and by the general difficulties in raising money. It holds a small collection of books and a substantial one of periodicals, including many foreign ones. Runs are erratic and often incomplete, but the material is often unique. The library also maintains a research register, and produces an occasional newsletter (no. 105) listing accessions. It is a sad reflection on the state of affairs in the UK that it is reduced to opening only one day a week.

105. *Feminist Library Newsletter*, irreg., 5 and 5a, Westminster Bridge Road, London SE1, 1984– .

Sadly diminished owing to the withdrawal of funding, this newsletter is hardly more than a token news-sheet, a sorry contrast to its sister publications across the Atlantic and the Channel. It was formerly the *WRRC Newsletter*.

106. INTERNATIONAL ARCHIEF VOOR DE VROUWEN-BEWEGING/INTERNATIONAL ARCHIVES FOR THE WOMEN'S MOVEMENT, Keizersgracht 10, 1015 CN Amsterdam, Netherlands.

This important collection of over 40,000 books, archival materials and periodicals on the women's movement was founded in 1935. It provides a unique worldwide documentary source. In 1988 the IIAV (International Information Centre and Archives for the Women's Movement) was formed to provide a nationwide information service and networking organization, and is building an automated information system. It publishes *Lover* (no. 435), acquisitions lists, indexes of Dutch periodicals, bibliographies, etc.

107. SCHLESINGER LIBRARY, Radcliffe College, 10 Garden St, Cambridge, MA 02138.

Although the full title of this library is the 'Arthur and Elizabeth Schlesinger Library on the History of Women in America' the collections have acquired a wider status over the nearly fifty years of their growth. Extensive MSS collections on American women are now supported by a wider growing book and periodical collection. Special collection and projects include cookbooks and oral history projects. An unparalleled resource centre for women's studies.

108. KING, Patricia Miller, 'Forty years of collecting on women: the Arthur and Elizabeth Schlesinger Library on the History of Women in America, Radcliffe College', *Special Collections*, vol. 3, no. 3/4, pp. 75–100, 1986.

This article covers the history of the library, describes the holdings, both MSS and books and periodicals, and mentions the culinary collection and other special projects.

109. SOPHIA SMITH COLLECTION, Smith College Library, Northampton, MA.

A special collection of contemporary and historical material, including college archives.

110. MURDOCK, Mary-Elizabeth, 'Exploring women's lives: historical and contemporary resources in the college archives and the Sophia Smith collection at Smith College', *Special Collections*, vol. 3, no. 3/4, pp. 67–74, 1986.

A brief article describing the collections and facilities.

111. WOMEN'S HISTORY RESEARCH CENTER LIBRARY.

This noteworthy collection, founded in Berkeley, CA by Laura X, was actively acquiring material from 1969–1974. Much of it was then microfilmed as three major collections; Women and Health, Women's Serials and Women and Law. These have been bought by many libraries.

The original collection is now divided up, the major holding of serials being at Northwestern University, Evanston IL. More detail is given in Turner (no. 99) and in Searing (no. 14).

For entries describing more specialized collections see the following:

ARCHIVES AND SPECIAL COLLECTIONS ON WOMEN IN MEDICINE. (no. 877)

BIBLIOTHEQUE MARGUERITE DURAND. (no. 398)

BOSTON WOMEN'S HEALTH COLLECTIVE. (no. 878)

CANADIAN WOMEN'S MOVEMENT ARCHIVES/ARCHIVES CANADIENNES DU MOUVEMENT DES FEMMES. (no. 507)

DOKUMENTASJONSTJENESTEN FOR LITTERATUR OM KVINNER/DOCUMENTATION SERVICES FOR LITERATURE ABOUT WOMEN. (no. 437)

GÖTEBORG UNIVERSITY LIBRARY: WOMEN'S HISTORY COLLECTIONS. (no. 445)

KVINDEHISTORISK SAMLING/WOMEN'S HISTORY ARCHIVE. (no. 388)

LESBIAN ARCHIVE. (no. 784)

LESBIAN HERSTORY ARCHIVES. (no. 785)

NATIONAL ARCHIVES FOR BLACK WOMEN'S HISTORY. (no. 633)

WOMEN ARTISTS SLIDE LIBRARY (WASL). (no. 575)

WOMEN'S HEALTH AND REPRODUCTIVE RIGHTS INFORMATION CENTRE (WHRRIC). (no. 879)

Catalogues

112. ARTHUR & ELIZABETH SCHLESINGER LIBRARY ON THE HISTORY OF WOMEN IN AMERICA, *The Manuscript Inventories and the Catalogs of Manuscripts, Books and Periodicals*, 10 vols, G.K. Hall, Boston, 2nd rev. and enl. ed., 1984.

One of G.K. Hall's mammoth library catalogues, this is basically a reproduction of the card catalogue at the Schlesinger Library of Radcliffe College, Harvard University. Volumes 1–7 cover the cards from A–Z, dictionary style. At the end of Vol. 7 and continuing to 8, cards beginning with 'woman' or 'women' are grouped separately as titles, subjects and corporate authors. At the end of Vol. 8 are periodical cards. Volumes 9 and

10 contain the manuscript inventories and catalogue cards to the huge collections of papers housed in the library; plus a chronological catalogue to the manuscript collection.

113. BIBLIOFEM, *BiblioFem: The Joint Catalogues of the Fawcett Library and the Equal Opportunities Commission, Together with a Continuing Bibliography on Equal Opportunity and Women*, City of London Polytechnic, London, 1978–1986.

BiblioFem is a combined catalogue and continuing bibliography on women, produced on microfiche. Its core is the holdings of the Fawcett Library and the Equal Opportunities Commission Library, but much of the material is culled from Library of Congress and British Library records. It was continuously updated until 1986 when it ceased publication. However, it remains the most comprehensive record of publications related to women in the widest sense. There are two sequences – alphabetic (author/title/series) and classified (arranged by Dewey), accessed by means of an index. A handbook 'Using BiblioFem' is provided, giving instructions on use.

114. GERRITSEN COLLECTION, *The Gerritsen Collection of Women's History, 1543–1945*, 3 vols, University Microfilms International, Ann Arbor, MI, 1983.

The Gerritsen Collection, 'possibly the greatest single source for the study of international women's history and the feminist movement', was begun in the late nineteenth century by Dr Aletta Jacobs and her husband, Carl Gerritsen. In 1903 she sold 2000 volumes to the John Crerar library in Chicago. The Crerar library added many new titles, but broke up the collection in 1954. Fortunately most of it (about 4000 vols) went to the University of Kansas which maintains it as a research collection. The material was supplemented for microfilming by a collection from the University of North Carolina at Greensboro, which includes much British ephemera and American Southern material. This guide to the collection organizes titles by language in Vol. 1, by subject in Vol. 2, and Vol. 3 covers the 256 serials in the collection, with author and title indexes.

115. INTERNATIONAL ARCHIEF VOOR DE VROUWEN-BEWEGING. Library, *Catalogue of the Library of the International Archives for the Women's Movement (Internationaal Archief voor de Vrouwenbeweging)*, Amsterdam, 4 vols, G.K. Hall, Boston, 1980.

Another whopping G.K. Hall catalogue in four huge volumes. Volumes 1 and 2 reproduce the card catalogue, twenty-one to a page in author order, Vols 3 and 4 are described as a 'systematic' catalogue, which is basically a subject list according to the fairly broad groups used by the archive and explained in the front of Vol. 3. Now also available on microform.

116. SOPHIA SMITH COLLECTION, *Catalogs of the Sophia Smith Collection, Women's History Archive, Smith College, Northampton, Massachusetts*, 7 vols, G.K. Hall, Boston, 1975.

Reproduction of the collection's card catalogue, in three parts: Author Catalog (2 vols), Subject Catalog (3 vols) and Manuscript Catalog (2 vols).

Thesauri

117. CAPEK, Mary Ellen S., *A Women's Thesaurus: An Index of Language Used to Describe and Locate Information by and about Women*, 1052 p., Harper & Row, New York, 1987.

This is a monumental enterprise. The compiler sets out to construct a non-sexist subject terminology which will enable information on all aspects of women to be retrieved, pointing out that the language of standardized indexing and classification systems tends to lump much important information under 'women', thereby making it difficult or impossible to find. The application is intended to be for indexing and cataloguing, but the compiler expresses the hope that it will also serve as an introduction to the language itself – 'reclaiming the power of naming'. The main, alphabetical listing of terms gives the main subject group into which each term falls, 'use for' terms, broader terms and related terms. There is also a separate rotated display, a hierarchical display, a subject group display, a use/do not use display, and a delimiters display. This is a complex work, easier to use than to describe, and clearly will become the standard classification of indexing terms for women.

118. DICKSTEIN, Ruth, Victoria A. MILLS, and Ellen J. WAITE, *Women in LC's Terms: A Thesaurus of Library of Congress Subject Headings Relating to Women*, 221 p., Oryx Press, Phoenix, AZ, 1988.

This work was designed to allow the retrieval of material on women using Library of Congress Subject Headings (LCSH), the standard system widely used in America and in many libraries elsewhere, by listing all those headings and cross-references which relate to women. There are over 3500 of them, and Chapter 1 provides an alphabetical list. The remaining eleven chapters give the headings used in broad subjects (e.g. Education, Literature, Law). Extremely valuable for any collection using LCSH, this is really a librarian's working tool. It does not seek to provide an alternative structure of subject headings like Capek (above) or a critique of LC like Marshall (no. 120).

119. MAGGIO, Rosalie, *The Nonsexist Wordfinder: A Dictionary of Gender-free Usage*, 210 p., Oryx Press, Phoenix, AZ, 1987.

A fascinating compendium of usage, historical development and feminist advice. Appendices contain guidelines for non-sexist writing, and selected readings from other publications on language, gender and sexism. Highly recommended.

120. MARSHALL, Joan K., *On Equal Terms: A Thesaurus for Nonsexist Indexing and Cataloging*, 152 p., Neal-Schuman, New York, 1977.

This is a work which developed from the gradual realization among feminist librarians in the early seventies of the full extent of sexism in the Library of Congress subject heading list. Although as a result of this awareness and pressure some changes were made in ways the subject headings referred to women, the extent to which the LC is tied to its catalogue for practical reasons and the pervasiveness of bias, not just sexual, prompted the development of this thesaurus. It is preceded by a set of principles for establishing subject headings, and by instructions for using the thesaurus. Mainly for librarians and information providers.

The book trade

PUBLISHING

There has been enormous growth in the publishing of books on women's issues in the last decade. The main feminist publishers of the late seventies (Virago and The Women's Press, both in London; the Feminist Press in New York; Women's Press in Toronto) have produced steady or increasing lists. They have been joined by many smaller feminist presses, some with specific briefs (like Onlywomen, the London based lesbian press), and all with financial problems. At the same time the growth of women's studies as an academic subject has led to increased interest by traditional publishing houses, many of which now have substantial series on women's issues. The invaluable

ARIEL, Joan, *Building Women's Studies Collections: A Resource Guide*. (no. 12)

contains lists of feminist publishers, of publisher's series in women's studies, of publishers with women's studies catalogues or lists, and of other organizations publishing on women's issues.
    The following are also good sources.

CLARDY, Andrea Fleck, *Words to the Wise: A Writer's Guide to Feminist and Lesbian Periodicals and Publishers*. (no. 33)

Directory of Women's Media (no. 611)

LEHMANN, Stephen and Eva SARTORI, *Women's Studies in Western Europe: A Resource Guide*. (no. 13)

The following entries contain information about publishers in a more specific subject or region:

Annuaire des Femmes du Canada/Canadian Women's Directory. (no. 497)

ALLEN, Jane *et al. Out on the Shelves: Lesbian Books into Libraries*. (no. 764)

CHAPMAN, Anne, *Feminist Resources for Schools and Colleges: A Guide to Curricular Materials*. (no. 665)

CRUIKSHANK, Margaret, *Lesbian Studies Present and Future*. (no. 767)

DOSS, Martha Merrill, *The Directory of Special Opportunities for Women: A National Guide of Educational Opportunities, Career Information, Networks, and Peer Counselling Assistance for Entry or Reentry into the Work Force.* (no. 1054)

MURPHY, Kate and LBC NEWS RADIO, *Women's London*. (no. 1027)

SCHMITZ, Betty, *Integrating Women's Studies into the Curriculum: A Guide and Bibliography*. (no. 183)

SCHNEIDER, Susan Weidman, *Jewish and Female: Choices and Changes in Our Lives Today*. (no. 1011).

VAID, Jyotsna, Barbara D. MILLER and Janice HYDE, *South Asian Women at Home and Abroad: A Guide to Resources*. (no. 331).

121. *Women in Publishing (WIP)*, c/o The Bookseller, 12 Dyott St, London WC1A 1DF.

To promote the status of women within publishing. Offers training for career and personal development. Publishes *WIPlash*, a monthly newsletter, and *WIP Directory*, an annual list of members.

BOOKSHOPS

ARIEL, Joan, *Building Women's Studies Collections: A Resource Guide*. (no. 12)

This is a good first stop for lists of bookstores with catalogues or lists, including two shops specializing in gay literature; she also includes lists of distributors (US only) and of book dealers in the US, UK and Australia.

Bookshops are also listed in Lehmann and Sartori (no. 13) for Western Europe, in Murphy (no. 1027) for London, and in the following:

CANADA. WOMEN'S PROGRAM, *Women's Resource Catalogue/Catalogue de Références de la Femme*. (no. 498)

Directory of Women's Media. (no. 611)

WYNNE, Patrice, *The Womanspirit Sourcebook*. (no. 997)

These two periodicals are important for current information:

122. *Feminist Bookstore News*, 6/yr, PO Box 882554, San Francisco, CA 94188, 1976- .

News of women's bookstores, publishers, book reviews, both US and international. Regular features include Writing wanted, Bestsellers, Subscription information.

123. *Radical Bookseller*, 6/yr, 265 Seven Sisters Rd, London N4 2DE, 1980– .

Although not specifically concerned with women's bookselling, this remains the most authoritative and up-to-date source on all happenings in the feminist book trade in the UK. As well as information on bookshops and publishers, it frequently includes feature articles on women's publishing and bookselling in particular places. Also lists Radical books of the month, of which many are feminist.

These are the two women's bookshops in London:

124.   SILVER MOON, 68 Charing Cross Rd, London WC2H 0BB.

125.   SISTERWRITE, 190 Upper St, London N1 1RQ.

ORGANIZATIONS

Women's organizations range from official international agencies to local groups with a few members addressing a very specific need. Most countries have official bodies dealing with women's issues at a governmental level, but the bulk of activity among women themselves occurs at a grassroots level. The level at which we have listed organizations in this book varies with the subject under scrutiny. Where a grassroots organization seems important within a subject we have included it. As a rule we have omitted official agencies except in one or two cases, since information on these is easily come by. On the whole we have relied on the fact that in the process of research, organizations are revealed in reference works and above all, journals and magazines. Therefore most of the information on organizations will be found under the subjects or topics in this book.

In this section we list a number of useful general works of which the bravest attempt is undoubtedly Shreir (no. 132), who manages a remarkably detailed international coverage. Other works by and large confine themselves to individual countries, regions or topics, and many are listed under the relevant subject in Parts II and III. Organizations come and go, and one suspects that they often remain in reference works long after their demise. When listing them we have tried as far as possible to ascertain that they are still active, but sometimes this has not been possible, and we have listed them nevertheless, using a secondary source as authority.

General works

126.   BUCHANAN, Mary, *World Directory of Women's Organizations*, 222 p., World Directory, London, 1953.

Of historic interest only, this is an amazing compilation of women's organizations, both national and international, of its time (countries go from Aden to Zanzibar). Information varies from entry to entry but at best includes address, membership, officers, and a summary of objectives and activities.

127. CHAMBERLAIN, Mariam K. and Debra L. SCHULTZ, *International Centers for Research on Women*, 25 p., National Council for Research on Women, New York, 1988.

A list of organizations and contact personnel, arranged by country. No other information is given, however, and the term 'international' is not defined, making it less useful than it might be. Many of the names of organizations are translated, and the vernacular version is not given – very odd in the case of countries where English is not a lingua franca.

128. COWLEY, Ruth, *What about Women?: Information Sources for Women's Studies*, 106 p., Fanfare Press, Manchester, 1985.

Section 1, which is the major part of the book, is a directory of organizations, of which 113 are in England, Scotland and Wales, Seven are international, twenty-two from other European countries and six from the US and Canada. Sections 2 and 3 are about developing a resource centre and include a selected list of materials and how to trace them, and an account of how to arrange and run a library.

129. DOSS, Martha Merrill, *Women's Organizations: A National Directory*, 301 p., Garrett Park Press, Garrett Park, MD, 1986.

A sizeable listing of organizations including details and a description. Provides indexes by type of organization and by state. Includes a list of women's directories.

130. *Everywoman Directory of Women's Co-operatives and Other Enterprises*, 24 p., Everywoman with ICOM Co-Publication, 34 Islington Green, London N1 8DU, 1987.

A useful 'yellow pages' of women's enterprises throughout Britain.

131. KLEIMAN, Carol, *Women's Networks: The Complete Guide to Getting a Better Job, Advancing your Career, and Feeling Great as a Woman through Networking*, 210 p., Lippincott & Crowell, New York, 1980.

Seventy pages of addresses in the United States are preceded by chapters describing networks and how they function, including business, professions, social support, health and sports, political and labour, arts and, of course, how to do it yourself.

132. SHREIR, Sally, *Women's Movements of the World* (Keesing's Reference Publications), 384 p., Longman, London, 1988. (Originally published by Oryx Press, 1987.)

This is a directory of women's organizations arranged in an alphabetical list by country. The editor describes it as a 'guide to the current status of women's issues and organisations throughout the world'. An introductory section is provided for each country giving a brief description of the political system and socio-economic conditions with special reference to women's issues. The length of these introductions varies from three or four lines to several pages. The organizations covered are not necessarily feminist, and include some government agencies and professional organizations 'where their activities seem to have . . . some broader significance for the position of women'. There is a list of international organizations at the end. Details of membership, activities, ideological orientation, publications, etc., are given as well as contact addresses. The selection on the whole seems remarkably comprehensive. This is a valuable reference work where one can find the details of women's organizations in countries from Afghanistan to Zimbabwe. An index of organizations would have been useful.

133. *Spare Rib Diary*, Available from Spare Rib, 27 Clerkenwell Close, London EC1R 0AT.

Contains a useful list of British women's organizations, which has the virtue of being updated yearly.

134. SPRINGBOARD, *A Directory of Women's Businesses and Organizations in the London Area*, 155 p., Springboard Pub. Ltd, PO Box 741, London NW6 4YP, 1988.

The idea for this directory is based on the American Los Angeles Women's Yellow Pages. It includes all sorts of information for women (e.g. A guide to your rights, What to do if you are assaulted, Finding a woman doctor, etc.). Different sections include Resources – survival guide, Children's resources, Training, Equal opportunities, followed by the Yellow Pages containing advertisers by subject. There is an index.

135. WOMEN'S ACTION ALLIANCE, *Women's Action Almanac: A Complete Resource Guide*, 432 p., Morrow, New York, 1979.

An excellent US resource guide but now desperately in need of updating were that enormous task possible. It nevertheless still gives useful leads into eighty-four topics and subjects areas, giving a brief outline of activity with publications and addresses. There is a supplementary list of US national women's organizations.

136. WOMEN'S NATIONAL COMMISSION, *Women's Organizations in Great Britain 1987/88*, 95 p., WNC, London, 1988.

Lists women's organizations divided by region (GB, Scotland, Wales), organizations concerned with pregnancy, children and families. The organizations selected are for the most part fairly traditional ones. Details of each organization's address, etc. are given, together with a description of its objects and a list of its publications.

See also:

Irish Women's Guidebook and Diary. (no. 384)

Wales Women's Directory/Cysylltiadur Merched Cymru: Women's Groups, Organizations and Businesses in Wales. (no. 387)

Funding organizations

137.   BOWMAN, Marion and Michael NORTON, *Raising Money for Women: A Survivors' Guide*, 128 p., Bedford Square Press/NCVO, London, 1986. (Published in association with *Directory for Social Change.*)

Designed to give 'practical help and advice on how to find a way through the maze of different sources of statutory and non-statutory funding'. Part 1 gives the background to the problems of raising money for women. Part 2 gives practical details, including preparation for raising money and sources of funds: first, the major official sources, such as local or central government, EC, etc., and secondly non-statutory sources such as grant-making trusts, companies, etc. There is also a section on developing other sources of funding. The book is full of advice on such matters as the methods of making applications for funding and presenting the case. It was written for the National Council for Voluntary Organizations' Women's Organizations Interest Group.

138.   SCHLACHTER, Gail Ann, *Directory of Financial Aids for Women 1987–1988*, 421 p., Reference Services Press, Redwood City, CA, 1987.

Third edition of a biennial publication listing sources of financial aid open exclusively to women. The first section lists financial aid programmes and grant-giving bodies under the subsections Scholarships, Fellowships, Loans, Grants, Awards and Internships. The second section lists state sources of information on educational benefits. The third section is an annotated bibliography of general financial aids directories, and the fourth contains indexes. The coverage is international in scope, but the focus is on programmes open to American citizens or tenable in the United States.

STATISTICAL INFORMATION

The field of statistics is one in which women have never wanted for recognition, gender of course being one of the primary divisions of the population for many demographic purposes. The many suspect implicit assumptions in these divisions have been challenged in a number of works. We include here surveys and presentations of data of a general nature, some of which are in the form of atlases which present the information in graphic form. Although it is beyond our brief in this book to list material not specifically on women, it is worth mentioning that British statistical sources on women can be accessed by consulting the *Guide to Official Statistics* (HMSO, 1986). Shreir (no. 132) also contains much statistical information on the status of women country by country.

139.   BOULDING, Elise *et al.*, *Handbook of International Data on Women*, 468 p., Wiley, New York, 1976.

A huge collection of statistics relating to women, covering economic activity, literacy and education, migration, marital status, life, death and reproduction, political and civic participation. Based on a survey of United Nations data on the position of women.

COMMISSION OF THE EUROPEAN COMMUNITIES, *Men and Women of Europe in 1987*. (no. 362)

COMMISSION OF THE EUROPEAN COMMUNITIES, *Women in Statistics*. (no. 363)

CURTIN, Leslie, *Status of Women: A Comparative Analysis of Twenty Developing Countries*. (no. 234)

140.   EQUAL OPPORTUNITIES COMMISSION, *Women and Men in Britain: A Research Profile*, 79 p., HMSO, London, 1988. (Previous editions entitled *Women and Men in Britain: A Statistical Profile*.)

This is a digest of statistics which have been gathered from a number of different sources. They are mainly British but include some comparative European material, and some of the data is drawn from unpublished sources. The data is divided into six broad subject areas: Population, Education and training, Employment, Income, Consumer affairs and Politics, public life and employment in the public service. The data is presented in tabular and graphic form with a narrative explanation. The 1988 edition contains considerably more data than previous editions.

GIBSON, Anne and Timothy Fast, *The Women's Atlas of the United States*. (no. 508).

141.   INTERNATIONAL   LABOUR   ORGANISATION/IN-STRAW, *Women in Economic Activity: A Global Statistical Survey (1950–2000)*, 170 p., INSTRAW, Santo Domingo, Dominican Republic, 1985.

'This publication presents a global statistical survey of women's economic activity, by geographical and economic region as well as by country . . . carried out as part of the effort to implement the objectives of the UN Decade for Women.' The data is presented with extensive narrative comment, divided by region: Africa, Asia, Latin America & the Caribbean, European Market economy countries, North America, Oceania, Eastern Europe. A preliminary chapter provides comparative Profiles of working women, with an appendix on Trends in employment and unemployment in developing and developed countries (1976-1980). A final chapter contains Statistical sources on women and work: selected bibliographical references (1976-1985). This is a valuable resource.

INTER-PARLIAMENTARY UNION, *Participation of Women in Political Life and in the Decision-Making Process: A World Survey as at 1 April 1988.* (no. 717)

142. MINTEL, *Women 2000* (Mintel Special Report), 315 p., Mintel Pubs Ltd, London, 1988.

'This report attempts to look at women's lives as they are today and to examine the factors which are effecting changes in women's lives.' A series of statistics on women are divided into sections on subjects such as Women and work, Women and health, Women and their aspirations, etc. The statistical tables are presented with narrative summaries of the findings and an introductory overview for each section.

143. SEAGER, Joni and Ann OLSON, *Women in the World: An International Atlas*, 128 p., Pluto, London, 1986. (Paperback ed. published by Pan Books. American ed. by Simon & Schuster.)

One of the splendid series of polemical Pluto atlases, this gives a visual dimension to statistical data on women by means of brilliant graphics. A series of maps and diagrams illustrate the position of women worldwide, covering numerous topics such as motherhood, work, welfare, authority, each of these being further subdivided into narrower topics. There is a subject index and a very useful bibliography.

SHORTRIDGE, Barbara Gimla, *Atlas of American Women.* (no. 510)

144. SIVARD, Ruth Leger, *Women: A World Survey*, 44 p., World Priorities, Box 25140, Washington, DC 20007, 1985.

A very useful publication providing statistical and factual information on the situation of women in the world today, in an accessible and abbreviated form. The material is presented narratively and in tabular or graphic form, and is divided into Perspectives, Background of change, Women's work, Women's health, Government and the laws, and National profiles and gender comparison.

UNITED NATIONS, Dept of International Economic and Social Affairs, Statistical Office, *World Survey on the Role of Women in Development.* (no. 235)

145. UNITED NATIONS, Statistical Office, *Women's Indicators and Statistics Database (WISTAT)*, United Nations, New York. (Available from the Sales Section, Publishing Division, Room DC 2-853, UN, New York, NY 10017.)

Seventy-two microcomputer spreadsheet files covering 178 countries or areas over a wide range of topics, including population, marital status, fertility, housing conditions, health, political participation, crime, national production and expenditure, etc.

146.   *Women of the World*, 5 vols, US Dept of Commerce, Bureau of the Census, Washington, DC, 1984–5.

The first four volumes cover respectively Latin America and the Caribbean, Sub-Saharan Africa, Near East and North Africa, Asia and the Pacific. They provide statistical summaries, charts and histograms covering population, literacy, economic activity, domestic arrangements, fertility and mortality. Volume 5 is a summary of the data in the four preceding volumes. As collations of statistics relating to women, these books are useful and reasonably current. However, they suffer from the 'official' nature of such statistics, and from the conceptual framework (male, western) in which they were gathered.

NON–BOOK MATERIAL

Audiovisual material

147.   ISIS INTERNATIONAL, *Powerful Images: A Women's Guide to Audiovisual Resources*, 210 p., Isis International, Rome, 1986.

Describing audiovisuals as 'a valuable tool for grassroots organizing', this work is primarily a catalogue of films, videos, slide-shows, etc. made by women all over the world. They are arranged under their subject matter, and listed by country. This is followed by a list of distributors, film-makers and grassroots organizations, and preceded by introductory articles most of which detail experiences in making audiovisuals for different feminist causes. The focus is predominantly Third World, although not exclusively.

148.   NORDQUIST, Joan, *Audiovisuals for Women*, 145 p., McFarland, Jefferson, NC, 1980. (Distributed by Bailey & Swinfen.)

Lists recent material, divided into 16mm films, videotapes, filmstrips, slides, recordings/spoken word; recordings/music, contemporary film-makers' works with brief descriptions of many of them. Directory of distributors, and list of further resources precede the subject index.

For an international list of audiovisual resource centres see the following:

RFR/DRF RESOURCES FOR FEMINIST RESEARCH, 'Women's Art/L'Art des Femmes'. (no. 525)

Microforms

Microfilming is a popular way of increasing access to primary sources and ensuring their survival, and women's studies is no exception to this activity. A useful list of microfilm publishers is given in Ariel (no. 12). Searing (no. 14) gives good descriptions of several major sources. Many libraries have growing collections on microforms, as purchasing power allows. The Women's History Research Center Library (no. 111) used this method to guarantee the permanence of their collection and its wider availability.

149. PATTERSON, Elizabeth, 'Women's studies resources in microform', *Microform Review*, vol. 15, pp. 99–102, Spring 1986.

Gives a useful summary of availability of resources.

Databases

Up until recently there have been no general databases relating specifically to women. Now the following three entries indicate considerable progress.

150. ISIS INTERNATIONAL WOMEN'S DATA BASE, Isis International, Casilla 2067, Correo Central 2067, Santiago, Chile, 1988–.

Our information on this suggests that it is a printed publication containing bibliographic citations with abstracts, with five indexes: thematic, individual or institutional author, geographic area, conferences and periodicals. A *List of Descriptors on the Theme of Women* is available to subscribers.

151. UNESCO, Division for the Advancement of Women, *Information System on Women (WIS)*, Division for the Advancement of Women, Centre for Social Development and Social Affairs, Vienna International Centre, PO Box 500, 1400 Vienna, Austria.

Computerized bibliographic information system for operation on IBM PCs, with a database management system. It lists more than 700 documents produced since January 1986, and provides searches for government and research institutions. Its major objective is tracking implementation of the Forward-Looking Strategies for the Advancement of Women. News of the database is given in the newsletter *Women 2000* (no. 208).

NATIONAL COUNCIL FOR RESEARCH ON WOMEN (NCRW). (no. 512)

This organization is compiling a database on work-in-progress using the Capek thesaurus (no. 117) as a basis for subject organization. The work is described in the first issue of *Women's Research Network News* (no. 84).

General databases, not specific to women, are listed clearly, with an indication of their subject coverage in:

ARIEL, Joan, *Building Women's Studies Collections: A Resource Guide*. (no. 12).

SEARING, Susan, E., *Introduction to Library Research in Women's Studies*. (no. 14)

For other data on women, but with a more limited subject orientation, see the following:

ADA, *A Database of Women Artists*. (no. 563)

CATALYST, *Catalyst Resources for Women (CRFW)*. (no. 1046)

CENTRE FOR RESEARCH ON EUROPEAN WOMEN (CREW). (no. 366)

UNITED NATIONS, Statistical Office, *Women's Indicators and Statistics Database (WISTAT)*. (no. 145)

CHAPTER 2

Biographical information

Here we have tried to mention, one way or another, all the works in this guide with a major biographical component. Books whose *raison d'être* is biographical, like general dictionaries and directories, have their main entry here. Works, often bio-bibliographical in form, which are predominantly concerned with a subject area – arts or literature are good examples – are in the main given a cross-reference here.

DICTIONARIES AND INDEXES

General

152.   IRELAND, Norma Olin, *Index to Women of the World from Ancient to Modern Times: Biographies and Portraits*, 573 p., Scarecrow, Metuchen, NJ, 1970. (Originally published by Faxon.)

Some 900 collective biographies were analysed for this work, yielding entries for about 13,000 women. Entries are brief, giving simply dates, country and occupation, plus a list of the biographical collections which include the women. Worth trying for hard-to-trace women. A 700 page supplement, published in 1988, analyses a further 380 collective biographies to bring the material up to date.

153.   UGLOW, Jennifer, *The Macmillan Dictionary of Women's Biography*, 621 p., Macmillan, London, 2nd ed., 1989. (Published in the USA as *The Continuum Dictionary of Women's Biography* by Crossroad/Continuum, New York; previous edition as *The International Dictionary of Women's Biography*.)

In her introduction the editor describes this as a response to 'a request for heroines'. A wonderfully eclectic compilation, with worldwide coverage spanning from the earliest times to today. A subject index groups the women in various categories. There is a useful introduction with an extensive bibliography of reference sources. The new edition contains over 1700 entries, including 250 new ones.

154.   WEISER, Marjorie P.K. and Jean S. ARBEITER, *Woman List*, 500 p., Atheneum, New York, 1981.

An exhaustive list of women of all times and places (but inevitably mainly American) in various somewhat unorthodox categories: Out of the ordinary, What's the difference, Show of courage, Love & marriage, M is for . . . and other family connections, She's the boss, Persons at work, Thirsting for knowledge, Arms & the woman, The search for adventure, That's entertainment, Music in the air, In their own write, For art's sake, In the money, Fads & fashions, Victims, Games women play, Words of wisdom & otherwise, Horrors. There is a bibliography and an index of names and subjects. Each woman gets a few lines of biographical information. There is a bibliography at the end of the book, but no specific bibliographical references for each woman. Includes many hundreds of women.

155.   *World Who's Who of Women*, 764 p., Melrose Press, Ely, Cambs., 1987. (Published in US by Reference Services Press)

Regularly produced directory of around 4000 women, with addresses.

American

156.   HERMAN, Kali, *Women in Particular: An Index to American Women*, 740 p., Oryx Press, Phoenix, AZ, 1984.

Arranged as four indexes: Field and career; Religious affiliation; Ethnic and Racial; Geographical; with subdivisions within each, and one A–Z index to the whole work. Information given about each woman is limited to name, dates, career description and sources, referring the reader on to various biographical reference works. No specific bibliographic references are made. Over 20,000 women are indexed.

157.   *Notable American Women, 1607–1950: A Biographical Dictionary*, 4 vols, Belknap Press of Harvard University, Cambridge, MA, 1971–80. (Volume 4 entitled *Notable American Women: The Modern Period*.)

Volumes 1–3 include 1359 women who died before 1951. Volume 4 includes 442 women who died between 1951–75, with particular efforts to include minority women. Entries are lengthy and include much detail, often based on papers held at the Schlesinger Library, Radcliffe College.

British

158.   BANKS, Olive, *The Biographical Dictionary of British Feminists*, 239 p., Wheatsheaf, Brighton, 1985. (Volume 1: 1800–1930.)

Long, well-documented entries on women (and a handful of men) active in various feminist causes of the nineteenth and twentieth centuries. Volume 2, post 1930, is forthcoming.

159.   *The Europa Biographical Dictionary of British Women: Over 1000 Notable Women from Britain's Past*, 436 p., Gale Research, Detroit, MI, 1983.

Entries of variable length, frequently including bibliographical details.

BIBLIOGRAPHIES OF PERSONAL WRITINGS

160.   ADDIS, Patricia K., *Through a Woman's I: An Annotated Bibliography of American Women's Autobiographical Writings, 1946–1976*, 607 p., Scarecrow, Metuchen, NJ, 1983. (A subsequent work is planned to cover material published prior to 1946.)

A fascinating compilation of 2217 autobiographies, diaries, letter collections, journals, travel reminiscences, etc., each descriptively annotated. The main arrangement is A–Z; indexes cover authors by 'profession or salient characteristic', 'narratives by subject matter' and titles. See also Rhodes (no. 165).

161.   CLINE, Cheryl, *Women's Diaries, Journals and Letters: A Historical Guide*, c.900 p., Garland, New York, 1989.

'This is the first comprehensive listing of women's personal writings that covers material from 1100 AD to the present . . . Anthologies, published collections of family papers, bibliographies and guides, and approximately 2000 diaries and collections of letters are included in this primary and secondary bibliography. The work is arranged alphabetically within these sections: bibliographies, critical works, anthologies, family collections, diaries, journals, and letters.' (From publisher's announcement.)

162.   DAVIS, Gwenn and Beverly A. JOYCE, *Personal Writings by Women to 1800: A Bibliography of American and British Writers*, 294 p., Mansell, London, 1989.

Personal writing is defined as covering 'a range of types and genres,' from spiritual autobiography to accounts of lawsuits, from explorations of the African continent to diaries of domestic life in villages'. The bibliography consists of nearly 5000 entries, arranged alphabetically by author. An appendix lists the authors chronologically, in fifty or twenty-five year groupings. The index gives access by subject, but some of the more general subject terms give rise to long lists of numbers.

163.   GOODFRIEND, Joyce D., *The Published Diaries and Letters of American Women: An Annotated Bibliography*, 230 p., G.K. Hall, Boston, 1987.

A chronological listing of published diaries and letters by American women, from the seventeenth century to 1982. The main criterion for inclusion is the personal and immediate nature of the material: works written retrospectively (i.e. autobiographies) or for public consumption have been excluded. The excellent and readable annotations give brief biographical details and a description of the themes revealed in the works. These are picked up in the subject index. There is also an index to authors.

164.   HUFF, Cynthia, *British Women's Diaries: A Descriptive Bibliography of Selected Nineteenth-Century Women's Manuscript Diaries*, 139 p., AMS Press, New York, 1985.

This work describes the diaries of fifty-nine women covering dates, places, the various formats and present location of the manuscript, the general content and stylistic features of each. The diarists are arranged by class, upper-class writers being subdivided into aristocracy and gentry, and middle-class into professional–commercial, intelligentsia and religious. There is a subject index and an index to diarists, plus a long introduction describing the diaries in a general way and discussing the possible light they throw on the role of women in the nineteenth century.

165.   RHODES, Carolyn H., *First Person Female American: A Selected and Annotated Bibliography of the Autobiographies of American Women Living After 1950*, 404 p., Whitston, Troy, NY, 1980. (First published as a special issue of *American Notes and Queries*, Sept. 1977.)

A charmingly idiosyncratic collection of lengthy annotations of 330 autobiographies of 224 women, compiled with a view to their usefulness to women's studies teachers and students, and with an eye to correcting the 'invisibility of women in the curricula of traditional departments'. An index of topics is given. There is a lot of overlap with Addis (no. 160) but some entries are unique to Rhodes, and in any case the annotations are much more detailed. The indexes are better in Addis.

See also:

BRADY, Anna, *Women in Ireland: An Annotated Bibliography.* (no. 381)

KANNER, Barbara, *Women in English Social History, 1800–1914.* (no. 712)

KOH, Hesung Chun, *Korean and Japanese Women: An Analytic and Bibliographical Guide.* (no. 347)

ROBINSON, Doris, *Women Novelists, 1891–1920: An Index to Biographies and Autobiographical Sources.* (no. 790)

SIMS-WOOD, Janet L., 'The Afro-American woman: researching her history'. (no. 643)

Women Live. (no. 83)

BIO-BIBLIOGRAPHICAL WORKS

The arts

AMBRUS, Caroline, *The Ladies' Picture Show: Sources on a Century of Australian Women Artists.* (no. 572)

BACHMANN, Donna G. and Sherry PILAND, *Women Artists: A Historical, Contemporary and Feminist Bibliography.* (no. 564)

CLAGHORN, Gene, *Women Composers and Hymnists: A Concise Biographical Dictionary.* (no. 551)

COHEN, Aaron I., *International Encyclopedia of Women Composers: Classical and Serious Music.* (no. 538)

HECK-RABI, Louise, *Women Film-Makers: A Critical Reception.* (no. 584)

HIXON, Donald L. and Don HENNESSEE. *Women in Music: A Biobibliography.* (no. 540)

LEPAGE, Jane Weiner, *Women Composers, Conductors and Musicians of the Twentieth Century: Selected Biographies.* (no. 543)

PETTEYS, Chris, *Dictionary of Women Artists: An International Dictionary of Women Artists Born Before 1900.* (no. 566)

PRATHER-MOSES, Alice, *The International Dictionary of Women Workers in the Decorative Arts: A Historical Survey from the Distant Past to the Early Decades of the Twentieth Century.* (no. 567)

SCHILPP, Madelon Golden and Sharon M. MURPHY, *Great Women of the Press.* (no. 614)

STERN, Susan, *Women Composers: A Handbook.* (no. 541)

ZAIMONT, Judith Lang and Karen FAMERA, *Contemporary Concert Music by Women: A Directory of the Composers and Their Works.* (no. 544)

History

BYRNE, Pamela R. and Susan K. KINNELL, *Women in North America: Summaries of Biographical Articles in History Journals.* (no. 692)

EMERSON, Kathy Lynn, *Wives and Daughters: The Women of Sixteenth Century England.* (no. 710)

FREY, Linda, Marsha FREY and Joanne SCHNEIDER, *Women in Western European History, First Supplement: A Select Chronological, Geographical and Topical Bibliography.* (no. 684)

GOODWATER, Leanna, *Women in Antiquity: An Annotated Bibliography.* (no. 707)

166. HUDAK, Leona M., *Early American Women Printers and Publishers 1639–1820*, 813 p., Scarecrow, Metuchen, NJ. 1978.

Detailed chapters on twenty-five American women covering biography and imprints with bibliographies collected together at the end of the book.

KANNER, Barbara, *Women in English Social History, 1800–1914.* (no. 712)

LEGGET, Jane, *Local Heroines: A Woman's Gazetteer to England, Scotland and Wales.* (no. 1026)

MANNING, Beverley, *Index to American Women Speakers, 1828–1978.* (no. 702)

MANNING, Beverley, *We Shall Be Heard: An Index to Speeches by American Women 1978-1985*. (no. 703)

SIMS-WOOD, Janet L., 'The Afro-American woman: researching her history'. (no. 643)

Literature

BETSKO, Kathleen and Rachel KOENIG, *Interviews with Contemporary Women Playwrights*. (no. 842)

FRIEDRICHS, Elisabeth, *Die deutschsprachigen Schrifstellerinnen des 18. und 19. Jahrhunderts: Ein Lexikon*. (no. 822)

ROBINSON, Doris, *Women Novelists, 1891-1920: An Index to Biographies and Autobiographical Sources*. (no. 790)

SCHLUETER, Paul and June SCHLUETER, *Encyclopedia of British Women Writers*. (no. 791)

TODD, Janet, *A Dictionary of British and American Women Writers, 1660-1800*. (no. 793)

WILSON, Katharina, *Encyclopedia of Continental Women Writers*. (no. 794)

Science and medicine

BULLOUGH, Vern L., Olga CHURCH and Alice P. STEIN. *American Nursing: A Biographical Dictionary*. (no. 883)

GRINSTEIN, Louise and Paul CAMPBELL, *Women of Mathematics: A Biobibliographic Sourcebook*. (no. 967)

167. HERZENBERG, Caroline L., *Women Scientists from Antiquity to the Present: An Index; An International Reference Listing and Biographical Directory of Some Notable Women from Ancient to Modern Times*, 200 p., Locust Hill Press, West Cornwall, CT, 1986.

The main sequence is A–Z. Information given is name, dates, nationality and source code, which refers to a bibliography of biographical dictionaries, etc. There is an index listing the women by field of activity. 'Scientist' is interpreted fairly widely, and nurses, midwives, anthropologists, cartographers, foresters and home economists are included along with traditional science fields. An excellent resource in a sparsely documented field.

KAUFMAN, Martin *et al.*, *Dictionary of American Nursing Biography*. (no. 884)

OGILVIE, Marilyn Bailey, *Women in Science: Antiquity through the Nineteenth Century: A Biographical Dictionary with Annotated Bibliography*. (no. 948)

168. SIEGEL, Patricia Joan, *Women in the Scientific Search: An American Bibliography 1724-1979*, 399 p., Scarecrow, Metuchen, NJ, 1985.

A list of general bibliographies is followed by well over a thousand entries arranged alphabetically by field of study from archaeology to zoology. Within each subject area women are listed alphabetically by name, with biographical and scholarly information. This is an example of painstaking bibliographical research which adds up to an invaluable resource.

Other

CENTER FOR THE AMERICAN WOMAN AND POLITICS, Rutgers University, *Women in Public Office: A Biographical Directory and Statistical Analysis*. (no. 747)

169. GACS, Ute *et al.*, *Women Anthropologists: A Biographical Dictionary*, 428 p., Greenwood, Westport, CT, 1988.

Fifty-eight women anthropologists are included here, each being given a substantial biographical entry including, as well as the usual biographical information, consideration of such matters as career difficulties, the state of the discipline, etc. Each entry has a bibliography (not comprehensive) of works by and about the subject. Most of the anthropologists are American.

HAMMACK, Mary, *A Dictionary of Women in Church History*. (no. 1014)

170. KERSEY, Ethel M., *Women Philosophers: A Bio-critical Source Book*, Greenwood, Westport, CT, 1979.

'Covers more than 170 women born before 1920 who wrote about or pondered questions of Western intellectual life. Using broad criteria, Kersey has included any woman who conducted serious work in the traditional fields of philosophy, including metaphysics, ethics, aesthetics, or logic.' (From publisher's announcement.)

171. LEAVITT, Judith A., *American Women Managers and Administrators: A Selective Biographical Dictionary of Twentieth-Century Leaders in Business, Education and Government*, 317 p., Greenwood, Westport, CT, 1985.

Lists alphabetically 226 twentieth-century American women prominent in business, education and government. The biographies are followed up by bibliographies of works by and about the subject. Preference in selection was given to presidents of companies and colleges, women who were 'firsts' in their fields, and women who were nationally prominent. An appendix lists the women in various categories, e.g. founders, 'firsts', presidents. There is a general bibliography and an index.

172. O'NEILL, Lois Decker, *The Women's Book of World Records and Achievements*, 798 p., Anchor Press/Doubleday, Garden City, NY, 1979.

Contrary to the impression given by the title, sport occupies only forty pages of this compilation, which is a survey of woman's activity to date in all possible spheres. Arranged in chapters such as politics, home and community, communication and military, various achievements are then described. The amount of detail varies, and the overall inclusion is a little idiosyncratic, but worth using as a source in broad areas, or for searching for particular women. There is a name index but no subject index.

REMLEY, Mary L., *Women in Sport: A Guide to Information Sources.* (no. 1035)

SHOEBRIDGE, Michele, *Women in Sport: A Select Bibliography.* (no. 1036)

STINEMAN, Esther, *American Political Women: Contemporary and Historical Profiles.* (no. 748).

173.　TINLING, Marion, *Women into the Unknown: A Sourcebook on Women Explorers and Travelers*, 416 p., Greenwood, Westport, CT, 1989.

'Portraits of some forty-five enterprising and intrepid women who have explored uncharted territory . . . The subjects include English, American, and continental European women. In addition to detailed biographical essays, the author presents comprehensive bibliographical data on the published and unpublished works of the subjects and the articles and books that have been written about them.' (From publisher's announcement.)

Women Directors: Who's Who in the World of Women Directors, compiled by Vivienne Kendall. (no. 1050)

PERIODICALS

Regular biographical features and articles are to be found in:

Trivia: A Journal of Ideas. (no. 64)

CHAPTER 3

Women's studies

Despite the title of this chapter, this whole book is of course about women's studies, in that all the items included are selected for their relevance to the needs of students, teachers, researchers and readers interested in any of the very varied aspects which are coming to characterize women's studies. This chapter therefore is limited to works dealing with women's studies as an 'entity' of some sort; books which are compiled with a conscious awareness of what it is to work in this area instead of another, and works which explicitly consider the problem of making sure (or trying to at any rate) that the work we do as feminists does not perpetuate unwittingly the patriarchal mind set or work from unconsciously androcentric viewpoints.

Much work in this area is tentative, almost exploratory, and there are therefore not many bibliographies or reference sources yet. Those we have found are divided into groups, roughly on a scale from 'pure' to 'applied'. Philosophies and theories on feminism and women's studies are followed by a group of works dealing directly with methods that distinguish feminist from non-feminist research. Then comes an important section on course development, and the effect of women's studies teaching on general curricula. These are sometimes limited to specific geographical areas or subjects, in which case cross references are made to the relevant chapters.

General women's studies journals often contain some articles which are centrally concerned with theories of women's studies, though usually the emphasis of the journal is more diverse. Such journals are listed in Chapter 1 (nos 44–71), and the individual articles should be sought via the bibliographies in this chapter, or for more recent material, in *Women Studies Abstracts* (no. 4). Periodicals listed in this chapter are limited to those, mainly news-letters, which are bulletins of women's studies associations, and which carry news and information about the activity of women's studies. Similarly, the organizations listed here are the 'umbrella' women's studies associations which often provide a first point of enquiry for anyone seeking information about activity within a country.

PHILOSOPHY AND THEORY

174. BOWLES, Gloria, Renate DUELLI-KLEIN and M. Erika HECKSCHER, 'Selected annotated bibliography of articles on theories of women's studies', in two parts in BOWLES, Gloria and DUELLI-KLEIN, Renate, *Theories of Women's Studies I & II*, Women's Studies, University of California, Berkeley, 1980, 1982, pp. 65–75 and pp. 131–152.

A useful collection of material on feminist methodology, mainly from late 1970s and early 1980s American sources.

175. HUMM, Maggie, *Dictionary of Feminist Theory*, c.256 p., Harvester/Wheatsheaf, Hemel Hempstead, 1989.

'The first fully cross-referenced guide to bring together, clarify and explain the concepts and ideas about women and their views of the world, which form the basis of feminist knowledge and theory . . . The Dictionary provides a comprehensive guide to the terminology and history of feminist theory relating the categories of feminist thinking to mainstream scholarship as it is practised in the western world. It provides succinct definitions of a wide range of terms and topics . . .' (From publisher's announcement.)

176. MORGAN, Kathryn Pauly, 'Bibliography of recent feminist philosophy and theory', *RFE/DRF Resources for Feminist Research*, vol. 16, no. 3, pp. 89–193, 1987.

A bibliography with the emphasis on books rather than articles (because articles may be readily accessed by using the Philosopher's Index), and special issues of periodicals. It is divided into General books and anthologies, 1970–present, Journals, History of philosophy, Methodology, Philosophy of language, Feminist aesthetics, Social and political philosophy, Philosophy of education, French feminist philosophy, and Special categories.

See also:

Hypatia: A Journal of Feminist Philosophy. (no. 56)
Newsletter on Feminism and Philosophy. (no. 77)

METHODOLOGY

177. EICHLER, Margrit, *Nonsexist Research Methods: A Practical Guide*, 182 p., Unwin Hyman, Boston, etc., 1988.

This immensely readable book is, despite its title, as much a critique of social science research as a guidebook, though the two are intertwined. She identifies four major problems – androcentricity, over-generalization, gender insensitivity and double standards – and three minor problems, and gives clear accounts and examples of each together with suggestions and ideas for avoiding them. The non-sexist Research Checklist provided as an appendix should be prominent in the planning of every project.

178.   FRANZOSA, Susan Douglas and Karen A. MAZZA, *Integrating Women's Studies into the Curriculum: An Annotated Bibliography*, 100 p., Greenwood, Westport, CT, 1984.

This is a fundamental collection of documents about the relationships between feminist theory and curriculum studies, providing some bases for the reassessment of traditional ways of teaching, to eliminate male bias. It covers material published between 1976 and 1983, with some earlier works, and is arranged in broad subject areas. Preliminary sections cover the general aspects of women's studies integration and bibliographic sources. There is an author index. A brief and lucid introduction explains the perspective from which the compilers selected entries, namely to 'question the assumptions used . . . [in] constructing and distributing knowledge'. See also Schmitz (no. 183) for a book of the same title.

179.   REINHARZ, Shulamit, Marti BOMBYK and Janet WRIGHT, 'Methodological issues in feminist research: a bibliography of literature in women's studies, sociology and philosophy', *Women's Studies International Forum*, vol. 6, no. 4, pp. 437–454, 1983.

Divided into ten sections with the publications listed chronologically within each section in order to show the development of ideas. Most references are drawn from sociological and psychological research and research in women's studies in general.

180.   SHREWSBURY, Carolyn M., 'Feminist pedagogy: a bibliography', *Women's Studies Quarterly*, vol. 15, no. 3/4, pp. 116–124, Fall/Winter 1987.

Part of a special issue on feminist pedagogy, this bibliography focuses on the process of teaching from a feminist point of view.

COURSES AND CURRICULA

181.   BRODRIBB, Somer, *Women's Studies in Canada*, 27 p., RFR/DRF Resources for Feminist Research, Toronto, 1987. (Special publication.)

As well as giving an overview of the state of women's studies in Canada, this also provides lists of women's studies programmes and their coordinators, associations, documentation centres and Canadian feminist periodicals.

182.   COMMISSION OF THE EUROPEAN COMMUNITIES, *Women's Studies* (Women of Europe Supplement no. 18), 93 p., Commission of the European Communities, Brussels, 1984.

Although is it now rather out of date, this publication is a very useful guide to women's studies in Western Europe, covering countries outside as well as in the European Community. Under each country there are descriptions of the research and teaching activity in women's studies, in both educational establishments and independent institutions. An appendix lists European Community research on women. The introduction contains an interesting comparison of the European and American models of women's studies, and of current developments in the USA, Canada and Europe. It can be expected that a new edition will be published soon.

183.   SCHMITZ, Betty, *Integrating Women's Studies into the Curriculum: A Guide and Bibliography*, 193 p., Feminist Press, Old Westbury, NY, 1985.

The first section describes two practical projects designed to move women's studies into higher education curricula, one at Montana State University and one known as the Northern Rockies Program on Women in the Curriculum. There is a directory of other projects too. This is followed by a bibliography and resource list which includes a lot of useful North American classroom material, course guides, course revision models, lists of periodicals, bibliographies and publishers, and a directory of programmes, consultants and organizations. It is disconcerting that two books with identical titles were published within a year of each other (the other being Franzosa and Mazza, no. 178).

See also:

CRUIKSHANK, Margaret, *Lesbian Studies Present and Future.* (no. 767)

DULEY, Margot and Mary EDWARDS, *The Cross-Cultural Study of Women: A Comprehensive Guide.* (no. 191)

ELWELL, Ellen Sue Levi and Edward R. LEVENSON, *The Jewish Women's Studies Guide.* (no. 1010)

HULL, Gloria T., Patricia Bell SCOTT and Barbara SMITH, *But Some of Us Are Brave: Black Women's Studies.* (no. 634)

LEHMANN, Stephen and Eva SARTORI, *Women's Studies in Western Europe: A Resource Guide.* (no. 13)

NORDIC ASSOCIATION FOR FEMINIST RESEARCH, *Women's Studies and Research on Women in the Nordic Countries.* (no. 370)

RICHTER, Werner, Liisa HUSU and Arnaud MARKS, *The Changing Role of Women in Society: A Documentation of Current Research: Research Projects in Progress 1984–1987.* (no. 361a)

An essential companion for anyone starting research in women's studies is:

SEARING, Susan E., *Introduction to Library Research in Women's Studies.* (no. 14)

This book provides an introductory overview of reference materials, and is a guide to library use.

PERIODICALS

184. *Australian Women's Studies Newsletter*, 3/yr, c/o Dr Robyn Rowland, School of Humanities, Deakin University, Geelong, Victoria 3217, Australia.

Contains news of all women's studies activities in Australian universities and colleges.

185. *NWSAction*, 4/yr, NWSA, University of Maryland, College Park, MD 20742-1325, 1988 - .

Newsletter of the National Women's Studies Association.

See also:

Chronique Féministe. (no. 374)

Etudes Féministes. (no. 404)

Fraueninformationsblatt. (no. 419)

Women's Research Network News. (no. 84)

ORGANIZATIONS

186. CANADIAN WOMEN'S STUDIES ASSOCIATION, Dept of Sociology, University of Winnipeg, Winnipeg, Manitoba R3B 2E9, Canada.

Network of women's studies scholars in Canada.

187. NATIONAL WOMEN'S STUDIES ASSOCIATION, University of Maryland, College Park, MD 20742-1325.

The network organization for women's studies in the US. It promotes feminist education through national and regional conferences, educational programmes, awards, etc. It has caucuses for different sub-groups. Publishes news of its activities in *NWSAction* (no. 185) and also a quarterly journal of feminist scholarship *NWSA Journal* (no. 58)

188. WOMEN'S STUDIES ASSOCIATION (NZ), PO Box 5067, Auckland 1, New Zealand.

Network for women scholars in New Zealand.

189.   WOMEN'S STUDIES ASSOCIATION OF IRELAND, Centre for Women's Studies, NIHE, Plessey, Limerick, Ireland.

A network for people involved in women's studies to further research and to disseminate information. Publishes an annual *Women's Studies Review* (no. 69) and sends out a quarterly newsletter to members.

190.   WOMEN'S STUDIES NETWORK (UK), c/o Women's Research and Resources Centre, Sheffield Polytechnic, 36 Collegiate Crescent, Sheffield S10 2BI.

Publishes a twice-yearly newsletter. Organizes conferences, workshops, etc.

See also:

NATIONAL COUNCIL FOR RESEARCH ON WOMEN (NCRW). (no. 512)

NATIONAL WOMEN'S EDUCATION CENTRE. (no. 324)

NORDIC ASSOCIATION FOR FEMINIST RESEARCH. (no. 369)

RESEARCH CENTRE FOR WOMEN'S STUDIES. (no. 326)

PART II

WOMEN IN THE WORLD

CHAPTER 4

International perspectives on women

In this part of the book we attempt to provide access to information on women's studies with an international perspective, and to what is happening in regions and countries across the world. It became apparent very early on that our original aim, which was to try to redress the anglocentric bias of the works we had come across, was a hopeless one. Without the resources to travel extensively we have had to rely on secondary sources available to us in Britain. Ironically, it proved easier to find out about activity in the continents of Asia, Africa and Latin America than in next-door Europe, and we were constantly frustrated by the non-availability in British libraries of sources which would have enabled us to dig deeper into the resources of other countries.

So what we have in this part is a rather incomplete and uneven survey of resources in women's studies across the world. Certain regions – notably Eastern Europe – are almost undocumented, while others are covered inconsistently, because, for example, while information was easily available for Scandinavian countries, it was absent for Portugal.

We must emphasize that the inconsistency reflects what has been published and to a large extent what is available for the researcher in Britain and America. We hope that the sources cited in the following chapters may give the researcher an entry into the areas she is interested in, and a base from which to start.

CROSS-CULTURAL APPROACHES

Bibliographies

191. DULEY, Margot and Mary EDWARDS, *The Cross-Cultural Study of Women: A Comprehensive Guide*, 439 p., Feminist Press, New York, 1986.

An excellent curriculum guide to 'research and issues in the cross-cultural study of women'. It is organized as a series of lecture outlines on topics within a broader subject, and supported by bibliographies. The bibliographies themselves distinguish between reading for students and for instructors, and there are also guides to reference sources. The book is in two sections: the first is on Theoretical perspectives (covering Biology and culture, Male dominance, Women, colonialism and development, Gender stratification and Women and religion). The second part is devoted to area studies. This is a carefully and clearly organized work. It is surprising that there is no index.

192.　JACOBS, Sue-Ellen, *Women in Perspective: A Guide for Cross-Cultural Studies*, 299 p., University of Illinois Press, Urbana, IL, 1974.

An extensive listing of some 3500 unannotated items, selected from an initial anthropological standpoint, although the selection goes far wider than that might suggest. The items are arranged in two sections: Part 1 consists of Geographical perspectives (a division by region and country), and Part 2 of Subject studies. Compiled in the early seventies this now shows its age, and its eclecticism has limited usefulness at a time of increasing specialization in the field.

193.　TIFFANY, Sharon W., 'Women in cross-cultural perspective: a guide to recent anthropological literature', *Women's Studies International Forum*, vol. 5, no. 5, pp. 497–502, 1982.

A 'short working guide' to recent anthropological literature on cross-cultural studies, mostly published between 1974 and 1981, and therefore updating Jacobs (no. 192). The bibliography is divided into general material and then by region. Not annotated.

194.　UNESCO, *Bibliographic Guide to Studies on the Status of Women: Development and Population Trends*, 292 p., Bowker, Epping, 1983. (Published in US by UNIPUB, New York.)

This book is really a collection of bibliographies covering different areas of the world, preceded by a general introductory section on labour force participation, education and demographic features. Each bibliography follows a standard format. Particularly useful in that it includes material on the under-documented region of eastern Europe, and thereby gives a world view.

Reference works

There are several important works providing data on women across the world:

BOULDING, Elise *et al.*, *Handbook of International Data on Women*. (no. 139)

CURTIN, Leslie, *Status of Women: A Comparative Analysis of Twenty Developing Countries*. (no. 234)

INTERNATIONAL LABOUR ORGANIZATION/INSTRAW, *Women in Economic Activity: A Global Statistical Survey (1950–2000)*. (no. 141)

SHREIR, Sally, *Women's Movements of the World.* (no. 132)

SIVARD, Ruth Leger, *Women: A World Survey.* (no. 144)

SEAGER, Joni and Ann OLSON, *Women in the World: An International Atlas.* (no. 143)

Women of the world, US Dept of Commerce, Bureau of the Census. (no. 146)

Periodicals

We have listed here periodicals which address themselves to international issues with a global perspective. Periodicals with a regional focus are found in the chapters on those regions.

195.   *Connexions: an international women's quarterly*, 4/yr, 4228 Telegraph Ave., Oakland, CA 94609, 1981–.

An interesting and unusual magazine, which publishes articles and creative writing selected from feminist periodicals from all over the world. The articles are translated if the language of origin is not English, and are arranged by country of origin. An international list of resources is included.

Crew Reports. (no. 364)

196.   *International Women's News/Nouvelles Feministes Internationales*, 4/yr, International Alliance of Women, PO Box 355, Valletta, Malta, 1904–.

Newsletter of the IAW, bilingual (English and French). News of the organization and articles of international interest.

ISIS INTERNATIONAL WOMEN'S DATA BASE. (no. 150)

197.   *Isis International Women's Journal*, 2/yr, Isis International, Via San Saba 5, 00153 Rome, Italy, 1984–86.

Originally published with *Women in Action* (no. 205) as its supplement, this is now superseded by *Isis International Book Series*, which provides two books a year in conjunction with a subscription to *Women in Action*.

Sisterlinks. (no. 868)

Third Woman. (no. 523)

198.   *Third World Women's Review*, Third World Communications, Kwame Nkrumah House, 173 Old St, London EC1V 9NJ, 1986–.

Magazine with articles and news on every aspect of Third World women, with a political focus.

199.   *Tribune (The): A Women and Development Quarterly*, 4/yr, International Women's Tribune Centre, 305 East 46th St, 6th Floor, New York, NY 10017, 1976–.

Full of international news, with a global coverage, and a grassroots approach. Less comprehensive than *WIN News*, but no doubt complementary. Organizations, campaigns, resources, etc.

200. *WID Bulletin*, Women in International Development, 202 International Center, Michigan State University, East Lansing, MI 48824.

Resource guide containing information about scholarships, conferences, employment opportunities, etc.

201. *WID Forum*, Women in International Development, 202 International Center, Michigan State University, East Lansing, MI 48824.

Short reports describing research projects and development programmes, and reviewing current policy issues.

202. *WIN News*, 4/yr, Women's International Network, 187 Grant St, Lexington, MA 02173, 1975–.

An excellent journal, packed with news and information from all over the world – a truly international coverage. Reports are culled from newspapers and periodicals, official and unofficial reports, oganizations and individuals, and are arranged under various headings, such as Women and the United Nations, Female circumcision, Women and health, etc. There are also sections for reports from different regions, and a clearinghouse for women and international affairs. This is a remarkable and energetic enterprise, a mine of information about organizations and goings on throughout the world, and of national and international campaigns (in particular against genital mutilation).

203. *Wiser Links*, irreg., WIRC, 173 Archway Rd, London N6 5BL, 1983–.

News of international interest across the world, with an emphasis on the Third World.

204. *Women and International Development Annual*, Annual, Westview Press, London, February 1989–.

'This series, published in cooperation with the Women in International Development Program at Michigan State University, uses a multidisciplinary approach to explore women's experiences across a wide range of geographical areas, economic sectors, and societal institutions. The articles . . . synthesize a growing volume of literature on key issues, suggest priorities for research, and propose changes in development policy and programming.' (From publisher's announcement.)

205. *Women in Action*, 4/yr, Isis International, Via San Saba 5, 00153 Rome, Italy, 1984–.

Started as a supplement to *Isis International Women's Journal* (ceased publication), both continuations of *Isis Women's International Bulletin*. *Women in Action* contains news of activities throughout the world. Subscription includes *Isis International Book Series* providing two titles a year.

Women in Europe. (no. 365)

206.   *Women News*, 8/yr, UN Division for the Advancement of Women, Vienna International Centre, PO Box 500, 1400 Vienna, Austria, 1986–.
Newsletter to promote the goals of the UN Decade for Women, with news of UN activities.

Women of Europe. (no. 361)

207.   *Women of the Whole World*, 4/yr, Unter den Linden 13, Berlin 1080, GDR, 1951–.
Journal of the Women's International Democratic Federation, a magazine containing articles, reports, interviews, etc., Eastern bloc viewpoint. Published in six languages.

208.   *Women 2000*, 3/yr, Branch for the Advancement of Women, UN Centre for Social Development and Humanitarian Affairs, Vienna International Centre, PO Box 500, 1400 Vienna, Austria, 1986–.
Newsletter published to promote the goals of the Nairobi Forward-Looking Strategies for the Advancement of Women. Contains news of UN activities.

209.   *Women's Watch (The)*, 4/yr, Women's Rights Action Watch, Humphrey Institute of Public Affairs, University of Minnesota, 309 19th Ave S, Minneapolis, MN 55455.
Reports law and policy changes affecting the status of women worldwide. Includes news stories concerning women appearing in the major media of many countries.

210.   *Women's World*, 4/yr Isis–WICCE, PO Box 2471, 1211 Geneva 2, Switzerland, 1983–.
Magazine full of news of Isis–WICCE activities, and campaigns, organizations, development programmes, resources and publications worldwide.

211.   *Working Papers in International Development*, Women in International Development, 202 International Center, Michigan State University, East Lansing, MI 48824.
Journal-length articles based on original research, theoretical analysis and evaluations of development programming and policy.

INTERNATIONAL ORGANIZATIONS

There is a vast range of international organizations concerned with women, and it has not been possible for us to include more than the tip of the iceberg. We have chosen to list here those which have a worldwide or regional focus, and which are concerned with women's rights and development. For the most part we have omitted official agencies. Organizations for a particular region will be found in the appropriate chapter, but some are included in this list. Ones concerned with specific subjects are under that subject.

We have deliberately excluded women's organizations in most individual countries, having rapidly realized that this would be an impossible task. Anybody conducting research on or in a particular country will find the names and addresses of organizations in many of the works listed below. The networking organizations described in this section also provide information on groups in different countries.

Information sources

The most comprehensive guide is undoubtedly the wonderful:

SHREIR, Sally, *Women's Movements of the World*. (no. 132)

This lists the principal organizations, official and unofficial, under each country, and also has a descriptive list of international organizations. It is the only source we know of covering all the countries of the world. Other valuable sources are listed below:

COMMISSION OF THE EUROPEAN COMMUNITIES, *Women and Development*. (no. 236)

FENTON, Thomas P. and Mary J. HEFFRON, *Women in the Third World: A Directory of Resources*. (no. 237)

ISIS INTERNATIONAL, *Powerful Images: A Women's Guide to Audiovisual Resources*. (no. 147)

WIN News. (no. 202)

Women's World. (no. 210)

List of international organizations

AFRICAN TRAINING AND RESEARCH CENTRE FOR WOMEN (ATRCW). (no. 273)

AFRICAN WOMEN LINK. (no. 274)

ARAB WOMEN'S SOLIDARITY ASSOCIATION. (no. 489)

212.   ASSOCIATED COUNTRY WOMEN OF THE WORLD, 50 Warwick Square, London SW1V 2AJ.

An old-established (1930) organization with a large membership throughout the world, working for development and training of women.

Works closely with UN. Publishes *The Countrywoman*, a bi-monthly newsletter.

ASIAN AND PACIFIC CENTRE FOR WOMEN AND DEVELOPMENT (APCWD). (no. 318)

ASSOCIATION OF AFRICAN WOMEN FOR RESEARCH AND DEVELOPMENT (AAWORD). (no. 275)

CENTRE FOR RESEARCH ON EUROPEAN WOMEN (CREW). (no. 366)

213. CHANGE, PO Box 824, London SE24 9JS.

Provides research and consultancy services on the condition and status of women all over the world. Publishes *Change International Reports*, a series each of which relates to a particular country, resource packs, handbooks, etc.

214. COMMONWEALTH SECRETARIAT: WOMEN AND DEVELOPMENT PROGRAMME, Marlborough House, Pall Mall, London SW1Y 5HX.

To advance the interests of women through research, training and educational programmes.

DAWN: Development Alternatives with Women for a New Era. (no. 466)

EUROPEAN NETWORK OF WOMEN (ENOW). (no. 367)

INSTITUTE FOR WOMEN'S STUDIES IN THE ARAB WORLD. (no. 490)

215. INTERNATIONAL ALLIANCE OF WOMEN, President's Office, PO Box 355, Valletta, Malta.

Originated as the Woman Suffrage Alliance in 1904. Has affiliated organizations all over the world, and works for equal rights status of women. Organizes workshops and seminars. Publishes *International Women's News* (no. 196) in English and French editions.

INTERNATIONAL ASSOCIATION FOR THE ADVANCEMENT OF WOMEN IN AFRICA. (no. 277)

INTERNATIONAL BLACK WOMEN'S CONGRESS (IBWC). (no. 651)

216. INTERNATIONAL CENTER FOR RESEARCH ON WOMEN, 1717 Massachusetts Ave. NW, Suite 501, Washington, DC 20036.

Aims to improve the productivity and incomes of poor women in developing countries by providing technical services, conducting policy research, and running educational programmes to improve understanding in the US. Publishes reports on development in the USA and abroad.

INTERNATIONAL COUNCIL OF AFRICAN WOMEN. (no. 652)

217. INTERNATIONAL FEMINIST NETWORK, Isis International, Via San Saba 5, 00153 Rome, Italy.

Organization for mobilizing support to fight cases of the violation of women's rights. Coordinated by Isis-WICCE and Isis International.

218. INTERNATIONAL RESEARCH AND TRAINING INSTITUTE FOR THE ADVANCEMENT OF WOMEN (INSTRAW), PO Box 21747, Santo Domingo, D.N., Dominican Republic.

Autonomous body within the UN. Set up to assist in the promotion of women's development by research, training and the gathering and exchange of information. Organizes seminars and research projects. Publishes *INSTRAW News*, reports, pamphlets, etc.

219. INTERNATIONAL WOMEN'S RIGHTS ACTION WATCH (IWRAW), Humphrey Institute, University of Minnesota, Minneapolis, MN 55455.

Supports research and publication on law and policy reforms worldwide in accordance with the principles of the Convention on the Elimination of All Forms of Discrimination Against Women. Publishes *The Women's Watch* (no. 209).

220. INTERNATIONAL WOMEN'S TRIBUNE CENTER, 777 United Nations Plaza, New York 10017.

A worldwide communications network set up following International Women's Year in 1976. It links individuals and groups over the world, organizes workshops and provides technical assistance. Publications include resource packs, newsletters, reports, and *The Tribune* (no. 199).

221. ISIS INTERNATIONAL, Via San Saba 5, 00153 Rome, Italy; Casilla 2067, Correo Central, Santiago, Chile.

Worldwide information and communication service with offices in Italy and Chile. Operates resource centres, runs the International Feminist Network, and the Latin American and Caribbean Women's Health Network. Publishes *Women in Action* (no. 205), resource guides, etc.

222. ISIS WOMEN'S INTERNATIONAL CROSS-CULTURAL EXCHANGE (ISIS–WICCE), PO Box 2471, 1211 Geneva 2, Switzerland.

Formed in 1983, when the original Isis split into two organizations. It runs an international resource centre in Geneva, organizes its activities around a special theme each year. Publishes *Women's World* (no. 210), (French version as *Monde des Femmes*), reports, resource lists etc. Extensive networking activities throughout the world. Organizes (with Isis International) the International Feminist Network (no. 217).

KEGME: Mediterranean Women's Studies Institute. (no. 425)

PACIFIC AND ASIAN WOMEN'S FORUM. (no. 325)

REGIONAL INFORMATION NETWORK ON ARAB WOMEN (RINAW). (no. 491)

223. RESEAU FEMMES ET DEVELOPPEMENT, 15–21 rue de l'Ecole de Médecine, 75005 Paris, France.

Network for women and development organizations in France and the Third World. Publishes a quarterly *Bulletin de Liaison*.

THIRD WORLD MOVEMENT AGAINST THE EXPLOITATION OF WOMEN (TW-MAE-W). (no. 327)

224. THIRD WORLD WOMEN'S NETWORK, PO Box 6648, Washington, DC 20009.

Founded in 1986 to 'expand and facilitate communication among Third World women . . . and promote participation of Third World women in . . . development strategies'.

225. WOMANKIND, 122 Whitechapel High St, London E1 7PT.

A development agency founded in 1988, dedicated to financing and supporting women's initiatives in the Third World by providing grants for pilot projects and fund raising. Links women's groups in Britain and overseas.

226. WOMEN AND DEVELOPMENT PROGRAM, Institute of Social Studies, 251 Badiusweg, Box 90733, 2597 JR The Hague, Netherlands.

Research and teaching institution, publishing reports and bibliographies.

227. WOMEN IN INTERNATIONAL DEVELOPMENT (WID), 202 International Center, Michigan State University, East Lansing, MI 48824.

Aims to disseminate the rapidly growing body of work that addresses the lives of women in Third World countries undergoing change. Publishes *WID Forum* (no. 201), *WID Bulletin* (no. 200) and *Working Papers on Women in International Development* (no. 211).

228. WOMEN OF THE WORLD/FRAUEN DER WELT, Warendorferstr. 6, 5000 Cologne 91, W. Germany.

Subtitled 'Office for Intercultural Education and Encounter'. Tackles women's questions in the framework of international cooperation, mainly between Germany and the Third World, but also other European countries and non-European minorities in Germany. Planning a biannual magazine for 1992 called *Women International*.

WOMEN'S GLOBAL NETWORK ON REPRODUCTIVE RIGHTS. (no. 902)

229. WOMEN'S INTERNATIONAL DEMOCRATIC FEDERA-TION, Unter den Linden 13, 1080 Berlin, GDR.

The main Eastern bloc international women's federation, uniting women's organizations in Eastern Europe and the Third World. Publishes *Women of the Whole World* (no. 207) in six languages.

230. WOMEN'S INTERNATIONAL NETWORK (WIN), 187 Grant St, Lexington, MA 02173.

A communication network of women throughout the world, supporting equality and development everywhere. Campaigns include the eradication of female circumcision. Publishes *WIN News* (no. 202).

231. WOMEN'S INTERNATIONAL RESOURCE CENTRE, 173 Archway Rd, London N6 5BL.

Networking and resource centre, with links to women's groups worldwide. Organizes workshops. Publishes a bi-monthly newsletter *Wiser Links* (no. 203) and an annual report.

232. WOMEN'S INTERNATIONAL RESOURCE EXCHANGE (WIRE), 475 Riverside Drive, Room 570, New York, NY 10115.

'A clearinghouse and distribution center for the evaluation and dissemina-tion of materials on women in the Third World and Third World women in the US.' Conducts workshops and seminars, etc.

233. WORLD FEMINIST COMMISSION, 18261 Hamilton Rd, Detroit, MI 48203/11; Ave. des Scarabées, 1050 Brussels, Belgium.

Set up in 1974 as an international network of communication. Plans inter-national action focused on the UN and UNESCO. Aims to set up an International Women's Party. Coordinators in Belgium and Japan.

THIRD WORLD

Reference works

234. CURTIN, Leslie, *Status of Women: A Comparative Analysis of Twenty Developing Countries*, 60 p., Population Reference Bureau, Washington, DC, 1982.

Based on World Fertility Survey data, the work covers twelve Asian and Pacific and eight Latin American countries. The statistical data is presented in figures and tables with lengthy explanation, and covers educational attainment and employment patterns. The countries covered are: Mexico, Costa Rica, Panama, Colombia, Peru, Dominican Repub-lic, Jamaica, Guyana, Turkey, Jordan, Pakistan, Nepal, Bangladesh, Sri

Lanka, Malaysia, Thailand, Indonesia, Philippines and Republic of Korea.

235. UNITED NATIONS, Dept of International Economic and Social Affairs, Statistical Office, *World Survey on the Role of Women in Development*, 238 p., UN, New York, 1986.

The report of a statistical survey analysing 'the role of women in relation to key developmental issues . . . focusing in particular on trade, agriculture, industry, energy, money and finance, and science and technology'. In addition, there is material on women's contribution to economic development trends by participation in the labour force, the benefits accruing to women from development, and the concept of self-reliance and the integration of women into development.

See also the works listed under Cross-cultural approaches above in this chapter.

Resources

236. COMMISSION OF THE EUROPEAN COMMUNITIES, *Women and Development* (Women of Europe, Supplement no. 17), 118 p., Commission of the European Communities, Brussels, 1984.

This informative publication contains mainly material on European Community activity in Third World development as it relates to women. It includes particularly useful descriptions of the UN agencies involved in women's development, and also of official organizations in EC countries and of non-governmental organizations throughout the world. This is followed by an annotated bibliography, now inevitably somewhat out of date but still useful for background.

237. FENTON, Thomas P. and Mary J. HEFFRON, *Women in the Third World: A Directory of Resources*, 141 p., Orbis Books, Maryknoll, NY, 1987.

A very useful and comprehensive guide to organizations and information on Third World women, including publications and audiovisual resources. Most entries have good annotations and there are indexes to names, titles, subjects and geographical area. Addresses are included for every entry. This should be a constant companion for anyone doing research in this field.

238. INTERNATIONAL RESEARCH AND TRAINING INSTITUTE FOR THE ADVANCEMENT OF WOMEN (INSTRAW), *Training for Women: An Inventory of United Nations Sponsored Activities*, 125 p., United Nations, INSTRAW, New York, 1980.

This was produced after the setting up of INSTRAW in 1979 in order to monitor research and training activities of women, and contains details of training projects set up under the UN. These are analysed by agency, by type of project, by category and by region, and listed in detail under the four subject headings of employment, health, education and multifaceted activities.

239. ISIS INTERNATIONAL, *Women in Development: A Resource Guide for Organization and Action*, 226 p., Isis International, Rome, 1983.

Particularly valuable because it comes from within the women's movement and reviews literature, institutions and programmes from a feminist standpoint, 'selecting those resources we feel are really relevant to women'. Concentrates on 'multinationals, rural development and food production, including appropriate technology and income, generation, health, migration and tourism education and communication'. Each chapter consists of an overview, followed by a list of resources.

240. MAY, Nicky, *No Short Cuts: A Starter Resource and Handbook for Fieldworkers with Women's Groups* (Change Actbook 1), 56 p., Change, PO Box 824, London SE24 9JX, 1986.

'Designed to give ideas to start discussion and resources to follow them up.' The first three sections (How can a field worker support women's groups?, Women's group organization, Women's group activities) are followed by a section on resources, giving brief bibliographies, lists of funding bodies, organizations, contact people, etc.

STAFFORD, Beth, 'Best reference works for the study of minority and Third World women'. (no. 513)

Bibliographies

The majority of bibliographies on women in the Third World deal with issues of development. some of the broader-based bibliographies mentioned above under Cross-cultural approaches are also useful, notably Duley and Edwards (no. 191) and the UNESCO study (no. 194). Much of the material on development aims at a comprehensive coverage. Other works are designed for producing a source of reference for people working with development agencies or with grassroots organizations, in particular Townsend (no. 254), who has as her brief 'high practical application' and is critical of what she calls the 'ghettoisation of information' which makes much material inaccessible to women in the field. Many works listed in these bibliographies are unobtainable without writing to the organizations which produced them.

Many of the bibliographies on particular countries are designed specifically for fieldworkers and contain largely locally obtainable material (e.g. the ATRCW bibliographies on Africa).

ALAUDDIN, Talat K., *Status of Women and Socio-economic Development: A Selected and Annotated Bibliography*. (no 349)

241.   BAAS, Ettie, *Women in Development: A Bibliography*, 111 p., Institute of Social Studies, The Hague, 5th updated ed., 1980.

This partially annotated bibliography is drawn from holdings at the ISS Library, and is concerned with the 'social, economic, political and cultural situation of Third World women'. The references are divided into broad subjects such as Employment, Labour, Fertility, Family planning, etc.

242.   BUVINIC, Mayra *et al.*, *Women and World Development: An Annotated Bibliography*, 162 p., Overseas Development Council, Washington, DC, 1976.

An annotated bibliography of about 400 items arranged by subject. It also includes appendices of special issues of periodicals, and bibliographies

243.   BYRNE, Pamela R. and Suzanne R. ONTIVEROS, *Women in the Third World: A Historical Bibliography*, 152 p., ABC-Clio, Santa Barbara, CA, 1986.

Contains 600 abstracts of works published between 1970–1985, selected from ABC-Clio's history database. In broad geographical groups: Africa, Middle East, Asia, Pacific, Latin America and West Indies, and within that alphabetically by author. The distinguishing thing about this compilation is the complexity of its subject index, based on the main words of the abstract, giving multiple entries for each item. There is also an author index. A list of periodicals included would have been useful.

244.   CEBOTAREV, E.A. *et al.*, 'Annotated bibliography on women in agriculture and rural societies', *RFR/DRF Resources for Feminist Research*, vol. 11, no. 1, pp. 93–180, 1982.

An extensive bibliography, divided into Canada, Developing countries (subdivided by region), Bibliographies, Manuals, and Organizations & periodicals. The entries are either given annotations or references to a previous review or abstract in *RFR/DRF*.

245.   DANFORTH, Sandra C., *Women and National Development*, 35 p., Vance Bibliographies, Monticello, IL, 1982.

DESTA, Alem, *Women in Development: An Annotated Bibliography of Women and Development in Africa*. (no. 260).

246.   EPSKAMP, C., *Inequality in Female Access to Education in Developing Countries*, 42 p., Centre for the Study of Education in Developing Countries, The Hague, 1979.

About 400 unannotated references, mostly from the 1970s.

247.   'Femmes migrantes, 1982: Bibliographie internationale (1965–1982)', *Studie Emigrazione*, pp. 449–514, Rome, 1982.

248.   GILL, Dhara S., *A Bibliography on Effectiveness of Agricultural Extension Services in Reaching Rural Women in Developing Countries*, 14 p., Vance Bibliographies, Monticello, IL, 1988.

HAFKIN, Nancy J., *Women and Development in Africa: An Annotated Bibliography*. (no. 263).

249.   MWANOSIKE, E.O., *Third World Women and Rural Development: A Select Annotated Bibliography*, Institut Panafricain pour le Développement, Douala, 1984.

NELSON, Nici, *Why Has Development Neglected Rural Women? A Review of the South Asian Literature*. (no. 329).

250.   OFFICE OF WOMEN IN INTERNATIONAL DEVELOPMENT, *Women and International Development: Multidisciplinary Guide*, Office of Women in International Development, University of Illinois at Urbana-Champaign, Urbana, IL, 1985.

PAN AMERICAN HEALTH ORGANIZATION, *Women, Health and Development in the Americas: An Annotated Bibliography*. (no. 864).

251.   RADCLIFFE, Sarah, A., *Gender in the Third World: A Geographical Bibliography of Recent Work* (IDS Development Bibliography series, no. 2), 90 p., Institute of Development Studies, University of Sussex, Brighton, 1988.

An unannotated bibliography divided by region, and within in each region by topic (e.g. agricultural production, migration, policy and development, etc.). There is also a list of organizations with interests in women in developing areas. It is a pity that some of the entries are inaccurate, making them difficult to trace.

252.   RIHANI, May and Jody JOY, *Development as if Women Mattered: An Annotated Bibliography with a Third World Focus*, 143 p., Overseas Development Council, Washington, DC, 1978. (Prepared under the auspices of the Secretariat for Women in Development of the New TransCentury Foundation.)

For this bibliography 287 works, including many reports and unpublished material, have been annotated and evaluated. Arranged by subject, with an author index; includes mainly material from 1976 and 1977. Within subject areas material is arranged geographically, and there are extensive cross references.

253.   SAULNIERS, Suzanne Smith and Cathy A. RAKOWSI, *Women in the Development Process: A Select Bibliography on Women in Sub-Saharan Africa and Latin America*, 287 p., University of Texas, Austin, TX, 1977.

A large bibliography of nearly 3000 unannotated references compiled from English, French, Portuguese and Spanish sources published between 1900 and 1975. The appendices list the sources, many of the periodicals cited and many special issues of journals. The work is arranged by subject and within that by geographical area. There is no index.

254.   TOWNSEND, Janet, *Women in Developing Countries: A Select Annotated Bibliography for Development Organizations* (IDS Development Bibliography Series no. 1), 189 p., Institute of Development Studies, University of Sussex, Brighton, 1988.

This is a first-class bibliography of 524 items selected to be of 'high practical application, accessible in the UK, recent and in English'. It 'seeks to give workers in development organizations access to the items of immediate relevance to their work'. Organized by country and grouped by continent, the entries are concisely annotated, and are given a star rating to indicate their importance (essential, useful or wider background reading). Holdings of the IDS Library are indicated. There are subject and author indexes.

255.   WHITE, Karen, *Women in Development: An Annotated Bibliography for the World Bank*, International Center for Research on Women, Washington, DC, 1985.

'An excellent list of material (effectively available in Washington) with informative annotations.' (From Townsend (no. 254).)

Periodicals and organizations

These are included in the sections on Periodicals (no. 195–211) and International organizations (no. 273–233) earlier in this chapter.

CHAPTER 5

Africa

GENERAL BIBLIOGRAPHIES

256. AFRICAN TRAINING AND RESEARCH CENTRE FOR WOMEN, 'Women and development in Africa: an annotated bibliography', *Women's Studies International*, no. 3, pp. 32–34, 1984.

A list of ATRCW publications, with descriptions of each.

BERRIAN, Brenda, *Bibliography of African Women Writers and Journalists: Ancient Egypt - 1984*. (no. 809)

257. BULLWINKLE, Davis A., 'Women and their role in African society: the literature of the seventies', *Current Bibliography of African Affairs*, vol. 15, no. 4, pp. 263–291, 1982/3.

A single alphabetical list of about 450 references preceded by an explanatory article.

258. BULLWINKLE, Davis A., *African Women: A General Bibliography, 1976–1985*, 355 p., Greenwood, London, 1989.

'The roles and needs of African women have been largely neglected in Third World policy-making by governments and international organisations, despite the existence of recent research providing the basis and justification for new policies. This work, the first volume of a three-part bibliography, makes that research available to researchers and policy-makers.' (From publisher's announcement.)

259. DE LEY, Margo, *Women in French-speaking Africa: An Annotated Bibliography of French-language Materials* (Curriculum Guide no. 9), 24 p., Women and International Development, University of Illinois at Urbana-Champaign, Champaign, IL, 1985.

'Very useful teaching review; invaluable on French-speaking Africa.' (From Townsend (no. 254).)

260. DESTA, Alem, *Women in Development: An Annotated Bibliography of Women and Development in Africa*, 101 p., Institute of Social Studies, The Hague, 1983.

A useful bibliography, with a specifically feminist focus, based on material in English available in the Netherlands. The works are arranged under general studies, socio-cultural factors, rural development and urban development.

261. GEBHARDT, Marion and Heike ZANZIG, *Die Rolle der Frau in Afrika: Nachträge zur Auswahlbibliographie*, 81 p., Deutsches Übersee-Institut, Hamburg, 1987.

See entry under Zanzig (no. 265)

262. GIORGIS, Belkis Wolde, *A Selected and Annotated Bibliography on Women and Health in Africa* (AAWORD Bibliographic Series, no. 1), 98 p., Association of African Women for Research and Development, [Dakar, Senegal], 1986.

'The purpose of this bibliography is to draw together some relevant resource materials relating to women's health issues in Africa; to provide a brief critique by analysing the methodological and conceptual orientation of the existing literature; and to suggest alternative methodologies . . .' The bibliography is divided by subject (e.g. nutrition, mental health, female circumcision, etc.), with an introductory Critique of the literature.

263. HAFKIN, Nancy J., *Women and Development in Africa: An Annotated Bibliography* (ATRCW Bibliography Series, no. 1), 177 p., UN Economic Commission for Africa, African Training and Research Centre for Women, Addis Ababa, 1977.

The first of the bibliographies produced by the ATRCW, consisting of 568 annotated references, divided into the following sections: General studies, Rural development and women, Population studies, Education and training, Urban development and women, Situation of women, Women's organisations. Many of the references are to UN publications. Within each section the entries are subdivided by country, and there is a country and an author index.

264. KINLEY, Barbara and Yolanda T. MOSES, 'Women and development in Africa: a bibliography', *Sage*, vol. 3, no. 2, pp. 65–69, Fall 1986.

Short bibliography of some 140 titles, arranged under three headings: Women in African Agriculture; Women: agriculture, development, economics and technology, with practice and theory; Women: political and social life.

SAULNIERS, Suzanne Smith and Cathy A. RAKOWSI, *Women in the Development Process: A Select Bibliography on Women in Sub-Saharan Africa and Latin America.* (no. 253)

265. ZANZIG, Heike and Marianne WEISS, *Die Rolle der Frau in Afrika: Auswahlbibliographie/The Role of Women in Africa: A Selected bibliography*, 131 p., Institut für Afrika-Kunde, Dokumentations-Leitstelle Afrika, Hamburg, 1984.

A useful bibliography of over 500 items based on publications currently indexed by the Africa Documentation Centre. The works listed include books, periodical articles, contributions to collective works, and grey literature held in libraries in the Federal Republic of Germany. North African countries are excluded (covered by Otto and Schmidt-Dumont (no. 485). The bibliography covers the period 1970–1983, with some older titles of general interest included. A substantial number of the works are in English, but this does provide useful access to material in other languages. The annotations are in German. There are subject and author indexes, and a list of periodicals indexed. It is supplemented by Gebhardt and Zanzig (no. 261).

Older works

266.   AFRICAN BIBLIOGRAPHIC CENTER, *Contemporary African Women: An Introductory Bibliographical Overview and a Guide to Women's Organizations, 1960–1967*, 59 p., Negro Universities Press, New York, 1968.

Rather old guide to organizations and literature. Of historic interest.

267.   PERLMAN, M. and M.P. MOAL, 'Analytical bibliography'. In: *Women of Tropical Africa*, ed. Pauline Dennis. London, Routledge & Kegan Paul, 1963, pp. 231–299.

An extensive annotated bibliography on women in tropical Africa, of works published before 1960, drawn from world literature.

PERIODICALS

Many of the journals concerned with women and development listed in Chapter 4 (nos 195–211) also contain articles and news on Africa.

268.   *AA WORD Journal*, Association of African Women for Research and Development, BP 3304, Dakar, Senegal.

269.   *African Woman*: quarterly development journal, 4/yr, Akina Mama wa Afrika, London Women's Centre, Wesley House, 4 Wild Court, London WC2B 5AU, 1988–.

A London-based African magazine, with informative articles on development and political issues in Africa.

270.   *Ahfad Journal*, 2/yr, Ahfad University College for Women, PO Box 167, Omdurman, Sudan, 1984–.

English-language journal publishing research reports, historical or critical analyses, literature reviews and book reviews pertaining to the status of women in developing countries, and also news of Ahfad University.

271.   *Echo*, 4/yr, AAWORD, Dakar, Senegal.

Newsletter of AAWORD, with news of its activities, work in progress, etc.

ORGANIZATIONS

The following directory is still of some use, though out of date:

272.   AFRICAN TRAINING AND RESEARCH CENTRE FOR WOMEN, *Directory of African Women's Organizations*, 119 p., UN Economic Commission for Africa, African Training and Research Centre for Women, Addis Ababa, 1978.

Details of women's organizations are given under each country.

More up-to-date information on women's organizations in Africa can be found in the works mentioned in the section on International organizations (nos 212–233), and in the various bibliographies under specific countries in this chapter. We list here only those organizations with an academic or an international perspective.

273.   AFRICAN TRAINING AND RESEARCH CENTRE FOR WOMEN (ATRCW), ECA, PO Box 3001, Addis Ababa, Ethiopia.

Aims to 'promote the advancement of women as vital human resources for development in Africa'. In 1983 placed under the UN Economic Commission for Africa. Publishes *ATRCW Update*, reports and bibliographies.

274.   AFRICAN WOMEN LINK, PO Box 50795, Nairobi, Kenya.

Links individuals, groups, organizations and agencies concerned with development. Publishes a newsletter.

275.   ASSOCIATION OF AFRICAN WOMEN FOR RESEARCH AND DEVELOPMENT (AAWORD), B.P. 3304, Dakar, Senegal.

Undertakes research, creates networks among African women researchers. Organizes seminars. Publishes *Echo* (no. 271), *AAWORD Journal* (no. 268) and occasional papers.

276.   FEDERATION OF AFRICAN MEDIA WOMEN, c/o Zimbabwe Inter-Africa News Agency, PO Box 8166, Causeway, Harare, Zimbabwe.

FOUNDATION FOR WOMEN'S HEALTH RESEARCH AND DEVELOPMENT (FORWARD). (no. 872)

277.   INTERNATIONAL ASSOCIATION FOR THE ADVANCEMENT OF WOMEN IN AFRICA, 6 Ridge St, PO Box 5737, Accra North, Ghana.

Provides education and training in literacy, health care, farming skills, etc.

INTERNATIONAL COUNCIL OF AFRICAN WOMEN. (no. 652)

278. WOMEN'S RESEARCH AND DOCUMENTATION UNIT
(WORDOC), University of Ibadan, Institute of African Studies, Ibadan,
Nigeria.

Established in 1987 to provide a focus for women's studies, to establish a
network with scholars nationally and internationally, and to build a documentation centre for the use of researchers and other interested persons.
Publishes a newsletter.

NORTH AFRICA

Works dealing with Arab women as a whole are to be found in
Chapter 10. The following works specify North Africa:

AL-QAZZAZ, Ayad, *Women in the Middle East and North Africa: An Annotated
Bibliography*. (no. 483)

OTTO, Ingeborg and Marianne SCHMIDT-DUMONT, *Frauenfragen im
modernen Orient: Eine Auswahlbibliographie/Women in the Middle East and North
Africa: A Selected Bibliography*. (no. 485)

SOUTHERN AFRICA

279. DURBAN WOMEN'S BIBLIOGRAPHY GROUP, *Women in
Southern Africa: A Bibliography*, 107 p., Women's Bibliography Group, Dept
of African Studies, University of Natal, Durban, S. Africa, 1985.

'Southern Africa' in this work comprises South Africa, Botswana,
Lesotho, Swaziland and Namibia. Around 1000 entries are arranged by
broad subject headings, such as Love, marriage and divorce, Politics and
resistance, etc. The compilers have tried to include 'as much as we could
find, irrespective of ideological approach'. The works listed are not annotated, and are limited to the English and Afrikaans languages. No index.

AFRICAN COUNTRIES: BIBLIOGRAPHIES

Botswana

See also Southern Africa above.

280. HENDERSON, Francine I., *Women in Botswana: An Annotated
Bibliography*, 20 p., National Institute of Development and Cultural
Research, Documentation Unit, University of Botswana, Gaborone,
Botswana, 1981.

Eighty-six briefly annotatated references to mainly locally available materials.

281. HORN, Nancy and Brenda NKAMBULE-KANYIMA, *Resource Guide: Women in Agriculture: Botswana*, 126 p., Bean/Cowpea Collaborative Research Support Program, East Lansing, MI, 1984. (Available from: Bean/Cowpea CRSP, 200 Center for International Programs, Michigan State University, East Lansing, MI 48824–1035).

The bulk of this consists of a selected annotated bibliography. Other resources include a list of women's organizations as well as material on small farm agriculture and the Botswana project.

282. LEKALAKE, Liyanda, *Women and Development in Botswana: An Annotated Bibliography*, 60 p., Ministry of Home Affairs, Women's Affairs Unit, Gaborone, Botswana, 1985.

Arranged in eleven development categories (such as Agriculture, Legal rights, Migration and urbanisation, etc.) there are 241 references. Many not specifically on women, but all 'touch on the condition of women.' Most are locally published.

Cameroon

283. DACKEY, Michelle, *La Femme Camerounaise et le Développement: Bibliographie*, 70 p., UN Economic Commission for Africa, African Training and Research Centre for Women, Addis Ababa, 1981.

284. FERGUSON, Anne and Nancy HORN, *Resource Guide: Women in Agriculture: Cameroon*, 62 p., Bean/Cowpea Collaborative Research Support Program, East Lansing, MI, 1984. (Available from: Bean/Cowpea CRSP, 200 Center for International Programs, Michigan State University, East Lansing, MI 48824–1035.)

Half of this consists of an annotated bibliography to materials available on women's work in agricultural production, food processing and marketing. The introductory section includes information on women's organizations in Cameroon.

Egypt

285. NETWORK OF EGYPTIAN PROFESSIONAL WOMEN, *Egyptian Women in Social Development: A Resource Guide*, 346 p., American University in Cairo Press, Cairo, 1988.

A directory of 174 Egyptian professional women with contact addresses, educational background, employment experience and activity, affiliation, etc. Incidental to this is a good deal of information on programmes and activity in the field of women's status and development in Egypt.

Ethiopia

286. SELASSIE, Alasebu Gabre, *Women and Development in Ethiopia: An Annotated Bibliography*, 58 p., UN Economic Commission for Africa, African Training and Research Centre for Women, Addis Ababa, 1981. (ATRCW Bibliography).

A bibliography of 169 references, mostly locally published.

Kenya

287. BIFANI, Patricia, *The Impact of Development on Women in Kenya: An Annotated Bibliography*, 38 p., University of Nairobi, Nairobi, 1982. (Part of a 2 vol. work. Published with the assistance of UNICEF.)

This bibliography of sixty-six items with lengthy annotations was written to support the research report (published as vol. 1), and contains general material on women and development as well as specifically on Kenya.

PERIODICALS

288. *Kenya Woman*, National Council of Women, PO Box 4371, Nairobi, Kenya, 1976–.

289. *Viva*, PO Box 46319, Nairobi, Kenya, 1974–.

Lesotho

See also Southern Africa above.

290. LEWIS, S., M. MOLAPO and B. SEXWALE, *Women in Lesotho: An Annotated Bibliography*, Women's Research Collective, National University of Lesotho, 1984.

Mali

291. CAUGHMAN, Susan, *Women and Development in Mali: An Annotated Bibliography* (ATRCW Bibliography Series, no. 6), 34 p., UN Economic Commission for Africa, African Training and Research Centre for Women, Addis Ababa, 1982.

An extensively annotated listing of works on Malian women, much of it locally published.

Morocco

292. MARSHALL, M., *Selected Bibliography of Women in the Arab World with Particular Emphasis on Morocco*, Women and International Development Research & Information Centre, University of Minnesota, Minneapolis, MN, 1984.

Nigeria

293. COBBALD, Elizabeth, 'Muslim Hausa women in Northern Nigeria: an annotated bibliography', *Africa Research and Documentation*, vol. 32, pp. 22–29, 1983.

Thirty-nine annotated references, drawn mainly from academic literature.

294. COLES, Catherine M. and Barbara ENTWISLE, *Nigerian Women in Development: A Research Bibliography*, 170 p., Crossroads Press, Los Angeles, 1986.

An extensive bibliography, unannotated and unindexed, so that the broad headings are the only guide to the contents. There are, however, over 2000 items (many not specifically on women).

295. KISEKKA, Mere Nakteregga, *Women and Development in Nigeria: A Bibliography* (ATRCW Bibliography Series, no. 4), 122 p., UN Economic Commission for Africa, African Training and Research Centre for Women, Addis Ababa, 1981.

A bibliography divided by broad subject, with a sociological rather than an economic emphasis.

ORGANIZATIONS

296. WOMEN IN NIGERIA, PO Box 253, Samaru-Zaria, Nigeria.

Publishes *Women in Nigeria Newsletter*.

South Africa

See Southern Africa above.

Sudan

297. BETHEL, Kathleen E., *Women in the Sudan: A Bibliography of Recent Literature, 1978/1988*, 1988. (Presented at the conference of the Sudan Studies Association, Khartoum.)

Although this is as far as we know an unpublished conference paper, this unannotated bibliography of eighty-five items is included because it is an up-to-date source, and may come out in some publication in the future.

298. WOMEN'S STUDIES DOCUMENTATION UNIT, *Women in Sudan: Annotated Bibliography*, Studies and Research Centre, University of Khartoum, Khartoum, 1980.

Swaziland

See Southern Africa above.

Tanzania

299.   MASCARENHAS, Ophelia and Marjorie MBILINYI, *Women in Tanzania: An Analytical Bibliography*, 256 p., Scandinavian Institute of African Studies/Swedish International Development Authority, Uppsala/Stockholm, 1983. (Update of ATRCW publication of same name, Addis Ababa, 1980. Also published by Holmes & Meier, New York 1983.)

Includes material published up to 1981. Takes the form of review essays on each topic, followed by extensively annotated bibliographic entries. The work is opened by an essay on 'The Woman question' in Tanzania, and closes with a list of resources and an author index.

Zambia

300.   ANTKIEWICZ, Susan and Shimwaayi M. MUNTEMBA, *Women and Development in Zambia: An Annotated Bibliography* (ATRCW Bibliography Series, no. 8), 98 p., UN Economic Commission for Africa, African Training and Research Centre for Women, Addis Ababa, 1983.

Contains 145 items with lengthy annotations.

301.   ZAMBIA ASSOCIATION FOR RESEARCH AND DEVE-LOPMENT, *An Annotated Bibliography of Research on Zambian Women*, 159 p., ZARD, Lusaka, 1985.

Updates the ATRCW bibliography, covering writing from 1979–1985. The work is divided into Education and training opportunities of women, Women's economic contribution, Women's status, Access to factors of production, Women and development, and Miscellaneous (nutrition, health, etc.). The 169 items are extensively annotated.

Zimbabwe

302.   AFRICAN TRAINING AND RESEARCH CENTRE FOR WOMEN, *Women and Development in Zimbabwe: An Annotated Bibliography* (ATRCW Bibliography Series, no. 9), 50 p., UN Economic Commission for Africa, African Training and Research Centre for Women, Addis Ababa, 1984.

Contains 150 annotated entries, divided by subject such as Women in the the press, Women and the law, Education, Health, etc. The bulk of the material listed is published in Zimbabwe. Author index.

CHAPTER 6

Asia and the Pacific

GENERAL BIBLIOGRAPHIES

For other works see the sections on South Asia and South East Asia below.

303. ASIAN AND PACIFIC CENTRE FOR WOMEN AND DEVELOPMENT, *Bibliographies of APCWD Meetings*, 42 p., APCWD, Bangkok, 1980.

Lists thirteen meetings, conferences, workshops, etc. organized by the United Nations APCWD between 1978 and 1980, with bibliographies/reading lists for each meeting on the topic it covers, mainly in the area of development.

304. ECONOMIC AND SOCIAL COMMISSION FOR ASIA AND THE PACIFIC, *Reading Profile on the Status of Women in Asia and the Pacific*, 151 p., UN ESCAP, Bangkok, 1982.

305. THORBURG, Marina, *Identification of Priority Research Issues of Women in Asia and the Pacific: A Report on Research and Research Organizations with Bibliography: Part 2, Bibliography*, 139 p., Swedish Agency for Research Cooperation with Developing Countries (SAREC), Stockholm, 1986.

This contains nearly 2000 items divided by country. Useful, though many of the bibliographic details are somewhat sparse, mkaing the works difficult to trace.

PERIODICALS

Most of these periodicals have an international or regional focus, or are academic journals. We have not included ones with a purely local interests, which can be found in the bibliographies on particular countries or regions.

306. *Asian Woman*, 3/yr, Asian Women's Institute, Association of Kinnaird College for Women, Lahore-3, Pakistan, 1976–.

A magazine with news and articles on status of women in Asia.

307.   *Asian Women Workers Newsletter*, 4/yr, Committee for Asian Women, 57 Pekin Rd, 5/F, Kowloon, Hong Kong.

Reports on the living and working conditions of Asian workers. Useful for resources.

308.   *Committee on South Asian Women Bulletin*, 2/yr, CoSAW, Dept of Psychology, Texas A & M University, College Station, TX 77843, 1982–.

Contains essays, reports, reviews, creative work.

309.   *Diva: A Quarterly Journal of South Asian Women*, 4/yr, 253 College Drive, Unit 194, Toronto, Ontario M5T 1R5, Canada.

Objectives are 'to provide a platform where issues could be discussed to enable women within South Asia to struggle from outside their own countries.

310.   *Journal of Asian Women*, Research Center for Asian Women, Sookmyung Women's University, Seoul, Korea, 1960–.

A scholarly publication in Chinese containing papers of the Research Center for Asian Women on a variety of subjects, mainly sociological but including scientific. There are abstracts in English.

311.   *Manushi: A Journal about Women and Society*, 6/yr, C/202 Lajpat Nagar 1, New Delhi 110024, India, 1979–.

An Indian feminist magazine containing interesting articles on all aspects of women's life in India, correspondence, news, creative writing, reviews. Extensively distributed outside India.

312.   *National Women's Education Centre Newsletter*, 2/yr, Japan, 1983–.

In English, focusing on Japanese women, NWEC activities.

313.   *Samya Shakti: A Journal of Women's Studies*, Irregular, Centre for Women's Development Studies, B-43, Panchsheel Enclave, New Delhi 110 017, 1983–.

This journal publishes research articles on a wide variety of topics, with its main focus on women in India. There are also book reviews and a discussion forum, and reports of meetings and conferences.

314.   *Trinjan: A Women and Development Newsletter*, 12/yr?, PO Box 3328, Main Market, Gulberg-II, Lahore, Pakistan.

Associated with the Simorgh Women's Resource and Publication Centre; gives news of activities in Pakistan and South Asia.

315.   *WINAP Newsletter*, 2/yr, Women in Development Section, Social Development Division, ESCAP, Rajdamnern Ave, Bangkok 10200, Thailand.

Published by UN-ESCAP, carries articles on emerging issues on women in Asia and the Pacific.

316. *Women of China*, 12/yr, China International Book Trading (Distributor), PO Box 399, Beijing, China, 1953–.

An English-language Chinese magazine, apparently widely distributed across the Western and Third World. It is in a women's magazine format with chatty articles and lots of illustrations, but nevertheless contains some interesting information about women in China. It is clearly meant to dispel the stereotypes of Chinese society, and present a modern image of Chinese women.

317. *Womenews*, 4/yr, Women's Studies and Resource Center, c/o GABRIELA, Santos Bldg, 2nd Floor, Gen. Malvar Ext., Davao City, Philippines.

Articles, news, network news, etc., on women's issues.

ORGANIZATIONS

We have not attempted to list the multiplicity of women's organizations in Asia and the Pacific, but only those which concern themselves with regional or international matters, or scholarly research.

318. ASIAN AND PACIFIC CENTRE FOR WOMEN AND DEVELOPMENT (APCWD), c/o APCD, PO Box 2224, Kuala Lumpur, Malaysia.

Aim to encourage research and training in member countries of ESCAP (UN Economic and Social Commission for Asia and the Pacific), and now incorporated into APCD (Asian and Pacific Development Centre).

319. ASIAN WOMEN'S INSTITUTE, c/o Association of Kinnaird College for Women, Lahore-3, Pakistan.

Networking organization, established in 1975, works for equal opportunities and improvement in the status of women in Asia. Publishes *Asian Woman* (no. 306).

320. ASSOCIATION FOR THE ADVANCEMENT OF FEMINISM, Room 1202, Yam Tze Commercial Bldg, 17–23 Thomson Rd, Wanchai, Hong Kong.

Founded in 1984 to promote understanding and concern about problems facing women.

321. COMMITTEE FOR ASIAN WOMEN, CCA-URM, 57 Peking Road, 5/f, Kowloon, Hong Kong.

Especially concerned with the position of women workers in transnational corporations. Publishes *Asian Women Workers Newsletter* (no. 307).

322. COMMITTEE ON WOMEN IN ASIAN COUNTRIES, Association for Asian Studies, University of Minnesota, Minneapolis, MN 55455.

A specialized committee of the Association for Asian Studies, it is concerned with promoting research on women and understanding of gender in Asian countries, and cooperation between women professionals in Asian studies.

323. GABRIELA, Santos Bldg, 2nd Floor, Gen. Malvar Ext., Dalvao City, Philippines.

Affiliation of over 100 women's organizations. GABRIELA stands for General Assembly Binding Women for Reforms, Integrity, Equality, Leadership and Action. Campaigns for women's rights and support systems.

324. NATIONAL WOMEN'S EDUCATION CENTRE. 723 Sugaya, Ranzan-machi, Hiki-gun, Saitama Prefecture 355–02, Japan.

Institution attached to Ministry of Education. Lavishly funded information centre with conference facilities for use by women's groups, national and international. Publishes information about women's studies courses and women's groups in Japan.

325. PACIFIC AND ASIAN WOMEN'S FORUM, 4 Bhagwandas Rd, New Delhi 110001, India.

Informal network of women activists in Asia and the Pacific.

326. RESEARCH CENTRE FOR WOMEN'S STUDIES, SNDT Women's University, Juhu Rd, Santacruz, Bombay 400 054, India.

Founded in 1974 to promote women's studies through research and teaching, collection and dissemination of information, and organization of workshops and seminars.

327. THIRD WORLD MOVEMENT AGAINST THE EXPLOITATION OF WOMEN (TW-MAE-W), PO Box 1434, Manila 2800, Philippines.

To promote intercultural links among women, especially in the Third World.

EAST ASIA

CHUNG, Betty Jamie, *The Status of Women and Fertility in Southeast and East Asia: A Bibliography.* (no. 332)

SOUTH ASIA

328. BLEIE, Tone and Ragnhild LUND, *Gender Relations, the Missing Link in the Development Puzzle: A Selected and Annotated Bibliographic Guide to Theoretical Efforts and South Asian Experience* (DERAP Publication no. 184), 361 p., Chr. Michelsen Institute, Development Research and Action Programme, Bergen, Norway, 1985.

The purpose of this bibliography is 'to give an overview of the more recent theoretical studies within the field of comparative women's studies together with an overview of empirical studies directly related to women targeted aid. The former covers volumes and articles from all regions while the latter is limited to . . . the South Asian region.' There are over 1000 well annotated references, with author and country/region indexes.

329. NELSON, Nici, *Why Has Development Neglected Rural Women? A Review of the South Asian Literature*, 106 p., Pergamon, Oxford, 1979.

A critical review of the literature on rural women, concentrating on South Asia. Bibliography of *c.* 300 references at end. Designed at reflect the paucity of research on rural women.

330. SAKALA, Carol, *Women of South Asia: A Guide to Resources*, 517 p., Kraus International Pubs, Millwood, NY, 1980.

In two parts. Part 1, Published resources, is based on the holdings of the University of Chicago's Regenstein Library, with 4627 references covering general and historical material, and material by region and countries (India, Pakistan, Bangladesh, Sir Lanka and Nepal). All entries are annotated. In Part 2, Libraries, archives and other local resources, each chapter is on a different area, and by different authors, covering India, Pakistan, Bangladesh and the UK. Includes women's organizations. There is an author and subject index.

331. VAID, Jyotsna, Barbara D. MILLER and Janice HYDE, *South Asian Women at Home and Abroad: A Guide to Resources*, 88 p., Committee on Women in Asian Studies of the Association of Asian Studies, Syracuse, NY, 1984.

This useful publication includes a statistical overview of women in South Asia, bibliographic resources, sources on legal status, a list of organizations in both Asia and the West, a list of publishers and distributors, films, and a list of women with relevant research interests in Asia and the West.

SOUTH-EAST ASIA

332. CHUNG, Betty Jamie, *The Status of Women and Fertility in Southeast and East Asia: A Bibliography* (ISEAS Books/Monographs Series, no. 8), 167 p., Institute of Southeast Asian Studies, Singapore, 1977.

Addressing itself specifically to the question of the relationship of the status of women to fertility behaviour, this bibliography of 548 items attempts to be a comprehensive guide to the literature. Most of the entries, which are arranged alphabetically, are annotated, and subject access is provided by a subject index. There is a supplementary list of bibliographies consulted. Could do with being updated.

333.   DUBE, Leela, *Studies on Women In Southeast Asia: A Status Report Prepared for the Division of Human Rights and Peace, Sector for Social Sciences and Their Application*, 77 p., UNESCO, Office of Regional Adviser for Social Sciences in Asia and Oceania, Bangkok, Thailand, 1980.

Introduced by a review of research on women in ASEAN countries occupying half the book, the bibliography consists of an alphabetical list of some 400 works, mainly from the 1970s, many of them reports of official bodies. They are not annotated.

334.   FAN Kok-sim, *Women in Southeast Asia: A Bibliography*, 415 p., G.K. Hall, Boston, 1982.

This massive work of nearly 4000 entries aims at comprehensiveness, although the author admits limitations of language in some cases, and the need for selectivity in certain areas such as family planning, so as not to overwhelm the whole bibliography. The works listed are predominantly in English, Malay and Indonesian. Works in non-Latin alphabets are excluded. The arrangement is by subject, subdivided by country. The entries are not annotated; there is an author index but no detailed subject index. Somewhat indigestible, but a careful work, especially for users with knowledge of Indonesian or Malay. There is a list of Asian serials consulted.

PACIFIC

335.   SIMMONS, Donna Vasiti and Sin Joan YEE, *Women in the South Pacific: A Bibliography*, 124 p., University of the South Pacific Library, Suva, Fiji, 1982.

Attempts a comprehensive listing of materials up to 1982, including books, theses, unpublished papers and articles from both journals and collected works. Entries from a selection of newspapers are included. The entries are arranged in fourteen broad subject areas, each further divided geographically. This is a carefully compiled bibliography of over 100 items. They are not annotated.

ASIAN COUNTRIES: BIBLIOGRAPHIES

Bangladesh

See also the works listed under South Asia above.

336. ISLAM, Mahmuda, *Bibliography on Bangladesh Women with Annotation*, 63 p., Women for Women Research & Study Group, Dacca, n.d.

Contains annotated references divided by subject up to 1978, most of them locally published.

China

337. ALL-CHINA WOMEN'S FEDERATION, *Reference Materials and Statistics on Chinese Women Today*, Beijing, China, 1986.

Although we have been unable to locate this item, taken from a reference in *Women's Studies International Forum*, vol. 11, no. 5, 1988 (article by Wan Sheping), we include it on the basis of its title as it looks like an essential reference work for the study of women in China.

338. CHENG, Lucie, Charlotte FURTH and Hon-Ming YIP, *Women in China: Bibliography of Available English Language Materials*, 109 p., Center for Chinese Studies, Institute of East Asian Studies, University of California, Berkeley, CA, 1984.

'This bibliography is designed to provide an introductory resource for the growing number of students and scholars in both East Asian Studies and Women's Studies who want access to research materials on the women of China.' It includes 4000-odd entries covering all historical periods and all disciplines, published up to 1981. It is arranged by subject with author and name indexes. Not annotated.

339. WEI, Karen T., *Women in China: A Selected and Annotated Bibliography*, 250 p., Greenwood, Westport, CT, 1984.

Over 1000 entries, briefly described and evaluated, arranged in subject areas, with sections for bibliographies and special issues. Author and title indexes. Unique (but see Cheng, Furth and Yip, no. 338). Covers China and Taiwan; includes English material and Chinese writing when translated into English. Some other European languages occur. A further work is planned for Chinese material.

India

See also the works listed under South Asia above.

340. ANANT, Suchitra, Ramani RAO and Kabita KAPOOR, *Women at Work in India: A Bibliography*, 238 p., Sag, 1986. (Institute of Social Studies Trust. Sponsored by Ministry of Labour, Government of India.)

'Myth and ignorance', say the compilers, 'cloud and confound the profile of women everywhere, including India. The myth is difficult to deal with, but the ignorance can be tackled.' This work is an attempt to do just that, and covers a wide range of published and unpublished material on women and work from Independence (1947) to December 1985. The arrangement is by subject including a very detailed breakdown of occupations; there are author, subject and geographical indexes, and an introduction discussing some of the current issues for Indian women. Useful appendices list organizations and periodicals used in the bibliography, women's studies periodicals in India, and feminist publishers. Appendix 5 updates the main work. There are brief annotations where the title is not self-explanatory.

341. DASGUPTA, Kalpana, *Women on the Indian Scene: An Annotated Bibliography*, 391 p., Abhinav Publications, New Delhi, 1976. (A project sponsored by the YWCA of India.)

Starts with an article on the (then) current state of research on women in India. The bibliography of over 800 items, well annotated, is arranged in broad subjects: Society Economics, Politics, Law, Education, Arts, Biographies, and provides author and subject indexes. Appendices list periodicals used (mainly Indian), libraries, relevant legislation and theses at Indian universities.

342. LYTLE, Elizabeth Edith, *Women in India: A Comprehensive Bibliography*, 29 p., Vance Bibliographies, Monticello, IL, 1978.

Contains 386 citations to material published between 1881 and 1978, half of them after 1950.

343. PANDIT, Harshida, *Women of India: An Annotated Bibliography*, 278 p., Garland, New York, 1985.

A substantial compilation of English-language material mostly published in India. The arrangement is by subject, including sections on Legal status, Social problems, Art forms and Psychological studies. An interesting addition is a list of films about women, with an indication of availability in North America. There are also lists of bibliographies and of English-language periodicals and an author index.

344. *Women's Studies Index 1986: A Guide to Indian Periodical Literature*, 82 p., Shreemati Nathibai Damodar Thackersey Women's University Library, Bombay, 1987. Sponsored by the Research Centre for Women's Studies, SNDT Women's University.

A list of articles on women from nearly 130 Indian periodicals, in English, Hindi, Marathi and Gujarati. They are arranged in an alphabetical list by subject descriptor.

345. YAGIN Anwarul, *Protection of Women under the Law: An Annotated Bibliography*, 200 p., Deep & Deep, New Delhi, 1982.

Indonesia

See also the works listed under South-East Asia above.

346.   POSTMA, Nel *et al.*, *Bibliografi Wanita Indonesia*, 2 vols, Kantor Menteri Muda Urusan Peranan Wanita, PDIN-LIPI, Jakarta, Indonesia, 1980–1983.

In Indonesian, with English translation of titles, divided by subject.

Japan and Korea

347.   KOH, Hesung Chun, *Korean and Japanese Women: An Analytic and Bibliographical Guide*, 962 p., Greenwood, Westport, CI, 1982. (Published under the auspices of the Human Relations Area Files.)

This is an enormously complex and unusual bibliography. It might take an hour to learn how to use it, but the rewards would be great. Based on a system known as Human Relations Area Files Automatic Bibliographic System at Yale University, it provides exceptionally thorough access to a collection of documents which are annotated in 'Book 2'. The indexes in 'Book 1' cover subject, time, location, role profiles and author profiles, reference materials, periodicals, and a special analysis of Japanese autobiographical material. Material is in English, Japanese and/or Korean, and spans the last 200 years. Unfortunately the work is tiresome to use physically as much of it is printed sideways on, in very small type.

Nepal

See also the works listed under South Asia above.

348.   SHRESTHA, Indira, *Annotated Bibliography on Women in Nepal*, 69 p., Centre for Economic Development and Administration, Tribhuvan University, Kathmandu, Nepal, 1979. (Part 4 of *The Status of Women in Nepal*, vol. 1: *Background Report*.)

This bibliography is part of a lengthy research project on women and development in Nepal. There are 223 references, some extensively annotated, others simply cited, mostly referring specifically to Nepal and from Nepalese sources, hence their interest in spite of the age of the work. The entries are divided into broad subjects such as economics, education, anthropology, law, health and population.

Pakistan

See also the works listed under South Asia above.

349.   ALAUDDIN, Talat K., *Status of Women and Socio-economic Development: A Selected and Annotated Bibliography*, 125 p., Pakistan Institute of Development Economics, Islamabad, 1977.

Contains 1169 references. Attempts worldwide coverage, but of most interest for the material on Pakistan, comprising the first 200 entries. Subject index.

350.   AYUB, Nighat, *Women in Pakistan and Other Islamic Countries: A Selected Bibliography with Annotations*, 203 p., Women's Resource Centre/ Shirkat Gah, Karachi, 1978.

A bibliography of 900 annotated items. Broad in scope, mostly from Pakistani sources. Now rather out of date.

Philippines

351.   ANGANGCO, Ofelia Regala, Laura L. SAMSON and Teresita M. ALBINO, *Status of Women in the Philippines: A Bibliography with Selected Annotations*, 98 p., Alemar-Phoenix Pub. House, Quezon City, Philippines, 1980.

Lists over 800 publications, arranged by format, with annotations for the 200 most significant in broad subject categories.

352.   VELEZ, Maria Cristina, *Images of the Filipina: A Bibliography*, 219 p., Ala-Ala Foundation, Manila, 1975.

Nearly 600 references, arranged by form.

Sri Lanka

See also the works listed under South Asia above.

353.   WANASUNDERA, Leelangi, *Women of Sri Lanka: An Annotated Bibliography*, 140 p., Centre for Women's Research, 16 Elliott Place, Colombo, Sri Lanka, 1986.

CHAPTER 7

Australia and New Zealand

LIBRARIES AND ARCHIVES

354.   DANIELS, Kay, Mary MURNANE and Anne PICOT, *Women in Australia: An Annotated Guide to Records*, 2 vols, Australian Government Publishing Service, Canberra, 1977.

A list of archival sources relevant to the history of women in Australia, with detailed annotations. There is a brief general section, but the work is mainly devoted to archival material state by state. Under each state are listed relevant holdings in the state archives or record offices, university and other libraries, and private collections. The documents listed are given relevance by the descriptive annotations. The bulk of material consists of official publications.

PARKINSON, Phil, 'Lesbian and gay archives in New Zealand: a minority gathers its history'. (no. 786)

355.   REED, Janet and Kathleen OAKES, *Women in Australian Society 1901-1945: A Guide to the Holdings of Australian Archives Relating to Women, 1901-1945*, 121 p., Australian Government Publishing Service, Canberra, 1977. A descriptive listing of the holdings of the Australian Archives related to women.

BIBLIOGRAPHIES

ADELAIDE, Debra, *Australian Women Writers: A Bibliographic Guide*. (no. 818)

AMBRUS, Caroline, *The Ladies' Picture Show: Sources on a Century of Australian Women Artists*. (no. 572)

BETTISON, Margaret and Anne SUMMERS, *Her Story: Australian Women in Print, 1788-1975*. (no. 708)

356.   HEINZ, N., *Women in New Zealand: A List of Material Issued, 1950-1978*, 106 p., Auckland University Library, Auckland, 1980. (Intended to complement Koopman-Boyden's *A Bibliography of the New Zealand Family* and Seymour's *Women's Studies in New Zealand, 1974-1977*)

A retrospective listing of nearly 2500 references to women in New Zealand, divided by subject. Some entries are briefly annotated.

PERIODICALS

Australian Feminist Studies. (no. 43)

Australian Women's Studies Newsletter. (no. 184)

357.   *Broadsheet*, 10/yr, 228 Dominion Rd, PO Box 56–147, Auckland 3, New Zealand, 1972–.
A radical feminist magazine, main focus on New Zealand women. Contains articles and news.

Hecate: a women's interdisciplinary journal. (no. 55)

358.   *Minymaku Council, Kulintja*, Pitjantjatjara Women's Council, PO Box 2189, Alice Springs, NI, Australia, 1985–.
Aboriginal women's magazine.

Lilith: a Feminist History Journal. (no. 678)

Sistership. (no. 1038)

359.   *Womanspeak*, 4/yr, Box 103, Spit Junction, Sydney 2008, Australia, 1974–.
Australian feminist magazine, with articles, creative writing, news.

ORGANIZATIONS

360.   RESEARCH CENTRE FOR WOMEN'S STUDIES, University of Adelaide, Box 498 GPO, Adelaide, SA 5001, Australia.
A women's studies association founded in 1982. Publishes *Australian Feminist Studies* (no. 43).

WOMEN'S STUDIES ASSOCIATION (NZ). (no. 188)

CHAPTER 8

Europe

In many ways, European countries are less accessible to the UK than the rest of the world, certainly the anglophone world. The women's movement in Britain has largely derived its inspiration from America, and relatively little research on women in Europe has been done in the anglophone countries. This is changing, however, and the greater integration of Britain into Europe on the one hand, and the opening of Eastern Europe on the other, will surely mean a growth in exchange of experience and ideas among women in Europe and the rest of the world in future.

GENERAL REFERENCE WORKS

Many of the works in Chapter 4 are also important for study on Europe.

Resources

The following resource guides are recommended as starting points for research on or in Europe:

COMMISSION OF THE EUROPEAN COMMUNITIES, *Women's Studies*. (no. 182)

LEHMANN, Stephen and Eva SARTORI, *Women's Studies in Western Europe: A Resource Guide*. (no. 13)

In addition the following publication is essential for keeping abreast of developments in European Community countries:

361. *Women of Europe*, 6/yr, Commission of the European Communities, rue de la Loi 200, 1049 Brussels, Belgium, 1977–.

This useful publication contains news and information on activities in the field of the advancement of women in the European Community countries. Published in the nine languages of the Community. Regular supplements are produced each dealing with a specific topic, some of them on a regular basis (e.g. Women and Men of Europe) and some one-off studies of, for example, women in a particular country, women and music, etc.

Research

The following work only came to our attention in the last stages of compiling this book:

361a.   RICHTER, Werner, Liisa HUSU and Arnaud MARKS, *The Changing Role of Women in Society: A Documentation of Current Research: Research Projects in Progress 1984–1987*, 713 p., Akademie-Verlag, Berlin, 2nd ed., 1989. (Edited for the European Cooperation in Social Science Information and Documentation (ECSSID). Compiled at the Scientific Centre for Research and of the Academy of Sciences of the GDR.)

This unique work is an inventory of research on women completed and in progress in twenty-two European countries, East and West. It lists over 700 research projects under fourteen subjects headings, mainly within the social sciences. It includes any work on women, not necessarily in the field of what we would define as 'women's studies', chiefly in academic institutions. Each entry, with the title in English, contains details of the research project such as scope, commissioning body, methodology, funding and project results, etc. An introduction presents a comparative analysis of the work being done in different countries and in Eastern and Western Europe, and makes a forceful claim for the necessity for supranational cooperation and for looking at activity outside the narrow confines of one's own academic tradition. The final section contains a series of national reports giving an overview of socio-economic conditions and the state of women's studies and the position of women in each country. This is an important source for access to institutions and researchers in Europe.

Statistical information

Statistics on women in Europe can be found in the main worldwide statistical sources listed in Part I (nos 139–146). In addition, the following sources are specific to Europe:

362.   COMMISSION OF THE EUROPEAN COMMUNITIES, *Men and Women of Europe in 1987* (Women of Europe Supplement no. 26), 63 p., Commission of the European Communities, Brussels, 1987.

New editions of this work (previously entitled *Women and Men of Europe!*) are produced every five years or so as supplements to *Women of Europe*. Statistics derived from identical questionnaires sent to all Community member countries are arranged in two parts: The place of woman in society, and Women and politics.

363. COMMISSION OF THE EUROPEAN COMMUNITIES, *Women in Statistics* (Women of Europe Supplement no. 14), 29 p., Commission of the European Communities, Brussels, 1984.

Tables of statistics on the economic and social situation of women in Community countries, arranged under Population, Vocational activity, and Education and training. It is an update of Women of Europe Supplement no. 10 with the same title.

LIBRARIES AND ARCHIVES

INTERNATIONAAL ARCHIEF VOOR DE VROUWENBEWE-GING/INTERNATIONAL ARCHIVES FOR THE WOMEN'S MOVEMENT. (no. 106)

The most important international collection on the history of the women's movement.

PERIODICALS

Periodicals from or about a particular country are listed under the country.

364. *CREW Reports*, 12/yr, Centre for Research on European Women, 38 rue Stévin, 1040 Brussels, Belgium, 1981.

Monthly bulletin of EC and general European news in the field of social and employment policy relating to women.

365. *Women in Europe*, 8/yr, Commission of the European Communities, 8 Storey's Gate, London SW1P 3AT, 1985-.

News and views about women and the European Community, with a British focus.

Women of Europe. (no. 361)

ORGANIZATIONS

Regular information on women's organizations in the European Community countries can be found in *Women of Europe* (no. 361).

366. CENTRE FOR RESEARCH ON EUROPEAN WOMEN (CREW), 38 rue Stévin, 1040 Brussels.

Set up to provide information on women and employment issues. Offers consultancy services, and has set up a databank of its documentation on EC and Member States. Publishes *CREW Reports* (no. 364).

367. EUROPEAN NETWORK OF WOMEN (ENOW), 38 rue
Stévin, 1040 Brussels, Belgium.

A grassroots pressure group within the European Community which
monitors the impact of EC legislation on women, and works for improving
the situation of women in the Community. Carries out research, organizes
seminars. Publishes a newsletter, *Network News*.

EASTERN EUROPE

Resources

RICHTER, Werner, Liisa HUSU and Arnaud MARKS, *The Changing
Role of Women in Society: A Documentation of Current Research: Research Projects in
Progress 1984-1987*. (no. 361a)

This major source on Eastern Europe is fully described earlier in this
chapter. It provides information on research projects, mainly in the social
sciences, in Bulgaria, Czechoslovakia, the GDR, Hungary, Poland, the
USSR and Yugoslavia as well as Western European countries. The
introduction contains an interesting comparative analysis of research
activity in Eastern and Western Europe. It is particularly useful in that it
lists the sponsoring institutions and researchers, thereby providing points
of contact for anyone interested in women's studies in the communist
countries. The work was compiled in East Germany, and is in itself an
interesting example of East-West cooperation.

Bibliographies

368. TRYFAN, Barbara, 'Research on the status of women, development and population trends in Eastern Europe: an annotated bibliography'. In: UNESCO, *Bibliographic Guide to Studies on the Status of Women*
(no. 194), pp. 113-139.

The most undocumented region of the world as far as women are
concerned. This bibliography is the only one that we have found on women
in Eastern Europe. About 100 works are listed, none of them published
after 1979. They are divided into General works, Work and labour force
participation, Family and household, Education and Demographic
features. Institutions undertaking research on women are listed at the end.

Periodicals

Soviet Woman. (no. 441)

Women of the Whole World. (no. 207)

Organizations

There is a list of the Academies of Science and Institutes in the Eastern European countries which carry out research on women at the end of Tryfan (no. 368). Also included are the international organizations supporting research on Eastern Europe. The following lists organizations by country:

SHREIR, Sally, *Women's Movements of the World*. (no. 132)

For the main Eastern bloc organization see:

WOMEN'S INTERNATIONAL DEMOCRATIC FEDERATION. (no. 229)

SCANDINAVIA

Women's studies in Scandinavia are excellently organized and funded. Centralized information is easy to come by, and much material is published in English. See also the individual countries below.

Bibliographies

New Literature on Women/Ny Litteratur om Kvinnor. (no. 1)
This gives bibliographic access to research on women in Scandinavia.

Organizations

369. NORDIC ASSOCIATION FOR FEMINIST RESEARCH, Centre for Feminist Research and Women's Studies, University of Copenhagen-Amager, Njalsgade 106, 2300 Copenhagen S, Denmark.

Established in 1981 by feminist scholars in Denmark, Norway, Sweden, Iceland and Finland to 'share theories, methods and insights . . . facilitate the exchange of scholars . . . work towards an international network of feminist scholars'. It has published a guide to women's studies in the Nordic countries (see no. 370).

370. NORDIC ASSOCIATION FOR FEMINIST RESEARCH, *Women's Studies and Research on Women in the Nordic Countries*, 45 p., Centre for Feminist Research and Women's Studies, University of Copenhagen-Amager, 1988. (Available from the Centre, Njalsgade 106, 2300 Copenhagen S, Denmark.)

Publication issued in connection with the Nordic Forum, a conference of all women's organizations in the Scandinavian countries. It describes the organization of women's studies in the separate countries, and lists individual institutions and contacts.

EUROPEAN COUNTRIES

Austria

PERIODICALS

371. *Auf: eine Frauenzeitschrift*, 4–6/yr, Verein zur Förderung Feministischer Projekte, Postfach 817, 1011 Vienna, Austria.
Articles on issues concerning women.

ORGANIZATIONS

372. DOKUMENTATION FRAUENFORSCHUNG, Institut für Wissenschaft und Kunst, Berggasse 17/1, 1090 Vienna, Austria.
A historical research and documentation centre on the Austrian women's movement, forming part of the IWK. The IWK's *Mitteilung* from time to time produces an issue on women.

Belgium

PERIODICALS

373. *Cahiers du GRIF*, Groupe de Recherche et d'Information Féministe, 29 rue Blanche, 1050 Brussels, Belgium, 1972–.
Social and cultural issues concerning women; news and reviews.

374. *Chronique Féministe*, 5/yr, Université des Femmes, 1a place Quetelet, 1030 Brussels, Belgium, 1983–.
Feminist journal with articles, news, reviews, etc., and information on the Université des Femmes programme.

ORGANIZATIONS

375. GROUPE DE RECHERCHES ET D'INFORMATIONS FEMINISTES (GRIF), 29 rue Blanche, 1050 Brussels, Belgium.
Documentation and information centre publishing *Cahiers du GRIF* (no. 373).

British Isles

Most of the material on Britain will be found elsewhere in this book. We list here some of the general British organizations and reference works, as well as bibliographies on Scotland and Ireland.

GREAT BRITAIN

Statistical information

See also the section on Statistics in Part I (nos 139–146).

EQUAL OPPORTUNITIES COMMISSION, *Women and Men in Britain: A Research Profile*. (no. 140)

Resources

Everywoman Directory of Women's Co-operatives and Other Enterprises. (no. 130)

SPRINGBOARD, *A Directory of Women's Businesses and Organizations in the London Area*. (no. 134)

Organizations

376. EQUAL OPPORTUNITIES COMMISSION, Overseas House, Quay St, Manchester M3 3HN.

A government advisory body set up to monitor and promote equal opportunities and counter sex discrimination. Publishes reports, news releases, research reports and statistical data, and has a library/information centre (no. 100). It also has offices in Scotland and Wales, but the administrative centre is in Manchester. See also Equal Opportunities Commission for Northern Ireland (no. 385).

377. FAWCETT SOCIETY, 40/46 Harleyford Rd, London SE11 5AY.

Old-established organization with origins in the suffrage movement, acts as a pressure group for women's rights. It founded the Fawcett Library and is still closely associated with it although the administration has passed to City of London Polytechnic.

378. LONDON WOMEN'S CENTRE, Wesley House, 4 Wild Court, off Kingsway, London WC2B 5AU.

Base for about fifteen women's groups and events, including evening classes for women. Publishes a newsletter, *News Update*.

379. NATIONAL ALLIANCE OF WOMEN'S ORGANISATIONS, c/o 36 Bedford Square, London WC1.

A broad grouping of diverse organizations, both feminist and traditional, covering a wide range of women's interests.

380. WOMEN'S NATIONAL COMMISSION, Government Offices, Great George St, London SW1P 3AQ.

A government advisory committee, 'made up of 50 women elected or appointed by national organizations with a large and active membership of women'. These include the women's sections of the major trade unions, political parties and churches, and some business and professional organizations.

IRELAND

Bibliographies

381. BRADY, Anna, *Women in Ireland: An Annotated Bibliography*, 478 p., Greenwood, New York, 1988.

This welcome bibliography contains 2312 annotated items, and has to be the essential starting point for any research on Irish women. Very broad in its subject coverage, it is unusual in that about a quarter of it is devoted to autobiography and biography. The author claims under-representation of materials on Northern Ireland, partly because many of these pertain to Great Britain as a whole and were therefore excluded. Lists of doctoral and masters dissertations follow the main subjects, and there is a decent subject index. The work is less easy to use than it might be because of the exceptionally unsympathetic microdot computer typeface.

382. SMYTH, Ailbhe, 'Feminism in Ireland: selected reading and resource list', *Women's Studies International Forum*, vol. 11, no. 4, pp. 411–418, 1988.

A useful bibliography of some 300 references to publications from 1975–1987, divided by subject. It includes lists of resources, journals and organizations.

Periodicals

383. *Women's News*, ?6/yr, 185 Donegall St, Belfast BT1.

A feminist news magazine with lots of information about activities, publications, etc., both North and South of the border.

Women's Studies Review. (no. 69)

Organizations

384. *Irish Women's Guidebook and Diary*, Attic Press, Dublin.

Gives a full listing of Irish women's organizations and groups.

385. EQUAL OPPORTUNITIES COMMISSION FOR NORTHERN IRELAND, Chamber of Commerce House, 22 Great Victoria St, Belfast BT2 2BA.

Official body set up to monitor and campaign for equal opportunities for women in Northern Ireland. Operates independently from the EOC in England. Publishes annual reports, research reports, reports on cases of interest, press releases, etc.

WOMEN'S STUDIES ASSOCIATION OF IRELAND. (no. 189)

SCOTLAND

Bibliographies

386. WOMEN IN SCOTLAND BIBLIOGRAPHY GROUP, *Women in Scotland: An Annotated Bibliography*, 65 p., Open University in Scotland, Edinburgh, 1988. (Available from 60 Melville St, Edinburgh EH3 7HF.)

Much of the material in this bibliography is unique to it: we have not come across it in other works. It includes a substantial section on oral and traditional culture and folklore, and much biographical/autobiographical material. One interesting section is on Women and foreign missions. A useful feature is the section on official statistics. This definitely fills a gap.

Reference works

HUNTER, Eveline, *Scottish Women's Handbook*. (no. 733)

WALES

Reference works

387. *Wales Women's Directory/Cysylltiadur Merched Cymru: Women's Groups, Organizations and Businesses in Wales*, 62 p., Women's Enterprise Bureau, Bangor, Gwynedd, 1984.

Bilingual directory of organizations in Wales.

Denmark

See also Scandinavia above.

LIBRARIES AND ARCHIVES

388. KVINDEHISTORISK SAMLING/WOMEN'S HISTORY ARCHIVE, The State Library, Universitetsparken, 8000 Aarhus C, Denmark.

Material from the Danish women's movement, also functioning as a centre of documentation for women's studies.

PERIODICALS

389. *Forum for Kvindeforskning*, 4/yr, Nyhavn 22, 1051 Copenhagen K, Denmark.

Quarterly magazine on women's studies, in Danish with English summaries.

390. *Kvinder*, Kvindehuset, Gothersgade 37, 1123 Copenhagen K, Denmark.

Feminist magazine with socialist perspective.

ORGANIZATIONS

391.   CENTER FOR KVINDEFORSKNING OG UNDERVIS-
NING/CENTRE FOR FEMINIST RESEARCH AND WOMEN'S
STUDIES, University of Copenhagen-Amager, Njalsgade 106, 2300
Copenhagen S, Denmark.

One of a number of centres for women's studies in Denmark which are
organized into a network supported by government funding. Information
on all women's studies activities can be obtained from this coordinating
institution. It publishes a newsletter five times a year, and publicity
material in English, and organizes the Forum for Kvindeforskere i
Danmark (National Forum for Feminist Scholars in Denmark.

392.   CENTER FOR SAMSUNDSVIDENSKABELIG KVINDE-
FORSKNING/WOMEN'S RESEARCH CENTRE IN THE SOCIAL
SCIENCES, Adelgade 49 st.tv., 1304 Copenhagen K, Denmark.

Independent institution founded in 1980, publishing a newsletter and a
series of working papers (some in English).

393.   KVINFO/CENTRE FOR INTERDISCIPLINARY INFOR-
MATION ON WOMEN'S STUDIES, Laederstraede 15, 2. sal, 1201
Copenhagen K, Denmark.

NORDIC ASSOCIATION FOR FEMINIST RESEARCH. (no. 369)

394.   WOMEN'S RESEARCH CENTRE IN SOCIAL SCIENCE,
Adelgade 49 st. tv., 1304 Copenhagen K, Denmark.

An independent institution founded in 1980, publishing a newsletter and a
series of working papers (some in English).

Finland

See also Scandinavia above.

PERIODICALS

395.   *Naisten Aani*, 5/yr, Bulevardi 11a, Vastauslahetys, Sopimus
00120/66, 00003 Helsinki, Finland.

Finnish feminist magazine, formerly entitled *Akkavaki*.

396.   *Naistukimus*, Finland, 1988–.

New scholarly women's studies journal. No details as yet.

ORGANIZATIONS

397.   COUNCIL FOR GENDER EQUALITY, PO Box 267, 00171
Helsinki, Finland.

Parliamentary advisory body set up in 1972 to promote equality and coordinate research. Publishes research reports and a newsletter on women's studies.

France

LIBRARIES AND ARCHIVES

398. BIBLIOTHEQUE MARGUERITE DURAND, 70 rue Nationale, 75013 Paris, France.

Founded in 1931, this is the major feminist collection in France, containing over 20,000 books, documentary materials and periodicals, mainly French, on and by women. It publishes an annual list of acquisitions.

BIBLIOGRAPHIES

GUILBERT, Madeleine, Nicole LOWIT and Marie-Hélène ZYLBER-BERG-HOCQUARI, *Travail et Condition Féminine: Bibliographie Commentée.* (no. 1043)

399. SMYTH, Ailbhe, 'Le féminisme contemporain en France: essai d'orientation bibliographique: travaux récentes', *RFR/DRF: Resources for Feminist Research*, vol. 12, no. 4, pp. 1–17, 1983/4.

A bibliography of some 600 or so items of writing by French feminists, from 1970 to 1983. Divided into twenty-three subject headings. A useful overview of French feminism.

400. WEITZ, Margaret Collins, *Femmes: Recent Writings on French Women*, 245 p., G.K. Hall, Boston, 1985.

Intended as an introduction to French feminist research, the main part of this book contains material published in France between 1970 and 1979 and not available in English at the time of publication. A bibliography of works from 1830 to 1969 is appended. The arrangement is by subject according to the main concerns of French feminists, and there are author and subject indexes.

PERIODICALS

401. *Bulletin du CRIF*, 4/yr, Centre de Recherches de Réflexion et d'Information Féministes, 1 rue des Fossés-St-Jacques, 75005 Paris, France.

Most of this publication is a current awareness bulletin reproducing the contents pages of a worldwide range of feminist periodicals.

402. *Cahiers du Féminisme*, 4/yr, PEC, 2, rue Richard-Lenoir, 93108 Montreuil, France.

Feminist magazine, eclectic selection of articles, news, comment.

403. *Des Femmes en Mouvement Hebdo*, 52/yr, 6 rue Mezières, 75006 Paris, France.

Feminist weekly magazine, containing much news of the international women's movement.

404. *Etudes Féministes*, 3/yr, 2ter passage du Marais, 75010 Paris, France, 1983-.

France's first national women's studies newsletter, with articles, news, discussion, information about women's studies throughout France.

405. *Femmes Informations*, 6/yr, CODIF, 81 rue Sénac, 13100 Marseille, France.

Magazine of the Centre d'Orientation de Documentation et d'Information Féminin, contains articles.

Lesbia: Revue Lesbienne d'Expressions, d'Information, d'Opinions. (no. 775)

406. *Nouvelles Questions Féministes*, 4/yr, 59–61 rue Pouchet, 75017 Paris, France, 1981-.

Describing itself as the only international women's studies review in the French language, it includes general information on women in France and the world, articles of feminist analysis and methodology, news of the activities of feminist movements in France and abroad, and bibliography, book reviews, etc. Frequently has double issues on special topics.

Pénélope: pour l'histoire des Femmes. (no. 679)

ORGANIZATIONS

407. CENTRE D'ORIENTATION, DE DOCUMENTATION ET D'INFORMATION FEMININS, 81 rue Sénac, 13001 Marseille, France.

An advice and information centre created in 1974. Publishes *Femmes Informations* (no. 405).

408. CENTRE DE RECHERCHES DE REFLEXIONS ET D'INFORMATION FEMINISTES (CRIF), 1 rue des Fossés-St-Jacques, 75005 Paris.

Centre for feminist research, communication network. Publishes a current awareness *Bulletin du CRIF* (no. 401).

409. CENTRE LYONNAIS D'ETUDES FEMINISTES, I.R.I.S.H., Université Lyon 2, ave. Pierre-Mendès-France, Case 11, 69676 Bron Cedex, France.

Women's studies research and resource centre.

RESEAU FEMMES ET DEVELOPPEMENT. (no. 223)

German Democratic Republic

See Eastern Europe above.

Germany

BIBLIOGRAPHIES

ARENDT, Ingrid and Hans-Jurgen ARENDT, *Bibliografie zur Geschichte des Kampfes der deutschen Arbeiterklasse für die Befreiung der Frau und zur Rolle der Frau in der deutschen Arbeiterbewegung: Von den Anfangen bis 1970.* (no. 716)

410. BOCK, Ulla and Barbara WITYCH, *Thema Frau: Bibliographie der deutschsprachigen Literatur zur Frauenfrage 1949–1979*, 293 p., AJZ, Bielefeld, 1980.

A bibliography of over 4000 German-language items, comprehensive in scope, and including theses as well as books and articles. It is divided by subject. Although translations of major works from other languages are included, this is predominantly a listing of German material, and therefore extremely useful for the study of the West German women's movement. There is an author index and a list of journals, and a list of libraries and archives in West Germany. There is also an appendix of late additions to the bibliography and an extensive introductory article on women's writing since World War II.

411. DELVENDAHL, Ilse and Doris MAREK, *Die Frauenfrage in Deutschland: Bibliografie*, Saur, Munich, 1981–.

Two volumes cover 1790–1930 and 1931–1980. Further volumes regularly update this bibliographic series.

412. NEW GERMAN CRITIQUE, 'Bibliography', *New German Critique*, no. 13, 14, pp. 197–229, 143–177, Winter 1978, Spring 1978.

The two parts of this bibliography are continuous, and are linked to a special Feminist issue of *New German Critique* (a journal published at the University of Wisconsin). They offer an overview of German feminist literature, arranged by topic. The entries each have page-long annotations.

413. PETERS, Anke and Maria GAWOREK-BEHRINGER, *Frauenerwerbstatigkeit: Literatur und Forschungsprojekte*, 400 p., Institut für Arbeitsmarkt- und Berufsforschung, Nuremberg, 1984.

PERIODICALS

414. *Emma: Das Magazin von Frauen für Frauen*, 12/yr, Frauenverlags Gmbh, Kolpingplatz 1a, 5000 Cologne 1, 1976–.

German feminist alternative magazine with nationwide circulation, also reaching women in Austria, Switzerland and the Netherlands with the idea of getting a wide circulation.

415. *Ergebnisse der Frauenforschung*, Freie Universität Berlin, Königin-Luise-Strasse 34, 1000 Berlin 33, W. Germany.

Journal published under the auspices of the University Centre for the Promotion of Women's Studies and Research on Women (no. 422).

416. *Eule (Die)*, 2/yr, H. Heinz, Augustastrasse 123, 5600 Wuppertal 1, W. Germany.

Articles on modern theories of feminism, psychoanalysis, philosophy.

417. *Feminist (Der):Beiträge zur Theorie und Praxis*, Christrosenweg 5, 8000 Munich 70, W. Germany, 1976-.

Contains articles on feminist theory and practice, promoting feminist party.

418. *Feministische Studien*, 2/yr, Deutscher Studien Verl., Weinheim, W. Germany, 1982-.

Academic women's studies periodical, most issues covering a special subject.

419. *Fraueninformationsblatt*, 3/yr, Freie Universität Berlin, Zentraleinrichtung für Förderung von Frauenstudien und Frauenforschung, Königin-Luise-Strasse 34, 1000 Berlin 33, W. Germany.

Information about women's studies courses, conferences, research projects, etc.

Frauen und Film. (no. 599)

420. *Informationen Für die Frau*, 12/yr, Sudstrasse 125, 5300 Bonn 2, W. Germany.

Monthly periodical of the National Council of German Women's Organizations, dealing with political topics of concern to women.

421. *Women in Germany Yearbook*, Annual, University Press of America, Lanham, MD, 1985-.

A scholarly publication, subtitled *Feminist Studies in German Culture*.

ORGANIZATIONS

422. UNIVERSITY CENTRE FOR THE PROMOTION OF WOMEN'S STUDIES AND RESEARCH ON WOMEN/ZENTRALEINRICHTUNG ZUR FÖRDERUNG VON FRAUENSTUDIEN UND FRAUENFORSCHUNG, Freie Universität Berlin, Königin-Luise-Strasse 34, 1000 Berlin 33, W. Germany.

Set up as an organization dedicated to the elimination of discrimination and the promotion of women's studies at institutional level, it also offers services throughout and outside the Federal Republic, including counselling and guidance, bibliographic and documentation services, etc. Publishes *Fraueninformationsblatt* (no. 419) and *Ergebnisse der Frauenforschung* (no. 415) as well as reports, etc.

Greece

PERIODICALS

423.   *Dini*, 2/yr, 95–97 Zoodochou Pighis St, 11473 Athens, Greece.

Exchange of ideas of the Greek and the international feminist movement.

424.   *Mediterranean Women KEGME Review*, 2/yr, Mediterranean Women's Studies Institute, 192/B Leoforos Alexandras, 11521 Athens, Greece.

English-language magazine which reports on research, women's studies projects and other activities of women's groups in the Mediterranean region.

ORGANIZATIONS

425.   KEGME: Mediterranean Women's Studies Institute, 192/B Leoforos Alexandras, 11545 Athens, Greece.

A research organization to study the position of Mediterranean women. Runs an information centre. Publishes *Mediterranean Women KEGME Review* (no. 424).

426.   EGE/WOMEN'S UNION OF GREECE, 8 Ainianos St, 10432 Athens, Greece.

A socialist feminist organization founded in 1976 as a response to the inequality of women in Greece, working for equal rights, participation, etc.

Iceland

See also Scandinavia above.

PERIODICALS

427.   *Vera*, 5–6/yr, Laugavegur 17, 101 Reykjavik, Iceland.

Feminist magazine produced by the Women's Alliance.

ORGANIZATIONS

428. AHUGAHOPUR UM ISLENSKAR KVENNARANN-SOKNIR/FORUM FOR ICELANDIC WOMEN'S STUDIES, Haskoli Islands, 101 Reykjavik, Iceland.

Network of women scholars, academics and students in Iceland.

Italy

BIBLIOGRAPHIES

429. BANISSONI, Maria, *Bibliografia sulla Condizione Feminile: Articoli, Saggi, Ricerce Psicologico-Sociali*, 206 p., Bulzoni, Rome, 1978.

A bibliography of multilingual sources, general in scope, divided into two sections. The first has general publications on the condition of women, and the second includes socio-psychological research on women and the women's movement. For the English-speaking reader this bibliography will be of most use for its Italian works. Now out of date.

430. CATALUCCI, Emanuela and Rita SARINELLI, *Donna e Lavoro: Bibliografia 1970–1981*, 122 p., Bulzoni, Rome, 1982.

Some 500 entries, almost exclusively Italian sources. Divided into broad subjects dealing with aspects of women's work, such as rural work, domestic work, etc. Within each subject the entries are divided by form (books and articles). The articles are sub-arranged by periodical scanned.

PERIODICALS

431. *Donna e Società*, Corso Rinascimento 113, 00186 Rome, Italy.

432. *DWF: Donna Woman Femme*, 4/yr, via S. Benedetto in Arenula 6, 00186 Rome, Italy, 1976–.

Publishes original Italian and significant foreign research on women, mainly concerned with literature and the arts.

433. *Effe: Mensile Feminista Autogestito*, 12/yr, Piazza Campo Marzio 7, 00186 Rome, Italy, 1972–.

Italian feminist magazine.

ORGANIZATIONS

434. CENTRO DI STUDI STORICI SUL MOVIMENTO DI LIBERAZIONE DELLA DONNA IN ITALIA, Via Romagnosi 3, 20121 Milan, Italy.

Netherlands

LIBRARIES AND ARCHIVES

INTERNATIONAAL ARCHIEF VOOR DE VROUWENBEWE-GING. Library, *Catalogue of the Library of the International Archives for the Women's Movement (Internationaal Archief voor de Vrouwenbeweging), Amsterdam.* (no. 115)

PERIODICALS

435. *Lover*, 4/yr, IIAV, Keizergracht 10, 1015 CN Amsterdam, Netherlands.

Review and resources quarterly for the women's movement with review articles, contents of feminist scholarly journals, bibliography of recent publications, books, articles, reports, research projects, etc.

ORGANIZATIONS

WOMEN AND DEVELOPMENT PROGRAM, Institute of Social Studies, The Hague. (no. 226)

Norway

See also Scandinavia above.

PERIODICALS

436. *Nytt om Kvinneforskning*, 5/yr, Secretariat for Women and Research, NAVF, Sandakerveien 99, 0483 Oslo, Norway.

Feminist newsletter, produced by the Norwegian Research Council for Science and Humanities, Secretariat for Women and Research.

ORGANIZATIONS

437. DOKUMENTASJONSTJENESTEN FOR LITTERATUR OM KVINNER/DOCUMENTATION SERVICES FOR LITERATURE ABOUT WOMEN, University Library, University of Bergen, 5000 Bergen, Norway.

Documentation and dissemination of literature on women.

438. KVINNE FRONTEN, Boks 53 Bryn, 0611 Oslo 6, Norway.

Independent organization with sixty-five groups around the country, founded in 1972 to fight the oppression of women. Publishes *Kvinnejournalen* magazine.

439. NAVF'S SEKRETARIAT FOR KVINNEFORSKNING/SECRETARIAT FOR WOMEN AND RESEARCH, Sandakerveien 99, 0483 Oslo 4, Norway.

Has national responsibility for coordinating research on women in Norway, under the auspices of NAVF (Norwegian Research Council for Science and the Humanities). Publishes *Nytt om Kvinneforskning* (no. 436).

440. SENTER FOR KVINNEFORSKNING/CENTRE FOR RESEARCH ON WOMEN, University of Oslo, p.b. 1040 Blindern, 0315 Oslo 3, Norway.

Interdisciplinary women's research unit.

Soviet Union

See also Eastern Europe above.

PERIODICALS

441. *Soviet Woman*, 12/yr, Komitet Sovetskikh Zhenshchin, Izdatel'stvo Pravda, Ul. Pravdy 24, Moscow 125047, USSR, 1945–.

Illustrated magazine with news of women in USSR and elsewhere; publishes editions in thirteen different languages.

Spain

BIBLIOGRAPHIES

442. IGLESIAS DE USSAL, Julio, *Elementos para el Estudio de la Mujer en la Sociedad Española: Análisis Bibliográfico, 1939–1980*, 210 p., Dirección General de Juventud y Promoción Socio-Cultural, Subdirección General de la Mujer, Madrid, ?1980.

PERIODICALS

A new periodical, *Desde el Feminismo*, has been announced, but we have not been able to verify its address.

443. *Mujer Feminista (La)*, Calle Almagro 28, 28010 Madrid, Spain.

News of national and international events related to women.

444. *Mujeres*, Instituto de la Mujer, Ministerio de Cultura, Almagro 36, 2a planta, 28010 Madrid, Spain, 1984–.

Spanish magazine with an international focus (especially on Latin America).

Sweden

LIBRARIES AND ARCHIVES

445. GÖTEBORG UNIVERSITY LIBRARY: WOMEN'S HISTORY COLLECTIONS, Box 5096, 402 22 Göteborg, Sweden.

Collections started thirty years ago by women librarian/scholars. Publishes *New Literature on Women* (no. 1) quarterly.

PERIODICALS

446. *Kvinnovetenskaplig Tidskrift*, 4/yr, Sf Eriksgatan 7, 112 39 Stockholm, Sweden, 1979–.

Interdisciplinary feminist journal which presents theory, debate and information within women's studies. There are English summaries for the major articles.

New Literature on Women/Ny Litteratur om Kvinnor. (no. 1)

ORGANIZATIONS

447. CENTRE FOR WOMEN SCHOLARS AND RESEARCH ON WOMEN, Uppsala University, 752 37 Uppsala, Sweden.

Supports and coordinates work done by women scholars, and initiates and conducts research. Publishes a newsletter *Sofia* with information on activities and courses, and a series of working papers calles *Uppsala Women's Studies, Women in the Humanities*, part of the university series Acta Universitatis Upsaliensis.

448. COMMISSION FOR RESEARCH ON EQUALITY BETWEEN MEN AND WOMEN (JAMFO), Drottninggatan 6 2tr, 111 51 Stockholm, Sweden.

Supports research, organizes seminars, and publishes reports. Monitors the position of women in research and at the universities.

449. KVINNOFRONTEN, 163 04 Stockholm, Sweden.

Swedish feminist organization with international links.

Switzerland

PERIODICALS

450. *Femmes Suisses et le Mouvement Féministe*, 12/yr, CP 323, Carouge, Geneva, Switzerland.

Magazine focusing on political and social issues for women in Switzerland and Europe, and on feminist research.

451. *Frauenfragen/Questions au Féminin/Problemi Feminile*, 4/yr Bundesamt für Kulturpflege, Box Office, 3000 Berne 6, Switzerland.

Trilingual journal monitoring equal rights in Switzerland.

Turkey

BIBLIOGRAPHIES

452. AREN, Munise, *Turk Toplumunda Kadin: Bibliyografya . . . (Women in Turkish Society)*, 153 p., Dernek, Ankara, 1980. (In Turkish.)

Lists 1000 titles, mainly periodical articles, in Turkish with some English ones. Arranged by subject groups with author index.

453. LYTLE, Elizabeth Edith, *Women in Turkey: A Selected Bibliography*, 14 p., Vance Bibliographies, Monticello, IL, 1979.

Lists 177 citations to periodical articles, monographs, dissertations and government documents, published between 1837 and 1976 (two-thirds of them before 1940), mainly in English.

ORGANIZATIONS

454. TURK KADININI GUCLENDIRME VE TANITMA VAKFI/FOUNDATION FOR ADVANCEMENT OF TURKISH WOMEN, Ataturk Bulvardi 219/14, Kavaklidere, Ankara, Turkey.

Objective is 'to advance and enhance the economic, social and cultural solidarity among Turkish women . . . to promote the social, cultural and economic achievements of today's Turkish women worldwide.'

CHAPTER 9

Latin America and the Caribbean

GENERAL BIBLIOGRAPHIES

455.   ASHBY, Jacqueline A. and Stella GOMEZ, *Women, Agriculture and Rural Development in Latin America*, 171 p., International Fertilizer Development Center/Centro Internacional de Agricultura Tropical, Muscle Shoals, AL/Cali, Colombia, 1985.

Introduced by an extensive essay, this bibliography consists of forty-five items, some with lengthy annotations and some unannotated. A large amount of the material is in Spanish.

456.   DE LEY, Margo and Maria SILVA, *An Annotated Bibliography of Spanish-language Materials on Women in Latin America* (Curriculum Guide no. 8), 20 p., University of Illinois at Urbana-Champaign, Champaign, IL, 1985.

'Very useful teaching review with long annotations.' (From Townsend (no. 254).)

457.   KNASTER, Meri, *Women in Spanish America: An Annotated Bibliography from Pre-Conquest to Contemporary Times*, 696 p., G.K. Hall, Boston, 1977.

An extensive (2500 entries) bibliography covering material in Spanish and English about women in Spanish-speaking Latin America. Covers the period up to 1974, arranged by subject, and within that by country. There are separate lists of dissertations, both masters and doctoral, and useful lists of periodicals scanned and reference works and libraries used. Completed by subject and author indexes. This is an excellent work, limited now by its age.

PAN AMERICAN HEALTH ORGANISATION, *Women, Health and Development in the Americas: An Annotated Bibliography*. (no. 864)

SAULNIERS, Suzanne Smith and Cathy A. RAKOWSI, *Women in the Development Process: A Select Bibliography on Women in Sub-Saharan Africa and Latin America*. (no. 253)

458.   STONER, K. Lynn, *Latinas of the Americas: A Source Book*, 650 p., Garland, New York, 1988.

'Coverage is interdisciplinary, with traditional disciplines and new topical categories serving as the basis for the book's organization . . . Research from all of the Americas and Europe is documented and includes Spanish-, English-, Portuguese-, French-, and German-language articles, unpublished papers, dissertations and theses . . . Indexes by country and period.' (From publisher's announcement.)

PERIODICALS

We have listed here a representative selection of journals and magazines. There are many others, information on which can be found in the sources described in Part I (nos 32–41), and also in the guides to international organizations in Chapter 4.

459. *Fem*, 6/yr, Universidad 1855–4 piso, Col. Oxtopulco-Universidad, CP 04310, Mexico DF, Mexico, 1976–.

Each issue has a theme, e.g. work, health, marriage, etc. Concerned with women in Mexico and Latin America.

460. *Mujer Fempress*, 12/yr, Unidad de Comunicación Alternativa de la Mujer, Casilla 16–637, Santiago 9, Chile.

Feminist magazine with contributions from all over Latin America.

461. *Mulherio*, 6/yr, Fundação Carlos Chagas, Av. Prof. Francisco Morato, 1565, CEP 05513, São Paulo, Brazil, 1981–.

Feminist newspaper.

462. *Quehaceres*, 12/yr, Centro de Investigación para la Acción Feminina (CIPAF), Santo Domingo, Dominican Republic, 1980–.

News-sheet format magazine.

Third Woman. (no. 523)

463. *Vamos Mujer*, Casa de la Mujer, Carrera 18 no. 59–60, Bogotá, Distrito Especial, Colombia.

Feminist publication dealing with women's issues in Latin America.

464. *Viva: Revista Feminista*, irreg., Painque Herman Velaide no. 42, Lima, Peru, 1984–.

Feminist magazine with articles on the activities of the Peruvian women's movement.

ORGANIZATIONS

Most Latin American women's organizations are of a grassroots nature, and there are a great many of them. These can be found listed in the sources mentioned in Chapter 4 under International organizations. The following publication may also be of use:

465. INTERNATIONAL WOMEN'S TRIBUNE CENTER, *A Guide to Women's Centers in Latin America*, IWIC, 777 United Nations Plaza, New York, NY 10017, 1989.

The first in a projected series of guides to women's centres throughout the world.

The following organizations have a region-wide focus:

466. DAWN: Development Alternatives with Women for a new Era, IUPERJI, Rua Paulino Fernández 32, Botafogo 22260, Rio de Janeiro, Brazil.

Founded in 1984 to act as a catalyst for Third World development projects. Publishes a quarterly newsletter called *DAWN Informs*.

467. SERVICIO ESPECIAL DE LA MUJER LATINO-AMERICANA (SEMLA), Apartado 70–10001, San José, Costa Rica.

Network of women journalists whose goal is to report information concerning the activities and situation of Latin American women around the world via Inter-Press Service.

CARIBBEAN

Bibliographies

BERRIAN, Brenda, *Bibliography of Women Writers from the Caribbean*. (no. 810)

468. COHEN STUART, Bertie A., *Women in the Caribbean: A Bibliography*, 2 vols, Dept of Caribbean Studies, Royal Institute of Languages and Linguistics, University of Leiden, Leiden, Netherlands, 1979–1985.

Contains 651 entries, supplemented by a further 993 in Part 2, subdivided into Bibliographies, Introductory works, Bibliographies of individual women, Lists of women's organizations, and Bibliography (the main part of the work, which is itself divided by broad subject such as Family and household, Politics and law). Each entry is given a code to identify its 'geographical unit', so that the area covered is immediately apparent. There are author and subject indexes. An excellently arranged bibliography, a model of how to construct one.

469. *Rural Women: A Caribbean Bibliography with Special Reference to Jamaica*, 29 p., Inter-American Institute of Agricultural Sciences, San José, 1980.

Periodicals

470. *Woman Speak!: A Newsletter about Caribbean Women*, 3/yr, WAND, Extra-Mural Dept, University of the West Indies, Pinelands, St Michael, Barbados.

Regional forum for information exchange between women's organizations in the Caribbean.

Organizations

471. CARIBBEAN ASSOCIATION FOR FEMINIST RESEARCH AND ACTION (CAFRA), PO Bag 442, Tunapuna Post Office, Tunapuna, Trinidad & Tobago.

Socialist feminist organization with membership of individuals and groups. Conducts research, acts as a communication network. Publishes *CAFRA News* quarterly.

472. CARIBBEAN WOMEN'S ASSOCIATION, PO Box 49, Basseterre, St Kitts.

For improving the status of Caribbean women through government legislative, social and economic programmes.

473. WOMEN AND DEVELOPMENT UNIT (WAND), c/o Extra-Mural Dept, University of the West Indies, Pinelands, St Michael, Barbados.

Networking organization for individuals, institutions and women's groups in the Caribbean, working closely with the UN Economic Commission for Latin America. Publishes *Woman Speak* (no. 470).

LATIN AMERICAN COUNTRIES: BIBLIOGRAPHIES

Bolivia

474. AGRAMONT VIRREIRA, Miriam, *Bibliografía de la Mujer Boliviana, 1920–1985*, 158 p., Ediciones CIDEM, La Paz, Bolivia, 1986.

Brazil

475. FUNDAÇAO CARLOS CHAGAS, *Mulher Brasileira: Bibliografia Anotada*, 2 vols, Editora Brasiliense, São Paulo, 1979.

A substantial annotated bibliography in Portuguese. Volume 1 covers History, Sociology, Ethnic groups and Feminism; Vol. 2 the Arts & media, Law, Work and Education. Material about Brazilian women is included up to 1976.

Chile

476. ARTEAGA, Ana Maria and Eliana Largo, *La Mujer en Chile: Bibliografía Comentada*, 284 p., Centro de Estudios de la Mujer, Santiago, Chile, 1986.

Guatemala

477. FERGUSON, Anne and Marina FLORES, *Resource Guide: Women in Agriculture: Guatemala*, 111 p., Bean/Cowpea Collaborative Research Support Program, East Lansing, MI, 1987. (Available from Bean/Cowpea CRSP, 200 Center for International Programs, Michigan State University, East Lansing, MI 48824–1035.)

In four parts: the first two consist of a general introduction to Guatemalan small-farm agriculture and the research programme. The third is a survey of women's organizations and organizations of relevance to women. The fourth is a selected bibliography on women's roles in agricultural production etc. in Guatemala, with lengthy and detailed annotations.

Mexico

478. BARTRA, Eli, *Mujer: Una Bibliografía Mexico*, 129 p., Universidad Autónoma Metropolitana, Mexico, 1983.

479. COMISIÓN NACIONAL DE LA MUJER (MEXICO), *Bibliografía sobre la Mujer*, 248 p., Consejo Nacional de la Población, Comisión Nacional de la Mujer, Mexico, 1986.

Venezuela

480. INSTITUTO LATINOAMERICANO DE INVESTIGACIONES SOCIALES, VENEZUELA, *Esterotipos y Roles Sexuales en Venezuela: Un Estudio Bibliográfico, 1975–1985*, 48 p., Ministerio de la Familia, ILDIS, Caracas, Venezuela, 1987.

CHAPTER 10

The Middle East

GENERAL BIBLIOGRAPHIES

481. AHDAB-YEHIA, May and May RIHANI, *A Bibliography of Recent Research on Family and Women in the Arab States*, Institute for Women's Studies in the Arab World, Beirut, 1976.
Included for its coverage of seventies material.

482. AL-BARBAR, Aghil M., *The Study of Arab Women: A Bibliography of Bibliophies*, 4 p., Vance Bibliographies, Monticello, IL, 1980.

483. AL-QAZZAZ, Ayad, *Women in the Middle East and North Africa: An Annotated Bibliography*, 178 p., Center for Middle Eastern Studies, University of Texas, Austin, TX, 1977.
This bibliography of some 270 English-language items is selected to cover the whole range of the Islamic position on women, as well as works dealing with more general socio-economic aspects. The lengthy annotations really amount to abstracts of the books and articles listed. They are arranged in a single alphabetical sequence by author, with a subject index under broad headings. A useful starting point, though now out of date, as the cut-off date is 1977. Most of the works listed were published in the 1970s. Marred by poor proofreading.

MARSHALL, M., *Selected Bibliography of Women in the Arab World with Particular Emphasis on Morocco.* (no. 292)

484. MEGHDESSIAN, Samira Rafidi, *The Status of Arab Women: A Select Bibliography*, 176 p., Mansell, London, 1980.
Includes mainly post-1950 material (1660 items), English and French, with some German, Italian and Spanish items. After a general section material is arranged by country. Includes Mauritania, Somalia and Oman, which Raccagni (no. 486) omits (though the latter has a special section on the Maghreb countries and on South Yemen). Author and subject indexes.

485. OTTO, Ingeborg and Marianne SCHMIDT-DUMONT, *Frauenfragen im modernen Orient: Eine Auswahlbibliographie/Women in the Middle*

East and North Africa: A Selected Bibliography, 247 p., Deutsche Orient-Institut, Dokumentation-Leitstelle Moderner Orient, Hamburg, 1982.

486. RACCAGNI, Michelle, *The Modern Arab Woman: A Bibliography*, 262 p., Scarecrow, Metuchen, NJ, 1978.

This multilingual bibliography includes nearly 3000 items in western languages (mainly English and French) as well as Arabic. It attempts comprehensive coverage up to 1976. After an initial general section it is arranged by country – Algeria, Bahrain, Egypt, Iraq, Jordan, Kuwait, Lebanon, Libya, the Maghreb, Morocco, Palestine, Saudi Arabia, South Yemen, Sudan, Syria, Tunisia, the United Arab Emirates and Yemen. Author and subject indexes follow. Some entries have brief annotations.

487. RUUD, Inger Marie, *Women's Status in the Muslim World: A Bibliographical Survey*, 143 p., E.J. Brill, Cologne, 1981.

Culled from material surveyed in libraries in Oslo, Uppsala, Copenhagen and London, this unannotated bibliography thus covers a good deal of European material and avoids the US bias often found in works on women. There is a good subject index and a geographical breakdown, but the main list is alphabetical. Over 1000 entries.

PERIODICALS

488. *Al-Raida*, 4/yr, Institute for Women's Studies in the Arab World, Beirut University College, PO Box 13, 5053, Beirut, Lebanon, 1976–.

English-language journal publishing current information on Arab women in the Middle East.

ORGANIZATIONS

489. ARAB WOMEN'S SOLIDARITY ASSOCIATION, 25 Murad St, Giza, Egypt.

Promotes social, economic and cultural status of Arab women.

490. INSTITUTE FOR WOMEN'S STUDIES IN THE ARAB WORLD, Beirut University College, PO Box 13, 5053 Beirut, Lebanon.

Research and resource centre to 'arouse general awareness of the needs, potential and responsibilities of women in development'. Acts as liaison between women's groups in Arab countries and elsewhere. Publishes *Al-Raida*. Organizes conferences, seminars, etc.

491. REGIONAL INFORMATION NETWORK ON ARAB WOMEN (RINAW), Social Research Center, American University in Cairo, PO Box 2511, 113 Sharia Kasr el-Aini, Cairo, Egypt.

MIDDLE EASTERN COUNTRIES: BIBLIOGRAPHIES

Iran

492.   MAHDI, Ali-Akbar, 'Women of Iran: a bibliography of sources in the English language', *RFR/DRF Resources for Feminist Research*, vol. 9, no. 4, pp. 19–24, 1981.

About 150 references on women in Iran; sources available in the US.

Israel

493.   CONANT, Barbara, 'Women in Israel: a bibliography',. *Creative Woman*, vol. 9, no. 2, p. 42, 1988.

A brief bibliography of twenty-six items, but including some recent material.

494.   LYTLE, Elizabeth Edith, *Women in Israel: A Selected Bibliography*, 14 p., Vance Bibliographies, Monticello, IL, 1979.

Contains 136 citations to books, articles, dissertations and government documents published between 1938 and 1978.

See also:

CANTOR, Aviva and Ora HAMELSDORF, *The Jewish Woman 1900–1985: A Bibliography*. (no. 1006)

HAMELSDORF, Ora and Sandra ADELSBERG, *Jewish Women and Jewish Law Bibliography*. (no. 1009)

RUUD, Inger Marie, *Women and Judaism: A Selected Annotated Bibliography*. (no. 1007)

PERIODICALS

495.   *Noga*, PO Box 21376, Tel Aviv 61213, Israel.

Only feminist magazine in Hebrew, covering information and research concerning women from an international perspective, including international news.

ORGANIZATIONS

496.   ISRAEL FEMINIST MOVEMENT, PO Box 33041, Tel Aviv, Israel

Networking organization for feminist groups in Israel, working for full equality for women.

CHAPTER 11

North America

CANADA

Women's studies are bibliographically well-organized in Canada, and anyone interested in the country can hardly do better than to peruse the excellent *RFR/DRF: Resources for Feminist Research*, a publication mentioned frequently in this book (see no. 8).

Resources

In addition to *RFR/DRF*, which gives a continous update on Canadian resources (among others), there are the following:

497. *Annuaire des Femmes du Canada/Canadian Women's Directory*, 308 p., Editions Communiqu'elles, Montreal, 1987.

Bilingual listing of 200 women's groups and associations across Canada, arranged by state. There are also lists of advisory councils, publishers, feminist periodicals and national organizations.

BRODRIBB, Somer, *Women's Studies in Canada*. (no. 181)

498. CANADA, WOMEN'S PROGRAM, *Women's Resource Catalogue/Catalogue de Références de la Femme*, 81, 68 p., Dept of the Secretary of State, Ottawa, 1984.

A French and English resource list in two complementary sequences, each listing largely different items, now in its third edition. Material is placed according to language of origin, and arranged by subject in small sections. No index. Extremely useful for sources of information about Canadian women. Lists organizations, periodicals, reports, audiovisual material, bookshops, etc.

RIELLY, Heather and Marilyn HINDMARCH, *Some Sources for Women's History in the Public Archives of Canada*. (no. 714)

Bibliographies

For material on politics and the law in Canada see Chapter 16. For historical works see Chapter 15.

499. FAIRBANKS, Carol and Sara Brooks SUNDBERG, *Farm Women on the Prairie Frontier: A Sourcebook for Canada and the United States*, 236 p., Scarecrow, Metuchen, NJ, 1983.

An illustrated work comprising both essays on prairie women and, in the second part, an annotated bibliography. The essay covers early settlement, pioneer women in the United States and Canada, and perspectives from fiction. The bibliography chapters are History and background, Nonfiction women's writing, Fiction by women and Literary backgrounds. There is a subject index. It is good to have US and Canadian material combined in one source here.

500. HAUCK, Philomena, *Sourcebook on Canadian Women*, 111 p., Canadian Library Association, Ottawa, 1979. (Author's note: 'An annotated guide to books, periodicals, pamphlets, audiovisual materials and general information sources directly or indirectly related to women and their concerns'.)

An attractively presented bibliography designed as 'useful for schools, junior colleges, women's groups, and all those interested in the socialisation of women and their (largely disregarded) role in Canadian life and history'. The annotations and the general presentation of the book are more like a newpaper review section than a bibliography, and none the worse for that. Describing itself as 'inclusive rather than exclusive' the bibliography is divided by broad subject, with an author/title index and a list of publishers' addresses. Now unfortunately out of date.

501. HOULE, Ghislaine, *La Femme au Québec* (Bibliographies québecoises, no. 1), 228 p., Bibliothèque Nationale du Québec, Ministère des Affaires Culturelles, Montréal, 1975. (Also issued under title *La Femme et la Société Québecoise*.)

A French-language bibliography arranged by subject with author and title indexes. Includes almost exclusively Canadian material, covering law, sexuality, politics, literature, biography and general themes, with appendices listing periodicals and organizations. Not annotated.

502. MAZUR, Carol and Sharon PEPPER, *Women in Canada: A Bibliography 1965–1982*, 377 p., OISE Press, Ottawa, 1983. (Rev. and exp. version of *Women in Canada 1965–75*.)

This is a large (over 7000 entries) unannotated bibliography arranged alphabetically by subject. The subject divisions are small and numerous – there is an extensive list at the front – which is at first curious because of the odd juxtapositions, e.g. Air pilots, Alcoholism, Architecture, Archives. However, this is a good solid reference work. An author index is provided. Special entries are made for bibliographies.

503. SAMSON, Marcelle Germain, *Des Livres et des Femmes*, 254 p., Conseil du Statut des Femmes, Gouvernement du Québec, Québec, 1978.

Over 1000 entries, occasionally annotated, covering the usual subjects but from a French-Canadian perspective. Also includes English-language works and much material published in France.

504. VEILLETTE, Denise, *Bibliographie thématique sur la condition féminine*, 255 p., Laboratoire de Recherches Sociologiques, Département de Sociologie, Faculté des Sciences Sociales, Université de Laval, Québec, ?1983.

Periodicals

Listed here are some of the periodicals published in Canada, all of which apart from one have their main entries elsewhere in this book:

Atlantis. (no. 42)

Breaking the Silence. (no. 70)

Canadian Journal of Women and the Law. (no. 725)

Canadian Woman Studies/Les Cahiers de la Femme. (no. 44)

Communiqu'elles. (no. 71)

CRIAW Papers. (no. 45)

Diva: A Quarterly Journal of South Asian Women. (no. 309)

Feminist Perspectives Féministes. (no. 49)

Fireweed. (no. 52)

Gallerie. (no. 579)

Healthsharing. (no. 867)

Hysteria: a magazine on feminist issues. (no. 74)

505. *Kinesis: News about Women That's Not in the Dailies*, 10/yr, Vancouver Status of Women, 301–170 Grant St, Vancouver, BC V5C 2Y6.
Feminist newspaper committed to social change.

Recherches Feministes (no. 60)

RFR/DRF: Resources for Feminist Research/Documentation sur la Recherche Feministe. (no. 8)

Spirals/Spirales: University of Ottawa Papers in Feminist Research. (no. 63)

Vox Benedictina. (no. 1021)

Women's Education des Femmes. (no. 668)

Women and Environments (no. 982)

Organizations

CANADIAN ASSOCIATION FOR WOMEN IN SCIENCE (CAWIS). (no. 956)

CANADIAN CONGRESS FOR LEARNING OPPORTUNITIES FOR WOMEN. (no. 669)

506.   CANADIAN RESEARCH INTITUTE FOR THE ADVANCE-MENT OF WOMEN (CRIAW)/INSTITUT CANADIEN DE RECHERCHES SUR LES FEMMES (ICREF), 151 Slater St, Suite 408, Ottawa K1P 5H3, Canada.

Sponsors and disseminates research. Publishes two series of working papers: *Criaw Papers* (no. 45) and *Feminist Perspectives Féministes* (no. 49).

507. CANADIAN WOMEN'S MOVEMENT ARCHIVES/ARCHIVES CANADIENNES DU MOUVEMENT DES FEMMES, PO Box 128, Station P, Toronto, Ontario M5S 2S7, Canada.

Founded in 1977 to collect material from the contemporary Canadian women's movement, the archive contains records from over 2000 women's groups, etc. in Canada, periodicals, sound recordings and posters, T-shirts and other ephemera. It produces a computerized database of Canadian women's groups called *Fem-Direct*.

CANADIAN WOMEN'S STUDIES ASSOCIATION. (no. 186)

NATIONAL ASSOCIATION OF WOMEN AND THE LAW/ASSOCIATION NATIONALE DE LA FEMME ET LE DROIT. (no. 742).

WOMEN'S HEALTH INTERACTION. (no. 875)

UNITED STATES

Most of the material on the USA is to be found elsewhere in this book, either in Part I or under subjects. We have included here material which is specific to the United States, most of which deals with minority groups. Apart from the few general works here, material on the political and legal system is in Chapter 16.

No research on American women would be complete without a mention of the many bibliographical and reference works of a general nature, most of which are largely American in focus – both because of the volume of writing, and because of the energy of the scholarly women's movement and the financial support for women who are gathering together this material to make it bibliographically accessible.

A good deal of research in United States is at a local level, and we have excluded these works. They are easily identified in the major reference sources.

Reference works

508.   GIBSON, Anne and Timothy FAST, *The Women's Atlas of the United States*, 248 p., Facts on File, New York, 1986.

A valuable book presenting information on women in the USA in map form – covers demographic information, education, family, health, crime and politics. The last map in the book is quite blank – it shows the birthplace of women presidents or vice-presidents.

509.   RIX, Sara, *The American Woman, 1987–88: A Report in Depth*, 350 p., Norton, New York, 1987.

Produced for the Women's Research and Education Institute of the Congressional Caucus for Women's Issues, this is planned to be an annual report 'on the status of women' in the USA 'to keep readers abreast of the changes in the roles of American women and their families, and to analyze the social, political and economic consequences of those changes'. It includes a review of the events of 1986, and summaries of women's position in various fields in a forty-page appendix called American women today: a statistical portrait.

510.   SHORTRIDGE, Barbara Gimla, *Atlas of American Women*, 164 p., Macmillan, New York, 1987.

Statistical information on women in the United States is presented here largely in narrative form, with small maps giving the data in graphic form. All the maps show the variations state by state. A useful and accessible source of statistics, with clear chapter headings dividing the data into subjects such as Demographics, Labor force, Sport, Pregnancy, and so on. There is a Graphics list, listing all the maps and tables under topic.

511.   *Women's Annual: The Year in Review*, 6 issues, G.K. Hall, Boston, 1980–1985.

A useful review of events affecting women in the past year, mainly in America. Each chapter is devoted to a particular subject and reviews the year's developments in both activities and theory. The topics chosen vary slightly from year to year, and cover such subjects as health, education, law, philosophy, etc. Now, sadly, discontinued.

Bibliographies

Many of the general bibliographies on women deal substantially with American women, and some of those that explicitly say so in fact include non-American material. So we have not thought it possible to identify any works which specifically address themselves to the subject of American women. Apart from the general works, in Part I, works on equal rights and the political and legal process are in Chapter 16, while bibliographies on other topics are under the relevant subject.

Organizations and periodicals

It is beyond our brief to attempt to identify all the American women's organizations here. Most of these of national or international importance will be found under the appropriate subject. The works listed in Part I under Organizations will also be useful for tracing American organizations. We list here only the following umbrella organization:

512. NATIONAL COUNCIL FOR RESEARCH ON WOMEN (NCRW), Sara Delano Roosevelt Memorial House, 47–49 E. 65th St, 5th Floor, New York, NY 10021.

A coalition of member research centres, aiming to produce collaborative research, exchange of information, etc.

Minority groups

Works on Black American women and women of colour in general are in Chapter 13.

RESOURCES

513. STAFFORD, Beth, 'Best reference works for the study of minority and Third World Women', *Special Collections*, vol. 3, no. 3/4, pp. 173–190, 1986.

Detailed descriptions of selected major bibliographies. Particularly useful for work on minority women in America.

NATIVE AMERICAN WOMEN

514. ANDERSON, Owanah, *Ohoyo One Thousand: A Resource Guide of American Indian/Alaska Native Women, 1982*, 290 p., Women's Educational Equity Act, US Dept of Education, Washington, DC, 1982. (Updated in 1983 by a 44 page supplement. Distributed by Ohoyo Resource Center, Wichita Falls, TX).

Lists more than 100 Native American and Alaska native women by name, activities, etc.

515. BATAILLE, Gretchen, 'Bibliography on Native American women', *Concerns*, pp. 16–27, 1980.

516. GREEN, Rayna, *Native American Women: A Contextual Bibliography*, 120 p., Indiana UP, Bloomington, IN, 1983.

Nearly 700 briefly annotated entries are arranged alphabetically, with date and subject indexes. A long introduction functions as a literature review pointing a path through the racism and sexism of much writing about Native women which she describes as 'selective, stereotyped and damaging'. Gradually during the sixties less distorted works appeared alongside the 'male-centered and inept', and works by Native women started appearing too. Green, herself a Cherokee, documents all this in the introduction which is an essential signpost to the bibliography.

517. KOEHLER, Lyle, 'Native women of the Americas: a bibliography', *Frontiers*, vol. 6, no. 3, pp. 73–101, 1981. (In a special issue on Native American women.)

Approximately 1000 items, attempting comprehensive coverage. Divided by subject (such as Native women in traditional and modern societies, Out-breeding across racial lines, Marriage and the family unit, Artists and craftswomen, etc.), with a lengthy introductory section on the study of Native American women. Entries are unannotated. Useful.

HISPANIC WOMEN

ALARCON, Norma and Sylvia KOSSNAR, *Bibliography of Hispanic Women Writers*. (no. 828)

518. CABELLO-ARGANDONA, Roberto, Juan GOMEZ-QUIN-ONES and Patricia Herrera DURAN, *The Chicana: A Comprehensive Bibliographic Study*, 308 p., Chicano Studies Center, University of California, Los Angeles, 1975.

Nearly 500 annotations, arranged by subject, with author and title index.

519. CHAPA, Evey, *La Mujer Chicana: An Annotated Bibliography*, 94 p., Chicana Research and Learning Center, Austin, TX, 1976.

Included for its coverage of earlier material, mainly from the sixties and seventies.

CORTINA, Lynna Ellen Rice, *Spanish-American Women Writers: A Bibliographical Research Checklist*. (no. 829)

520. LOEB, Catherine, 'La Chicana: a bibliographic survey', *Frontiers*, vol. 5, no. 2, pp, 59–74, 1980.

This is from a special issue 'Chicanas en el ambiente nacional/Chicanas in the national landscape' and is an excellent survey of late seventies literature on the Chicana.

STONER, K. Lynn, *Latinas of the Americas: A Source Book*. (no. 458)

521. SWEENEY, Judith, 'Chicana history: a review of the literature', In SANCHEZ, Rosaura and Rosa Martinez CRUZ, *Essays en la Mujer*, Chicano Studies Center, UCLA, 1977, pp. 99–122.

A useful historical review with a long bibliography. Includes a section of bibliographies and research guides covering older material.

522.   ZINN, Maxine Baca, 'Mexican heritage woman', *Sage Race Relations Abstracts*, vol, 9, no. 3, pp. 1–12, August 1984.

Covers recent scholarship about Chicanas as part of the larger American Hispanic population.

See also the following periodical:

523.   *Third Woman*, 2/yr, Chicano Studies, Dwinelle Hall 3412, University of California, Berkeley, CA 94720, 1981–.

A forum for creative and critical work of, or on behalf of, Hispanic and Third World women in general.'

WOMEN IN THE REGIONS

FAIRBANKS, Carol and Sara Brooks SUNDBERG, *Farm Women on the Prairie Frontier: A Sourcebook for Canada and the United States*. (no. 499)

FARR, Sidney Saylor, *Appalachian Women: An Annotated Bibliography*. (no. 696).

STEINER-SCOTT, Elizabeth and Elizabeth Pearce WAGLE, *New Jersey Women, 1700–1979: A Bibliography*. (no. 705)

TIMBERLAKE, Andrea *et al.*, *Women of Color and Southern Women: A Bibliography of Social Science Research*, *1975 to 1988*. (no. 646)

PART III

SPECIAL
SUBJECTS

CHAPTER 12

The arts and media

Most of the documentation on women in the arts is concerned with individual art forms. It is noticeable how this varies according to the demands of and the availability of sources for the particular art form. The more women have been an integral and necessary part of the art form the less has been the need to reclaim them or research them. Hence to our surprise we have found nothing on dance, very little on popular music. These will be catered for by the general material available on these subjects.

GENERAL WORKS

Organizations

There exist innumerable groups, workshops, studios, etc., concerned with women's arts, which can best be accessed by reading the various arts and general feminist magazines.

GUIDES TO ORGANIZATIONS

Directory of Women's Media. (no. 611)

This lists among other things women's groups in film, broadcasting, music, theatre and video.

ISIS INTERNATIONAL, *Powerful Images: A Women's Guide to Audiovisual Resources.* (no. 147)

This is invaluable for women's grassroots organizations involved in creating audiovisual material.

524. NAVARETTA, Cynthia, *Guide to Women's Art Organizations and Directory for the Arts: Multi-arts Centers, Organizations, Galleries, Groups, Activities, Networks, Publications, Archives, Slide Registries* . . ., 174 p., Midmarch Associates, New York City, 1982.

Basically a directory, with a supplementary bibliography, covering visual arts, dance, music, theatre, architecture and design, crafts, film and electronic print media, and writing. It includes information on many types of group including artists colonies, funding bodies, art business and resource and information agencies. There is even a section on health hazards. Covers North America only, and is unhappily now becoming out of date.

525.   RFR/DRF RESOURCES FOR FEMINIST RESEARCH, 'Women's art/L'art des femmes', *RFR/DRF Resources for Feminist Research*, vol. 13, no. 4, Dec/Jan 1984/5.

Special issue with articles, book reviews, research in progress, etc., and including an international list of audiovisual resource centres and persons.

GENERAL ARTS ORGANIZATIONS

526.   WOMEN IN ENTERTAINMENT, 7 Thorpe Close, London W10 5XL.

'A national organisation committed to creating better opportunities for women in the arts.' Produces a newsletter six times a year.

527.   WOMEN IN THE ARTS FOUNDATION, 325 Spring St, Room 200, New York, NY 10013.

Organization of women in the arts.

Periodicals

We have listed here arts journals and magazines apart from those which address themselves specifically to one art form. Many of the general feminist periodicals also contain material on the arts, of course, and it is a feature of feminist publishing that drawings, poems and other creative works are frequently published in journals which otherwise are concerned with a particular topic.

We have deliberately excluded 'little magazines' containing only creative work.

528.   *Chrysalis: A Magazine of Women's Culture*, 4/yr, The Woman's Building, 1727 N Spring St, Los Angeles, CA 90012, 1977–. (Ceased publication.)

A magazine publishing material on all the arts, with a strong emphasis on the visual arts. It is a mixture of creative work and critical writing, eclectic in nature, so that some of the material is wider in interest than the arts as such. It includes resource listings.

Creative Woman. (no. 72)

529.   *FAN: Feminist Arts News*, irreg., Distrib. by Central Books, 14 The Leathermarket, London SE1 3ER, 1980–.

A magazine containing all sorts of articles and information on the arts, very strongly based in the women's movement in Britain. Issues focus on a topic (e.g. Film and video). Invaluable for current information on feminist activity in the arts.

530.   *Genders*, 3/yr, University of Texas Press, Austin, TX.

'Essays in art, literature, film and history that focus on sexuality and gender.'

531.   *Helicon Nine: The Journal of Women's Arts and Letters*, 3/yr, PO Box 22412, Kansas City, MO 64113, 1979–.

Interdisciplinary arts journal containing articles, poetry, fiction, visual art, music.

532.   *Heresies: A Feminist Publication on Art and Politics*, 2/yr, PO Box 1306, Canal St Station, New York, NY 10013, 1977–.

'An idea-oriented journal devoted to the examination of art and politics from a feminist perspective.' Dominantly, but not exclusively, concerned with the visual arts.

533.   *Hot Wire: Journal of Women's Music and Culture*, 3/yr, Empty Closet Enterprises, 5210 N. Wayne, Chicago, IL 60640, 1984–.

Deals predominantly with (popular) music, but also includes articles on other art forms.

534.   *Hurricane Alice*, 4/yr, 207 Lind Hall, 207 Church St SE, Minneapolis, MN 55455, 1983–.

Contains creative writing, arts reviews.

535.   *Kalliope: A Journal of Women's Art*, 3/yr, 3939 Roosevelt Blvd, Jacksonville, FL 32205, 1979–.

'Medium of communication through which women artists may share their work, ideas and opinions.' Covers both verbal and visual art forms.

536.   *Women & Performance: A Journal of Feminist Theory*, 2/yr, New York University/ Tisch School of the Arts, 721 Broadway, 6th Floor, New York, NY 10003, 1983–.

Devoted to the performance arts, the journal includes articles, scripts, reviews and notes of resources, announcements and news. A special theme provides a focus for some issues.

MUSIC

It is notable that most of the works on women and music are concerned with classical music. The absence of any material specifically on popular music, apart from the works listed below on jazz, probably reflects the integration of women into the world of popular music. In addition, the majority of these works are about women composers rather than performers – women have traditionally been accepted as interpreters but not as creators.

No distinction has been made here between types of reference work. The majority of works are biographical indexes of one kind of another, catalogues of works or discographies, or a combination of all three. Bibliographical information is relatively scant. There are several important comprehensive works, among which Cohen (no. 538) and Frasier (no. 539) are outstanding, as well as a number confining themselves to particular countries, centuries or genres.

Comprehensive reference works

537. COHEN, Aaron, *International Discography of Women Composers*, 254 p., Greenwood, Westport, CT, 1984.

A companion volume to Cohen's *International Encyclopedia* (see no. 538) this work lists works by 468 women composers of classical and serious music available in recordings. The coverage is worldwide, and there is an index to record labels and companies, and of composers by country.

538. COHEN, Aaron I., *International Encyclopedia of Women Composers: Classical and Serious Music*, 896 p., Bowker, Epping, 1982.

A biographical dictionary of women composers from ancient times to the present containing 5000 composers from nearly 70 countries. Entries include biographical information, compositions, publications, bibliography, key to reference sources. There is an index by country and by century. A standard work.

539. FRASIER, Jane, *Women Composers: A Discography*, 300 p., Information Coordinators Inc., Detroit, MI, 1983.

Lists 337 composers of classical music and over 1000 discs indexed by record company, by title of work, and by genre. Although not as large as the Cohen (no. 537) discography, this work contains some composers omitted in Cohen.

540. HIXON, Donald L. and Don HENNESSEE, *Women in Music: A Biobibliography*, 347 p., Scarecrow, Metuchen, NJ, 1975.

An alphabetical list of musicians 'whose efforts have been directed toward "classical" music'. Each entry gives name, dates, field of musical activity, and lists sources for biographies. Full details of the forty-eight sources are given at the front. There is a classified list of musicians. An unusual and useful source.

541. STERN, Susan, *Women Composers: A Handbook*, 191 p., Scarecrow, Metuchen, NJ, 1978.

An alphabetical list of women 'classical' composers, culled from a number of sources (mostly music reference books, but some articles from journals). Each entry refers to the original source, in which biographical and other

information on the composer can be found. This has been largely
superseded by Cohen (no. 538) and Frasier (no. 539) but nevertheless is a
useful list.

542.   ZAIMONT, Judith Lang, Catherine OVERHAUSER and Jane
GOTTLIEB, *The Musical Woman: An International Perspective*, 2 vols,
Greenwood, Westport, CT, 1984, 1987. (Volume 1: to 1983; Vol. 2:
1984–5.)

These two volumes are each arranged in two sections: first a gazette covering performances, festivals, prizes, publications, discographies, and in
vol. 2 films and videos, conductors and deaths. The second section in both
volumes is a collection of essays – a sort of 'year's work in women's
music', and includes some fascinating material, such as an international
list of women's songs, compiled by Miriam Stewart-Green, and a detailed
article on curriculum creation by Carol Neuls-Bates. There are also some
extremely interesting and painstaking statistics on women in music,
including a survey of women in music textbooks.

Twentieth-century music

543.   LEPAGE, Jane Weiner, *Women Composers, Conductors and Musicians
of the Twentieth Century: Selected Biographies*, 3 vols, Scarecrow, Metuchen,
NJ, 1980–1988.

Together these three volumes provide substantial essays on fifty-two
women musicians, mostly Americans, including lists of compositions,
discography and addresses, but no bibliographical information.

544.   ZAIMONT, Judith Lang and Karen FAMERA, *Contemporary
Concert Music by Women: A Directory of the Composers and Their Works*, 355 p.,
Greenwood, Westport, CT, 1981.

Includes short biographies of seventy-eight women composers and
musicians submitted by the women themselves, printed with a photograph
and a page of handwritten music. Then follows a list of compositions,
divided into ten genres, an address list of publishers, composers, etc., a
discography and a composer index. Covers more women than LePage but
gives less information about them. It includes women from Italy, Belgium,
Germany and Australia as well as the USA.

American music

545.   BLOCK, Adrienne Fried and Carol NEULS-BATES, *Women in
American Music: A Bibliography of Music and Literature*, 303 p., Greenwood,
Westport, CT, 1979.

This work includes musicians from colonial times to the present (1973),
divided into five chronological sections, with preliminary chapters of
reference works and general historical works. It is unusual in that it

includes both literature and music, so each chapter ends with a section listing musical works. There are indexes to both the literature and the music
entries. The abstracts are more detailed than in Skowronski (no. 547).

546. HANDY, D. Antoinette, *Black Women in American Bands and
Orchestras*, 319 p., Scarecrow, Metuchen, NJ, 1981.

A survey arranged in topics – orchestras and orchestra leaders, string
players, wind and percussion players, keyboard players, administrators,
the younger generation. Each chapter consists of an essay followed by
profiles of women performers. There are many photographs, plus a bibliography and indexes.

547. SKOWRONSKI, JoAnn, *Women in American Music: A Bibliography*,
183 p., Scarecrow, Metuchen, NJ, 1978.

A briefly annotated bibliography covering all types of music in America in
1976. It is arranged in four chronological groups with extra sections on
general historical works and reference material. Something of a brief
overview, but useful for its breadth. Block and Neuls-Bates (no. 545) is
more thorough and easier to use.

Jazz

548. LEDER, Jan, *Women in Jazz: A Discography of Instrumentalists
1913–1968*, 305 p., Greenwood, Westport, CT, 1985.

Some 250 women players are identified in this discography, which is split
into two sections: the first is alphabetical by player and, within that,
chronological by recording session, and the second is a chronologically
listed section of recordings with two or more women players. There is an
index of players. The author admits problems in identifying women where
names are not gender-specific. The aim is to show the participation of
women in the instrumental side of jazz since its beginning. Since the cut-off
date of 1986 the number of women instrumentalists is thought have
doubled.

549. PLACKSIN, Sally, *Jazzwomen 1900 to the Present: Their Words, Lives,
and Music*, 332 p., Pluto, London, 1985. (Originally published in the USA
by Wideview Books, New York, 1982.)

This is 'a combined narrative/oral history portrait of women who played or
continue to play important roles in jazz'. It implicitly excludes many of the
'greats' (Billie Holliday, Ella Fitzgerald) but contains biographies of some
sixty jazz vocalists and instrumentalists. There is a selected discography.

Specialized works

550. BOENKE, Heide M., *Flute Music by Women Composers: An Annotated
Catalog*, 217 p., Greenwood, Hamden, CT, 1988.

An alphabetical listing of flute music by women composers from over forty countries and spanning three centuries. Provides biographical information on the composers, publishers, availability of works and annotations on the works themselves.

551. CLAGHORN, Gene, *Women Composers and Hymnists: A Concise Biographical Dictionary*, 288 p., Scarecrow, Metuchen, NJ, 1984.

A list of the concise biographies of 155 composers (of sacred music) and 600 hymnists. Mainly American, but includes English and a few from other countries. Complements Rogal (no. 554) well, as individual hymns are not listed here. The two works could be used together.

552. COOK, Susan and Thomasin LAMAY, *Virtuose in Italy 1600–1640: A Reference Guide*, 163 p., Garland, New York, 1984.

Arranged in three sections, this highly specialized guide has a chapter on the history of the virtuosa from 1580–1640, followed by a repertory of music for the female vocal ensemble, and then an annotated bibliography of musical sources. There is an appendix of female composers and performers.

553. MEGGETT, Joan M., *Keyboard Music by Women Composers: A Catalog and Bibliography*, 210 p., Greenwood, Westport, CT, 1981.

A catalogue of 290 women composers for piano and harpsichord, including brief biographical information and references to further sources, titles of keyboard music (excluding jazz, popular and rock music), bibliography. In the appendices composers are listed by period and by country of origin. There are lists of research libraries and organizations and discographies for the individual composers.

554. ROGAL, Samuel, *Sisters of Sacred Song: A Selected Listing of Women Hymnodists in Great Britain and America*, 162 p., Garland, New York, 1980.

An alphabetical list giving names, dates, nationality and denomination, plus titles of collected hymnals if any, and a list of first lines of hymns. Appendices classify hymnodists by nationality and by denomination, and index hymns by individual and collection titles. There is a long and interesting introduction.

555. STEWART-GREEN, Miriam, *Women Composers: A Checklist of Works for the Solo Voice*, 297 p., G.K. Hall, Boston, 1980.

Lists 3746 women from seventy-two countries, dating from as early as 600 BC. It excludes jazz and folk songs. There is a bibliography. This is a very precise, detailed work for the specialist.

Other works

556. COMMISSION OF THE EUROPEAN COMMUNITIES, *Women and Music* (Women of Europe, Supplement no. 22), 92 p., Commission of the European Communities, Brussels, 1985.

Includes a biographical index of some ninety women musicians 'who were not only well known to their contemporaries but have also made a lasting impression on the history of music'. The selection is described as arbitrary, and is mainly of composers, but includes a few instrumentalists and vocalists, and at least one non-musician (the ballerina, Anna Pavlova). A general bibliography includes books on women musicians, but is also highly selective. Jazz and popular music are mentioned, but not referred to in the biographical index and have only a few entries in the bibliography.

Organizations

There are a number of companies and groups specializing in the production and publishing of music by and for women. A more comprehensive listing will be found in the *Directory of Women's Media* (no. 611).

557. AMERICAN WOMEN COMPOSERS, 1690 36th St NW, Suite 409, Washington, DC 20007.

Organization to help women attain recognition as composers.

558. ARSIS PRESS, 170 NE 33rd St, Fort Lauderdale, FL 33334.

Press publishing serious contemporary music by women.

559. INTERNATIONAL LEAGUE OF WOMEN COMPOSERS, PO Box 42, Three Mile Bay, NY 13693.

A non-profit organization devoted to expanding opportunities for women composers of serious music.

560. LADYSLIPPER, PO Box 3130, Durham, NC 27705.

Supplier of women's music, with large mail-order list.

561. LEONARDA PRODUCTIONS, PO Box 124, Radio City Station, New York, NY 10101.

Company specializing in recording women's music (classical).

562. WRPM, 62 Woodstock Rd, Birmingham B13 8BN.

A distributor of recorded women's music (jazz, folk, rock). Produces a regular catalogue.

VISUAL ARTS

Art is a difficult area to research, and the subject is less well served with comprehensive reference works than, for example, music. The difficulty lies in the fact that exhibitions are not documented, and therefore research on them, and consequently the artists, becomes almost impossible to do outside of one's immediate orbit. It is therefore paradoxically easier to identify the historical than the contemporary, since there is some documentation of earlier periods, and international coverage then becomes possible. One might be inclined to deduce from some of the works listed that modern art is almost exclusively American. There are, however, a number of excellent magazines, and the impression given by these as a whole is more comprehensive.

We have interpreted the term 'visual arts' to cover craft and design as well.

Bio-bibliographical works

563.   ADA, *A Database of Women Artists*, 32 Eland Rd, London SW11 5JY.

A new database, which will hold comprehensive details of European women artists past and present. Available on disc for use on IBM PC compatible micros.

564.   BACHMANN, Donna G. and Sherry PILAND, *Women Artists: An Historical, Contemporary and Feminist Bibliography*, 323 p., Scarecrow, Metuchen, NJ, 1978.

The bibliography is in three sections, divided by century. The central section lists 161 women artists, and under each brief biographical data and works about them – both books and articles and references in standard histories and dictionaries/directories. Section 1 consists of a bibliography of general works, including books, periodicals and catalogues. Section 3 is a selected bibliography on needlework. The nineteenth and twentieth centuries are heavily biased towards American women artists – twenty-four out of forty-one in the nineteenth century and thirty-seven out of sixty-four in the twentieth century are American. The twentieth-century section is the least satisfactory, being extremely selective, and with a cut-off birth date of 1930.

565.   McQUISTON, Liz, *Women in Design: A Contemporary View*, 144 p., Trefoil Publications, London, 1988.

A beautifully produced book describing the work of forty-three designers in different fields and from various countries, who have made an impact on the design profession. They are a mixed collection of 'young and old, classic and controversial'. A presentation of their work is preceded by a biographical statement.

566.   PETTEYS, Chris, *Dictionary of Women Artists: An International Dictionary of Women Artists Born before 1900*, 851 p., G.K. Hall, Boston, 1985.

Thousands of women are listed here with brief biographical details, and a reference to the bibliographical source used. These sources are listed in an appendix.

567.   PRATHER-MOSES, Alice, *The International Dictionary of Women Workers in the Decorative Arts: A Historical Survey from the Distant Past to the Early Decades of the Twentieth Century*, 200 p., Scarecrow, Metuchen, NJ, 1981.

This is a goldmine of information on hundreds of artists and craftswomen, each given a paragraph of biographical and descriptive information. The sources consulted are listed but unfortunately not linked to the individual women and no further bibliographical leads are given. A subject index helps locate women who practised in particular art forms or places.

AMERICAN

568.   CHIARMONTE, Paula, 'Women artists: a resource and research guide', *Art Documentation: Bulletin of the Art Libraries Society of North America*, vol. 1, no. 5, pp. A3–A20, October 1982.

Covers organizations, print resources and non-print resources, including slide sets and registries, filmographies, video, galleries and performance art. Extremely useful.

569.   TUFTS, Eleanor, *American Women Artists, Past and Present: A Selected Bibliographic Guide*, 340 p., Garland, New York, 1984.

A list of 500 artists, including painters, sculptors, graphic artists, photographers and 'conceptual artists', born from colonial times to the mid-twentieth century. The artists are arranged alphabetically, with dates and main medium, followed by selected bibliographies of varying length.

570.   VALIANT, Sharon D., *American Women and Crafts: A Selective, Annotated Bibliography*, 250 p., Garland, New York, 1987.

'This bibliography focuses on the history of women and crafts in both the public and private sector, from the earliest American Indian work to today. Both primary and secondary English-language materials have been selected. A general introduction, chapter introductions, and subject index are provided.' (From publisher's announcement.)

571.   WATSON-JONES, Virginia, *Contemporary American Women Sculptors Bibliographical Directory*, 704 p., Oryx Press, Phoenix, AZ, 1986.

This beautiful book is a 'study of living American women sculptors, and provides a visual and written record of their achievements'. Arranged alphabetically by artist's name, the information includes biographical data, and whereabouts of works, exhibitions, collections, current teaching post and selected bibliography. There is a photograph of one work of art and a statement by the artist. Geographic and media indexes are provided.

AUSTRALIAN

572.   AMBRUS, Caroline, *The Ladies' Picture Show: Sources on a Century of Australian Women Artists*, 288 p., Hale & Iremonger, Sydney, 1984.

A well researched work, with a lengthy introductory chapter on

'Australian women artists between the wars: an unacknowledged generation'. The bibliography lists women artists (with a cut-off date excluding
women born after 1915), and each entry includes brief biographical notes,
awards and exhibitions, galleries and collections where the artist's work is
represented, primary sources (which include newspaper articles and
reviews) and secondary sources (including books). Nearly 400 women are
listed.

Bibliographies

573. BULLOCK, Graham, *Feminist Art and Design: A Bibliography*, 52 p.,
Art and Design Library, Hull College of Higher Education, Hull, 1984.

Although primarily a guide to the library, this is quite a useful general
bibliography on the subject. In eight sections covering books, dissertations, exhibitions held in the seventies and eighties, journals and articles,
film, video, audio and slides, organizations and events, and individual
artists.

574. OLIN, Ferris and Barbara B. MILLER, 'Women and the visual
arts: a bibliographical essay', *Women's Studies Quarterly*, vol. 15, pp. 62–66,
Spring/Summer 1987.

This valuable bibliography is unusual in that it includes a description of the
methods used to obtain the references (and the obstacles encountered in
retrieving information on women in the visual arts). 'We have tried to map
out a typical plan for locating materials' in a library. The works uncovered
by this technique fall into Survey books, Exhibition catalogues, In the
reference collection, Journals, Art education, Art history and Artists
(subdivided by form). There is a final miscellaneous section. The coverage
is confined to the US.

Resources

575. WOMEN ARTISTS SLIDE LIBRARY (WASL), Fulham
Palace, Bishop's Avenue, London SW6 6EA.

Collects information on women artists, past and present, in a reference
library which holds slides, books, catalogues, theses, cuttings and posters
of women in the visual arts. Organizes exhibitions. Publishes a newsletter
(no. 582).

Organizations

There are many local organizations, workshops, galleries, etc.,
which we have not included here, but which can be found by
reading the magazines.

576. SOCIETY OF WOMEN ARTISTS, 34 South Molton St, London
W1Y 2BP.

Founded in the mid-nineteenth century, the Society of Women Artists, although explicitly non-feminist, has been important in encouraging and showing the work of women artists for over 100 years. Holds an annual exhibition, currently at the Westminster Gallery in London.

577. UNION FEMININE ARTISTIQUE ET CULTURELLE: SALONS INTERNATIONAUX (UFACSI), 80 Blvd Louis Schmidt, Be. no. 2, 1040 Brussels, Belgium.

Worldwide federation of women artists, created in 1948 to promote the work of women. Organizes exhibitions, etc.

578. WOMEN'S CAUCUS FOR ART, Moore College of Art, 20th & the Parkway, Philadelphia, PA 19103.

A national organization with chapters throughout the United States, its membership consists of women actively engaged in the visual arts professions. It promotes equality of opportunity in the arts by educational and research programmes.

Periodicals

See also the general arts periodicals listed above (nos 528–536), in particular *FAN* (no. 529) and *Heresies* (no. 532).

579. *Gallerie*, 4/yr, 2901 Panorama Drive, North Vancouver, BC V7G 2A4, Canada, 1988–.

Gallerie Magazine appears three times a year, with the fourth issue made up of the book-length *Gallerie Annual*. Includes work by women artists and essays of art criticism.

580. *Women's Art Journal*, 2/yr, 7008 Sherwood Drive, Knoxville, TN 37919, 1980–.

A glossy art history journal, with scholarly articles on women painters, or themes related to women. Lengthy book reviews. A publication aimed at the international market, with no American bias.

581. *Women Artists News*, 12/yr, Midmarch Associates, PO Box 3304, Grand Central Station, New York, NY 10163, 1975–.

Each issue has a theme, and contains articles, reviews of books and exhibitions, obituaries, comment, news, letters. A lively American magazine.

582. *Women Artists Slide Library Journal*, 12/yr, Women Artists Slide Library, Fulham Palace, Bishop's Avenue, London SW6 6EA, 1986–.

'The most comprehensive and up-to-date publication about women's art and the theoretical issues surrounding all women's art practice everywhere.' This excellent and lively magazine contains articles about women artists and issues of women's art, reviews of exhibitions, etc., letters, listings of events. It is concerned with the Women Artists Slide Library, which is the archive for women's art in Britain.

FILM

Works on women and film cover both women as film-makers and the portrayal of women in film. There is obviously some overlap with television and other media, and more works will be found in the section on Media below. We have excluded material on non-sexist films for children.

Bio-bibliographical works

583.   FOREMAN, Alexa L., *Women in Motion*, 248 p., Bowling Green University Popular Press, Bowling Green, OH, 1983.

This is a list of 'the most representative women involved with motion pictures from the birth of films to the present'. Films are listed only if they are available for rent or sale. All films are 16mm. The women are listed in four categories: independent and avant-garde film-makers, directors, editors and screenwriters. Under each woman's name the films are listed with the title, release date, run time, colour/black and white, distributor. In Chapters 2–4 the cast and director precede a summary of the film; in Chapter 1 only the summary is provided. An appendix of filmographies is provided for some women. There is a list of distributors. Particularly useful for its inclusion of editors and screenwriters.

584.   HECK-RABI, Louise, *Women Film-makers: A Critical Reception*, 408 p., Scarecrow, Metuchen, NJ, 1984.

Intended by the author as 'an introductory salute to the women who in my judgement have made the best, most memorable films', this book contains chapters on film-makers Alice Guy-Blache, Germaine Dulac, Lois Weber, Dorothy Arzner, Leni Riefenstahl, Muriel Box, Maya Deren, Ida Lupino, Mai Zetterling, Shirley Clarke and Agnes Varda.

Filmographies

585.   DAWSON, Bonnie, *Women's Films in Print: An Annotated Guide to 800 16mm Films by Women*, 165 p., Booklegger Press, San Francisco, 1975.

A now classic compilation, listing films alphabetically by maker, with title and subject indexes, a list of distributors and a bibliography.

586.   ROOT, Jane, *Women's Film List*, 239 p., British Film Institute, London, 1985.

An update of previous lists issued by the BFI, this is a more ambitious project. It is divided into six sections: section 1, Films by subject, allowing the user to retrieve films by theme; section 2, Animated films by women; section 3, Formal/experimental films by women; section 4, Television; section 5, Other films by women; section 6, Women directors.

587.   OSHANA, Maryann, *Women of Color: A Filmography of Minority and Third World Women*, 338 p., Garland, New York, 1985.

'This book aims to acquaint the reader with English language films whose characters include a woman of color, specifically an American woman character who belongs to a minority group or a woman of the third world.' Includes films released from 1930–1983 – mostly American, some British. The woman of colour in the films is often actually played by a white woman. Films are listed A–Z by title, giving as much information as possible about them and the minority group they portray. A summary of the plot is given. The films are indexed by actress, by director, and by minority/Third World classification.

588.   OTHER CINEMA, *Women's Movement: A Film Catalogue*, ed. by Sue Clayton, 43 p., Other Cinema, London, 1982.

Substantial reviews of fifty-one feminist films available from the Other Cinema.

589.   SULLIVAN, Kaye, *Films for, by and about Women*, 2 vols, Scarecrow, Metuchen, NJ, 1980, 1985. (Later volume subtitled Series II.)

Together these two volumes are a massive resource for women's films. In each, films are listed by title, with substantial descriptions, particularly in the later volume, and are indexed by subject and director.

Bibliographies

590.   GALERSTEIN, Carolyn L., *Working Women on the Hollywood Screen*, c. 300 p., Garland, New York, 1989.

'This annotated bibliography examines how working women have been portrayed in American films over a forty-five year period. It presents a chronological, organized picture of the perceived role of women in American society as presented on screen from 1930 to 1975.' (From publisher's announcement.)

591.   KOWALSKI, Rosemary Ribich, *Women and Film: A Bibliography*, 278 p., Scarecrow, Metuchen, NJ, 1976.

Over 2000 entries, some described briefly, others more fully, arranged in four sections: Women as performers, Women as film-makers, Images of women, Women columnists and critics, plus index. Predominantly US and UK but not exclusively.

592.   NORMAN, Jenny, *Women and Film Bibliography*, 29 p., British Film Institute, London, 1977. (Extended version of Patricia Erens' biblio-

graphy in Sexual Stratagems – The World of Women and Film.)

Although out of date, this bibliography of some 700 items has some use for retrospective research. The entries, consisting of periodical articles, are unannotated. There are supplementary lists of books, pamphlets, programmes and special magazine editions, and women's film festivals.

593. SMITH, Prudence, *Women and Film Bibliography*, 132 p., British Film Institute, London, 1984.

This is an update and extension of the 1977 BFI publication by Norman (no. 592) but is really a completely new work, since as well as including publications up to 1983 its format is quite different. It is unconventionally arranged, eschewing a subject classification in favour of five different ways of accessing the material: 1 – a list of journal articles arranged alphabetically by journal title; 2 – the same articles arranged chronologically; 3 – articles containing interviews with film-makers arranged by film-maker's name; 4 – articles of feminist criticism and analytical writing on women and film arranged alphabetically by author; 5 – articles concerning specific films arranged by film title. The compiler's claim to provide a 'thorough research tool and a useful resource for Women and Film studies' is well sustained.

Organizations

Women film-makers and women's collectives concerned with the making and distribution of films are listed in the following publications:

ISIS INTERNATIONAL, *Powerful Images: A Women's guide to Audiovisual Resources*. (no. 147)

Directory of Women's Media. (no. 611)

See also the list of arts organizations in *RFR/DRF Resources for Feminist Research*, vol. 13, no. 4, 1984/5 (no. 525) which includes film-making collectives.

There is a growing number of women's film distributors, including the following:

594. CINEMA OF WOMEN, 31 Clerkenwell Close, Islington, London EC1 0AT.

Feminist film and video distributors of films by and about women.

595. CIRCLES, 113 Roman Rd, London E2 0HU.

Feminist distribution company founded in 1980 by women to promote and distribute women's films and video.

596. MAGENTA FILMS, Chelsea Reach, 2nd Floor, 78–89 Lots Rd, London SW10 0RN.

New women's production company, interested in encouraging women film-makers.

597.   WOMEN MAKE MOVIES, 225 Lafayette St, #12, New York, NY 10012.

Distributor for films by and about women. Also runs a Production Assistance Program to raise money for women's productions. Publishes study guides for films and a newsletter.

See also:

WOMEN'S FILM TELEVISION AND VIDEO NETWORK (WFTVN). (no. 625).

Periodicals

Film is also treated in some of the general arts journals listed above (nos 528–536), which often devote issues to the subjects, as well as in theoretical women's studies journals. Only two journals specifically on film have been traced:

598.   *Camera Obscura: A Journal of Feminism and Film Theory*, 3/yr, Johns Hopkins University Press, Baltimore, MD, 1976–.

Articles discussing film from a feminist theoretical perspective. Many of the issues are double or triple ones.

599.   *Frauen und Film*, 4/yr, Rotbuch Verl., Potsdamer Str. 98, 1000 Berlin 30, W. Germany, 1974–.

PHOTOGRAPHY

Resources

The Women Artists Slide Library (no. 575) is developing a black and white photography section.

Periodicals

600.   *Women Focusing: A Photography Newsletter for Women*, 4/yr, 90a Camberwell Rd, London SE5 0EG, 1988–.

A news and resources magazine.

ARCHITECTURE

Bibliographies

601. DOUMATO, Lamia, *Architecture and Women*, 288 p., Garland, New York, 1988.

'This is the first comprehensive bibliography of works by and about American women architects, architectural critics, writers on gardens and landscapes, housing reformers, planners, and women in the arts who have made a significant contribution to the field.' (From publisher's announcement.)

602. DOUMATO, Lamia, *Women: Architects of the Environment*, 12 p., Vance Bibliographies, Monticello, IL, 1981.

603. DOUMATO, Lamia, *Women Architectural Critics*, 13 p., Vance Bibliographies, Monticello, IL, 1982.

604. DOUMATO, Lamia, *Women as Architects: A Historical view*, 12 p., Vance Bibliographies, Monticello, IL, 1978.

605. JOHNSON, Carolyn, *Women in Architecture: An Annotated Bibliography and Guide to Sources of Information*, 25 p., Council of Planning Librarians, Monticello, IL, 1974.

606. HARMON, Robert B., *The Feminine Influence in Architecture: A Selected Bibliography*, 10 p., Vance Bibliographies, Monticello, IL, 1980.

Organizations

607. ALLIANCE OF WOMEN IN ARCHITECTURE, PO Box 5136, FDR Station, New York 10022.

Professional association to promote equal opportunity in architecture and related professions.

608. ASSOCIATION OF WOMEN IN ARCHITECTURE, 7440 University Drive, St Louis, MO 63130.

609. INTERNATIONAL UNION OF WOMEN ARCHITECTS/ UNION INTERNATIONALE DES FEMMES ARCHITECTES, 14 rue Dumont d'Urville, 75116 Paris, France.

Professional association for international communication between women architects.

610. MATRIX: Feminist Architectural Co-operative Ltd, 62 Beechwood Rd, London E8 3DY.

Non-profit-making architectural cooperative doing free work for women's groups and groups which benefit women. It also runs courses for women on reading architectural drawings and technical drawing, and provides a model-making and drawing service.

MEDIA

'Media' is a very fuzzy term and is often interpreted widely (see the entry on the *Directory of Women's Media* below). Relevant material will also be found elsewhere in this chapter, and also in Part I. We have chosen to include material on the mass media (broadcasting, journalism, advertising and popular culture in general).

Reference works

There is one pre-eminent work of reference on the media:

611.   *Directory of Women's Media*, Annual, Women's Institute for Freedom of the Press, 3306 Ross Place NW, Washington, DC 20008, 1972–.

Invaluable for its listings of women's media. These include a list of women's periodicals across the world, probably the most comprehensive published, also presses/publishers, news services, media organizations, public relations, bookstores, arts organizations, etc.

For audiovisual material see the following:

Directory of Women's Media (no. 611)

NORDQUIST, Joan, *Audiovisuals for Women*, (no. 148)

An earlier resource is:

612.   CEULEMANS, Mike and Guido FAUCONNIER, *Mass Media: The Image, Role and Social Conditions of Women: A Collection and Analysis of Research Materials*, 78 p., UNESCO, Paris, 1979. (Also published in French and Spanish.)

Although this is elderly, it is still of some interest because of its worldwide coverage. It is divided into three main sections: 1 – the image of women in mass media; 2 – the professional status of women in the media; 3 – conclusions, implications, recommendations. There is a bibliography of references at the end.

Bio-bibliographical works

BERRIAN, Brenda, *Bibliography of African Women Writers and Journalists: Ancient Egypt – 1984.* (no. 809)

613. *Foremost Women in Communications: A Bibliographical Reference Work on Accomplished Women in Broadcasting, Publishing, Advertising, Public Relations and Allied Professions*, 788 p., Foremost Americans Pub. Corp., New York, 1970.

This is now out of date, but is included for its use as a reference work for retrospective study. Nearly 8000 American women are listed, using the date supplied by the 'biographees' themselves. There is an index by geographical area, which is further broken down by industry or profession.

614. SCHILPP, Madelon Golden and Sharon M. MURPHY, *Great Women of the Press*, 248 p., Southern Illinois UP, Carbondale, IL, 1983.

Covers 18 women in American journalism: Timothy, Goddard, Royall, Hale, Fuller, Walter, Swisshelm, Croly, Nicholson, Tarbell, Gilmer, Barnett, Seaman, Bonfils, Dorr, Thompson, Bourke-White, Higgins.

Bibliographies

615. COURTNEY, Alice and Thomas WHIPPLE, *Sex Stereotyping in Advertising, An Annotated Bibliography*, 96 p., Marketing Science Institute, Cambridge, MA, 1980.

See next entry.

616. COURTNEY, Alice and Thomas WHIPPLE, *Sex Stereotyping in Advertising:* 239 p., Lexington Books, Lexington, MA, 1983.

The subject matter of these two works is the same, but the form and to a lesser extent the detailed content are different. The later work is an extensive literature review of sex roles and advertising, covering description, social attitudes, effectiveness, pressure for change, and regulatory mechanisms. There are lists of references in each chapter, and there is an unannotated unindexed twenty-two page bibliography at the end. The earlier work gives detailed annotations for 250 items, mainly American, but including some Canadian and British material, arranged by subject with an author index. Material is easier to trace in the annotated bibliography, but the literature review includes more items and is three years more recent. Both books cover mainly 1970s material.

617. FISHBURN, Katharine, *Women in Popular Culture: A Reference Guide*, 267 p., Greenwood, Westport, CT, 1982.

A nice resource guide presented as a series of review essays with substantial bibliographies following each, and appendices covering periodicals, lists of bibliographies and resource guides. There is also a chronology, from 1637, of important events and publications in the United States, and a list of institutions and research centers. The review essay topics include popular literature, magazine fiction, film, TV, advertising, fashion, sports, comics, and theories of women in popular culture.

618.   FRIEDMAN, Leslie J., *Sex-Role Stereotyping in the Mass Media: An Annotated Bibliography*, 324 p., Garland, New York, 1977.

Over 1000 entries from mainly North American periodicals and books, speeches, films and magazines from the academic to the popular. Arranged in sections covering advertising, broadcast media, film, print media, popular culture, minority women, men, children's media, and with a handful of references on the influence of stereotypes on occupation choices. Very interesting contents, needs updating.

619.   MONTGOMERY, Sarah, *Women and Television.Bibliography*, 18 p., British Film Institute, London, 1984.

Aims 'to bring together the relatively small amount of critical and analytical work on women and television'

620.   SIGNORIELLI, Nancy, *Role Portrayal and Stereotyping on Television: An Annotated Bibliography of Studies Relating to Women, Minorities, Aging, Sexual Behavior, Health, and Handicaps*, 214 p., Greenwood, Westport, CT, 1985.

Although not exclusively about women, half the entries in this work relate to women, sex roles or sexual behaviour/orientation. It covers material published through 1984 mainly from American books and articles. Author and subject indexes provided.

Organizations

The reference sources mentioned above are invaluable for their coverage of women's media organizations:

Directory of Women's Media. (no. 611)

ISIS INTERNATIONAL, *Powerful Images: A Women's Guide to Audiovisual Resources.* (no. 147)

Among the organizations listed below, we include women's writers' groups, since they cover journalism as well as creative writing.

FEDERATION OF AFRICAN MEDIA WOMEN. (no. 276)

621.   GENDER AND NEW INFORMATION TECHNOLOGIES (GRANITE), c/o Dept of Mass Communication, University of Amsterdam, Oude Hoogstraat 24, 1012 CE Amsterdam, Netherlands.

Group formed at a conference of the International Association for Mass Communication Research, aiming to put gender on the agenda of communication scholars involved in research about new information technologies, and to put new information technologies on the agenda of communication scholars involved in studies about gender.

622. INTERNATIONAL ASSOCIATION OF WOMEN IN RADIO AND TELEVISION, 43 Gainsborough St, Sudbury, Suffolk CO10 6EU.

Founded in 1951 for women to share their professional interests and experience. Conferences are held every two years, after which a Bulletin is published. Has an index of professional women willing to serve in communication projects or broadcasting organization in the Third World. Publishes a three-monthly newsletter.

623. NETWORK OF WOMEN WRITERS ASSOCIATION, 8 The Broadway, Woking, Surrey.

'Acts as a lifeline for all women who write.' Publishes a quarterly magazine featuring women's writing.

ORGANIZATION FOR RESEARCH ON WOMEN AND COMMUNICATION (ORWAC), (no. 857)

624. WOMEN IN MEDIA, 7 Winetavern St, Belfast BT1 1JQ, N. Ireland.

Publications and videos on women.

WOMEN IN PUBLISHING (WIP). (no. 121)

625. WOMEN'S FILM TELEVISION AND VIDEO NETWORK (WFTVN), 79 Wardour St, London W1V 3PH.

'Feminist network to provide support, advice, referrals and a free flow of information between women.' Publishes a quarterly newsletter and a directory of women working in film, TV and video.

626. WOMEN'S INSTITUTE FOR FREEDOM OF THE PRESS, 3306 Ross Place, NW, Washington, DC 20008.

A communications network for women working in the media, with the goals of 'feminizing world media'. Organizes conferences, research, etc. Publishes *Media Report to Women* (no. 630) and *Directory of Women's Media* (no. 611).

627. WOMEN'S MEDIA ACTION GROUP, c/o London Women's Centre, Wesley House, 4 Wild Court, off Kingsway, London WC2B 5AU.

Campaigns for the elimination of sexism in the media.

628. WORLD ASSOCIATION OF WOMEN JOURNALISTS AND WRITERS, 3945 Blvd St Martin Ouest, Chomedey, Laval, Quebec, H7T 1B7.

629. WRITERS GUILD WOMEN'S COMMITTEE, 430 Edgware Rd, London W2 1EH.

Concerned with issues involving women's writing. Liaises with other women's groups from the media. Members are women writing books and writing for TV, film, theatre and radio.

Periodicals

Directory of Women's Media. (no. 611)

630.   *Media Report to Women*, 6/yr, Women's Institute for Freedom of the Press, Communication Research Associates Inc., 10606 Mantz Rd, Silver Spring, MD 20903-1228.

'What women are thinking and doing to change the communication media.' Contains articles on the media, mostly in America.

631.   *Sexroles Within Mass Media*, School of Journalism and Communication Studies, University of Stockholm, Gjorwellsgatan 26, 112 60 Stockholm, Sweden.

A newsletter which gives information about research on sex roles within mass media in order to reach an increased knowledge of this field and further its theoretical and methodological development, and to exchange information.

Women and Language. (no. 856)

Women's Studies in Communication. (no. 855)

CHAPTER 13

Black women

Here are works concerning Black women specifically and women of colour in general. Inevitably the vast majority of them relate to Afro-American women. It is likely that the next decade will see a growth of material on Black women in Britain and other countries, where the Black populations are newer, and where the links are more clearly with the countries of origin.

Further works on ethnic minority women in America are noted under Minority groups in Chapter 11 (nos 513–523). For the most part material on minority women in other countries, though often extensive at grassroots level, is too localized to come within our scope.

ARCHIVES

632. COLLIER-THOMAS, Bettye, 'Towards Black feminism: the creation of the Bethune Museum archives', *Special Collections*, vol. 3, no. 3/4, pp. 43–65, 1986.

Describes the history and development of the National Archives for Black Women's History, currently housed at 1318 Vermont Avenue, Washington, DC, together with the Mary McLeod Memorial Museum. The major holdings are briefly described.

633. NATIONAL ARCHIVES FOR BLACK WOMEN'S HISTORY, 1318 Vermont Ave, Washington, DC 20005.

The major collection of the archives is the records of the National Council of Negro Women, but there are other special collections, and material on Black women's studies is also collected.

RESOURCES

634. HULL, Gloria T., Patricia Bell SCOTT and Barbara SMITH, *But Some of Us Are Brave: Black Women's Studies*, 401 p., Feminist Press, New

York, 1982. (Full title: *All the Women Are White, All the Blacks are Men, But Some of Us Are Brave*.)

An important collection of articles, bibliographies and course outlines, including sections of Black feminism, racism, education and literature.

THESES

SIMS-WOOD, Janet L., 'The Afro-American woman: researching her history'. (no. 643)

BIBLIOGRAPHIES

635.   AMOS, Valerie, 'Black women in Britain: a bibliographic essay', *Sage Race Relations Abstracts*, vol. 7, no. 1, pp. 1–11, Feb. 82.

Short article written from feminist point of view. Critical of much writing about Black women; useful for categorization of institutional material, and for emphasis given to work by Black women themselves.

636.   BROWN, Martha H., 'A listing of non-print materials on Black women', in HULL, Gloria T. *et al.*, *But Some of Us Are Brave* (no. 634), pp. 307–326, Feminist Press, New York, 1982.

This includes lists of 16mm instructional films, major studio films, videotapes, records or phonodiscs, cassette tapes, slides and prints, with a selected bibliography and index to distributors.

CHAPMAN, Dorothy H., *Index to Poetry by Black American Women*. (no. 833)

CREQUE-HARRIS, Leah, 'Literature of the diaspora by women of color'. (no. 834)

DANDRIDGE, Rita B., 'On the novels written by selected Black American women: a bibliographical essay'. (no. 835)

637.   DAVIS, Lenwood G., *The Black Woman in American Society: A Selected Annotated Bibliography*, 159 p., G.K. Hall, Boston, 1975.

An early bibliography of over 700 references to works on Black American women arranged by form: books, articles, reference works, periodicals, reports and government publications. Also includes lists of libraries with major holdings, organizations, notable individuals and some statistics. Indexed.

FERRIER, Carole, 'Black women's prose fiction in English: a selective bibliography'. (no. 836)

HANDY, D. Antoinette, *Black Women in American Bands and Orchestras*. (no. 546)

638. KLOTMAN, Phyllis R. and Wilmer H. BAATZ, *The Black Family and the Black Woman: A Bibliography*, 231 p., Arno Press, New York, 1978.

Primarily a list of the holdings of the Indiana University Library, again unannotated. In two sections: the Black family, covering slave narratives, historical background, twentieth century and children's literature; and the Black woman, covering biography, law, psychology, sociology, literature, arts and the professions. Books and articles are listed, with Indiana library call numbers.

639. REDFERN, Bernice I., *Women of Color in the United States: A Guide to the Literature*, 176 p., Garland, New York, 1989.

'Surveys the recent literature by and about Afro-American, Hispanic American, Asian American and Native American women in the United States . . . It organizes these materials by ethnic group with an introductory discussion of the literature of each group followed by the annotated bibliography'. (From publisher's announcement.)

640. RICHARDSON, Marilyn, *Black Women and Religion: A Bibliography*, 153 p., G.K. Hall, Boston, 1980.

An American-based compilation of some 700 items: first books and articles about Black women and religion, then fiction, drama, poetry, music, art, audiovisual materials, general reference materials and bibliographical information. Indexed.

ROBERTS, J.R., *Black Lesbians: An Annotated Bibliography*. (no. 770)

RUSHING, Andrea Benton, 'An annotated bibliography of images of Black women in Black literature'. (no. 837)

641. SCOTT, Patricia Bell, 'Selected bibliography on Black feminism', in HULL, Gloria T. *et al.*, *But Some of Us Are Brave* (no. 634), pp. 23–33, Feminist Press, New York, 1982.

An unannotated list covering biographies, general historical works, Black women's organizations, and the contemporary scene.

SHERMAN, Joan R., 'Afro-American women poets of the nineteenth century: a guide to research and bio-bibliographies of the poets'. (no. 838)

642. SIMS, Janet L., *The Progress of Afro-American Women: A Selected Bibliography and Resource Guide*, 378 p., Greenwood, Westport, CT, 1980.

Includes nineteenth-and twentieth-century materials on all aspects of the life of the Black American woman, listing over 4000 items but with no annotations. The arrangement is a mixture of categories, some subject, some form, including audiovisual, organizations, magazines, special collections, special periodical issues. Subject and author index. Thorough and useful.

643. SIMS-WOOD, Janet L., 'The Afro-American woman: researching her history', *Reference Services Review*, vol. 11, no. 1, pp. 9–30, Spring 1983.

An annotated bibliography of biographical autobiographical works on or by Afro-Amerian women. It is arranged in an alphabetical sequence by person, with a separate section on special periodical issues.

644. STEVENSON, Rosemary, 'Black women in the United States: a bibliography of recent works', *Black Scholar*, vol. 16, pp. 45–94, March/April 1985.

Contains 74 items, effectively updating an earlier work by Johanetta Cole ('Black women in America: an annotated bibliography', *Black Scholar*, 1971, pp. 42–53). Includes creative writing by Black women as well as works about them. Also complements and updates Sims (no. 642).

645. STEVENSON, Rosemary M., 'Black women in the United States of America: a bibliographical essay', *Sage Race Relations Abstracts*, vol. 8, no. 4, pp. 1–19, Nov. 83.

Covers some historical sources but mainly deals with works relating to current issues, particularly 1970s and early 1980s. Includes sections on bibliographic sources and on graduate research.

646. TIMBERLAKE, Andrea *et al., Women of Color and Southern Women: A Bibliography of Social Science Research, 1975 to 1988*, 264 p., Center for Research on Women, Memphis State University, Memphis, TN, 1988.

Includes Southern White women as well as women of colour. Nearly 2700 entries are arranged in six broad categories: Culture, Education, Employment, Family, Health, Political activism/social movements. Within each category the entries are arranged by ethnic group.

647. WILLIAMS, Ora, *American Black Women in the Arts and Social Sciences: A Bibliographical Survey*, 197 p., Scarecrow, Metuchen, NJ, 1978.

A well arranged but not annotated guide, covering reference material, fine and useful arts, anthologies, literature, history and audiovisual material. Gives bibliographies for fifteen women.

648. YELLIN, Jean Fagan, 'Afro-American women 1800–1910: a working bibliography', in HULL, Gloria T. *et al., But Some of Us Are Brave* (no. 634), pp. 221–244, Feminist Press, New York, 1982.

A useful bibliographic review-style essay listing many sources for the study of Black women in the US, both published works and reference collections.

FILMOGRAPHIES

OSHANA, Maryann, *Women of Color: A Filmography of Minority and Third World Women*. (no. 587)

PERIODICALS

649. *Black Scholar*, 6/yr, Black World Foundation, 300 Brannan St, San Francisco, CA 94107, 1970–.

A journal of Black scholarship, which frequently contains material on Black women, often in the form of special issues (e.g. Black women and feminism, the Black woman writer and the diaspora, etc.).

650. *Sage: A Scholarly Journal on Black Women*, 2/yr, Sage Women's Education Press, PO Box 42741, Atlanta, GA 30311–0741, 1984–.

An interesting and informative journal, publishing issues on special themes (e.g. the Diaspora, Mother/Daughter) and also some 'open' issues. It contains articles, reviews, interviews, resource lists and letters, and is well illustrated with photographs. A notable feature is its regular provision of bibliographies.

ORGANIZATIONS

Innumerable organizations exist for Black women, mainly at a grassroots level. We have listed here some which have a national or international perspective.

651. INTERNATIONAL BLACK WOMEN'S CONGRESS (IBWC), 1081 Bergen St, Suite 200, Newark, NJ 07112.

Aims 'to bring together, at an international level, women of African descent for the purposes of mutual support and socio-economic development'. Publishes quarterly *IBWC Newsletter*.

652. INTERNATIONAL COUNCIL OF AFRICAN WOMEN, PO Box 55076, Washington, DC 20011.

'African women dedicated to networking with women of color worldwide.'

653. NATIONAL INSTITUTE FOR WOMEN OF COLOR (NWIC), Suite 104, 1400 20th St, NW, Washington, DC 20036.

Organization to promote educational and economic equity for women of colour (Black, Hispanic, Asian American, Pacific Islander, American Indian and Alaska Native). Publishes *NWIC Network News*.

CHAPTER 14

Education

There are two clear aspects of education which are reflected in the literature. One is the major topic of the education of girls and women, and material relating to that is collected in this chapter. The other, slightly less easy to define and delimit, has to do with the questions of feminist teaching, of women's place in the curriculum, and of guarding against repeating patriarchal models in methods and behaviour. This we have called women's studies as a discipline, and reference material on this aspect of education will be found in Chapter 3. There is also the question of the role and conditions of women who work in education be it as teachers or students. This material is listed here either as a main entry or by cross-reference to Chapter 24.

GENERAL BIBLIOGRAPHIES

654. GRAMBS, Jean Dresden, *Sex Differences and Education*, *c*. 200 p., Garland, New York, NYP.

'A practical resource of English-language materials . . . organized by subject.' (From publisher's announcement.)

655. PARKER, Franklin and Betty June PARKER, *Women's Education: A World View*, 2 vols, Greenwood, Westport, CT, 1979–1981. (Volume 1: Annotated bibliography of doctoral dissertations; Vol. 2: Annotated bibliography of books and reports.)

Includes 'all available entries in English on many aspects of girls' and women's education worldwide'. Volume 1 is a single alphabetical list of Canadian and American theses. Volume 2 includes nearly 4000 briefly annotated entries arranged in a single alphabetical sequence. There is a subject index referring back to the item numbers, but the mere size of the work as well as the unfriendly computer-produced format make this cumbersome to use – you would have to be very persistent. 'The editors hope that [these volumes] will advance women's studies.' This remains to be seen.

656. RIDDELL, Sheila, 'Bibliography', in *World Yearbook of Education 1984, Women and Education*, ed. by Sandra Acker, Kogan Page, London/Nichols Pub. Co., New York.

This bibliography lists references on women and education, and some general works on women. It is in four parts: the first three list books, official publications and articles, and are not annotated. The fourth section contains annotations for thirty-one of the most significant entries in the preceding sections. English-language only, but with an international perspective.

657. WILKINS, Kay S., *Women's Education in the United States: A Guide to Information Sources*, 217 p., Gale, Detroit, MI, 1979.

An annotated bibliography of over 1000 items, divided into nineteen sections dealing with different aspects of education, the first two of which list reference works and special journal issues. Apart from the sections comprising past theorists of education for women, the works listed are mainly published between 1968 and 1978. There are subject, title and author indexes.

See also:

FAUNCE, Patricia Spencer, *Women and Ambition: A Bibliography*. (no. 1041)

SHREWSBURY, Carolyn M., 'Feminist pedagogy: a bibliography'. (no. 180)

HISTORY OF EDUCATION

658. LIDDLE, Madeline, *A Guide to the Literature of Formal Female Education in England and Wales from 1675 to the Present*, 201 p., Library Association, London, 1979. (FLA thesis.)

As one would expect in a thesis submitted for Fellowship of the Library Association, this is a meticulous work. It includes material published in Great Britain up to January 1987, and though the author disclaims it being a full bibliography, this is a result of her careful research rather than omission. The bibliography, which is preceded by a lengthy introduction, is divided into Reference works, Bibliographies, Official publications and local education authority publications, Theses, Publications of associations and organizations, Periodicals, Texts of girls' education, and Broader educational texts. Two appendices list specialized collections and useful addresses. There is a name index but no subject index. The typescript format inevitably makes this more cumbersome to use than if it was in published format, but it should be an essential starting point for any research on the subject.

659.   SCHNORRENBERG, Barbara Brandon, 'Education for women in eighteenth century England: an annotated bibliography', *Women and Literature*, vol. 4, no. 1, pp. 49–55, 1976.

A bibliography of contemporary works with extensive annotations.

EDUCATIONAL EQUITY AND AFFIRMATIVE ACTION

660.   PARKS, Beverly J. *et al.*, *Sourcebook of Measures of Women's Educational Equity*, 652 p., American Institute for Research in the Behavioral Sciences, Palo Alto, CA, 1979.

'A wide variety of questionnaires, rating scales, inventories . . . for use in examining procedures, progress and outcomes of educational equity programs and projects . . . The sourcebook may be used as a reference for 1, locating research studies related to women's educational equity; 2, identifying methods and ideas for project or program evaluation [etc.]'. The measures are described in detail. There is an annotated bibliography of additional measures.

661.   QUAY, Richard H., *In Pursuit of Equality of Educational Opportunity: A Selective Bibliography and Guide to the Research Literature*, 173 p., Garland, New York, 1977.

Not annotated and now somewhat outdated, most useful for its long list of bibliographies, many of them in report form and otherwise hard to find.

See also:

DOSS, Martha Merrill, *The Directory of Special Opportunities for Women: A National Guide of Educational Opportunities, Career Information, Networks, and Peer Counseling Assistance for Entry or Reentry into the Work Force*. (no. 1054)

EPSKAMP, C., *Inequality in Female Access to Education in Developing Countries*. (no. 246)

662.   SWANSON, Kathryn, *Affirmative Action and Preferential Admissions in Higher Education: An Annotated Bibliography*, 342 p., Scarecrow, Metuchen, NJ, 1981.

Over 1000 entries from American literature of the 1970s, including government publications, periodical and newspaper articles, and chapters from collected works. Arranged in three sections: The law and the courts, The academic community response, and The philosophical debate, with name and title indexes. Each section has an extensive analytical introduction.

WOMEN IN EDUCATION

663.   FLETCHER, Joan, *The Women Student's Handbook: How to Survive in Style at College, Polytechnic or University*, 142 p., Northcote House, Plymouth, 1987.

The book seeks to provide a comprehensive guide for women students on all aspects of higher education – grants, money, accommodation, courses, study, exams, social life, problems, helplines, careers and employment. Its brief is perhaps too wide to be really useful, since a book which is aimed at both intending students (still at school) and mature and overseas students and covering the whole span of college life can hardly reach all its targets. Nevertheless, it approaches the issues in a lively and sympathetic way.

664.   SHAKESHAFT, Charol, *Women in Educational Administration: A Bibliography*, 36 p., Vance Bibliographies, Monticello, IL, 1981.

The coverage is American, and includes 240 books and articles and 114 dissertations.

See also Chapter 24, nos 1054 to 1060, and in particular the following:

FARLEY, Jennie, *Academic Women and Employment Discrimination: A Critical Annotated Bibliography*. (no. 1062)

FEINBERG, Renee, *Women, Education and Employment: A Bibliography of Periodical Citations, Pamphlets, Newspapers, and Government Documents, 1970–1980*. (no. 1055)

CURRICULUM GUIDES

665.   CHAPMAN, Anne, *Feminist Resources for Schools and Colleges: A Guide to Curricular Materials*, 190 p., Feminist Press, New York, 3rd ed., 1986.

Expanded to twice its size from the previous edition, this bibliography of 445 items is designed to 'help teachers increase their own and their students' knowledge of the new scholarship on women'. The first section, Print resources, comprises a list of books divided by subject, with each item having detailed annotations. The emphasis is heavily American. Most valuable is section 2, Audiovisual resources, giving lists of films, slides, tapes, etc., for use in the classroom. There is a directory of publishers/distributors, and author/title and subject indexes.

See also:

CRUIKSHANK, Margaret, *Lesbian Studies Present and Future*. (no. 767)

DULEY, Margot and Mary EDWARDS, *The Cross-Cultural Study of Women: A Comprehensive Guide*. (no. 191)

ELWELL, Ellen Sue Levi and Edward R. LEVENSON, *The Jewish Women's Studies Guide*. (no. 1010)

FRANZOSA, Susan Douglas and Karen A. MAZZA, *Integrating Women's Studies into the Curriculum: An Annotated Bibliography*. (no. 178)

GOLUB, Sharon and Rita Jackway FREEDMAN, *The Psychology of Women: Resources for a Core Curriculum*. (no. 909)

HULL, Gloria T., Patricia Bell SCOTT and Barbara SMITH, *But Some of Us Are Brave: Black Women's Studies*. (no. 634)

PALUDI, Michele A., *Exploring/Teaching the Psychology of Women: A Manual of Resources*. (no. 910)

REESE, Lyn and Jean WILKINSON, *Women in the World: Annotated History Sources for the Secondary Student*. (no. 686)

SCHMITZ, Betty, *Integrating Women's Studies into the Curriculum: A Guide and Bibliography*. (no. 183)

SEXUAL HARASSMENT

CROCKER, Phyllis L., 'Annotated bibliography on sexual harassment in education', (no. 932)

PERIODICALS

666.　*Feminist Teacher*, 3/yr, Ballantine Hall, Indiana University, Bloomington, IN 47405, 1984–.

A journal for teachers; includes articles, news, resource lists, bibliographies.

667.　*Gender and Education*, 4/yr, Carfax Pub. Co., Abingdon, Oxon., 1989–.

A scholarly journal, publishing 'articles and shorter, more polemic "viewpoints" from throughout the world which contribute to feminist knowledge, theory, consciousness, action and debate.'

668.　*Women's Education des Femmes*, 4/yr, Canadian Congress for Learning Opportunities for Women, 47 Main St, Toronto, Ontario M4E 2V6, Canada, 1982–.

'A feminist connection to the world of learning and education'.

ORGANIZATIONS

669. CANADIAN CONGRESS FOR LEARNING OPPORTUNI-TIES FOR WOMEN, 47 Main St, Toronto, Ontario M4E 2V6, Canada.

'A national organization that promotes feminist education and the empowerment of women. Publishes *Women's Education des Femmes* (no. 668).

670. CENTRE FOR RESEARCH AND EDUCATION ON GENDER, Institute of Education, University of London, 20 Bedford Way, London WC1H 0AL.

'Networking and resource facility for researchers concerned with women's issues on gender and sexuality.'

CHAPTER 15

History

Historical study links the present women's movement very firmly to its roots, both in the suffragist movement and earlier. One of the most significant areas of activity in women's studies has been the attempt to redress the balance of historical stucy by reclaiming women's history. Consequently there are several major works of considerable significance in women's studies listed in this chapter which should be essential starting points for any research.

GENERAL WORKS

Archives and libraries

GUIDES TO COLLECTIONS

671. BARROW, Margaret, *Women, 1870–1928: A Select Guide to Printed and archival Sources in the United Kingdom*, 248 p., Mansell, London, 1980.

This essential guide to historical research is divided into four parts: Archives, Printed works, Non-book material and Libraries & record offices. Each part has a detailed list of contents. Part 1, Archives, is divided by major subject (Education, Emigration, Employment, First World War, Moral & social issues, Suffrage, and Diaries), within which the archives are described. Part 2, Printed works, includes a selection of books, pamphlets and periodicals arranged by type (e.g. Bibliographies, Biographies, Official publications, etc.). Within each division the arrangement is by the subject headings used in Part 1. Part 3, Non-book material, lists important collections of artefacts, films, illustrations, newspaper cuttings and oral history. Part 4, Libraries and record offices, describes the holdings of these, with the major part being devoted to a description of the archival collections in the Fawcett Library. There is a subject index and an author/title index.

672. HINDING, Andrea, *Women's History Sources: A Guide to Archives and Manuscript Collections in the United States*, 2 vols, Bowker, New York, 1979.

Volume 1 is a description of '18,000 archives and MS collections of primary sources relating to women', arranged alphabetically by state and city.

Volume 2 is the 400 page index to the entries. This is a massive work of great detail.

673.   KENNEY, Anne R., *Archival Sources for Women's History: An Annotated Bibliography of Guides, Inventories, and Catalogs to Archives and Manuscript Collections in the United States*, c. 125 p., Garland, New York, 1989.

'The first union list of guides to archival sources for women's history . . . offering comprehensive coverage for the years 1970–1986.' (From publisher's announcement.)

LIBRARIES AND LIBRARY CATALOGUES

We have listed here the major historical archives. Further details on these, and on other collections, will be found in Chapter 1.

FAWCETT LIBRARY. (no. 101)

GERRITSEN COLLECTION, *The Gerritsen Collection of Women's History, 1543–1945*. (no. 114)

SCHLESINGER LIBRARY. (no. 107)

ARTHUR & ELIZABETH SCHLESINGER LIBRARY ON THE HISTORY OF WOMEN IN AMERICA, *The Manuscript Inventories and the Catalogs of Manuscripts, Books and Periodicals*. (no. 112)

SOPHIA SMITH COLLECTION, *Catalogs of the Sophia Smith Collection, Women's History Archive, Smith College, Northampton, Massachusetts*. (no. 116)

674.   WEDBORN, Helena, *Women in the First and Second World Wars: A Checklist of Holdings of the Hoover Institution on War, Revolution and Peace*, Hoover Institution, Stanford University, Stanford, CA, 1988.

Microform collections

A number of companies produce microform collections of primary source material. We have not attempted to list these comprehensively, but a description of some of them will be found in Searing (no. 14). A useful overview is provided in Patterson (no. 149).

Directories

675.   JUSTICE, Joyce Allen, *Directory of Women Historians*, 141 p., American Historical Association, Washington, DC, 1975. (Supplement issued 1976.)

An A–Z list of women historians giving position, special interests and publications. Index to special interest provided.

Periodicals

676.   *Gender and History*, 3/yr, Blackwell, Oxford, 1989–.

'Founded as a response to the recent upsurge of interest in historical questions about femininity and masculinity and the roles of women and men in the past . . . The journal will cover all historical periods and a wide spectrum of national societies. It will publish features on methodological issues and source materials, as well as articles on specific topics.' (From publisher's announcement.)

677.   *Journal of Women's History*, 3/yr, Dept of Afro-American Studies, Indiana University, Bloomington, IN 47405, 1989–.

Publishes new historical research on women.

678.   *Lilith: A Feminist History Journal*, PO Box 154, Fitzroy, Melbourne, Victoria 3065, Australia.

Publishes historical articles and reviews informed by a feminist consciousness.

679.   *Pénélope: Pour l'Histoire des Femmes*, 2/yr, Paris, 1979–85.

French women's history journal, now ceased publication.

680.   *Women and History*, 4/yr, Haworth Press, New York, 1989–.

New women's history journal.

Organizations

681.   NATIONAL WOMEN'S HISTORY PROJECT, Box 3716, Santa Rosa, CA 95402.

Its goal is to 'promote the rediscovery and celebration of women in US history. As the originators and primary promoters of National Women's History Month, we also stress a multicultural approach.' It produces an inventory and catalogue of books and other items on women's history, and provides information, referral and consultation services.

682.   WOMEN'S HISTORY NETWORK, Box 3716, Santa Rosa, CA 95402.

A network of around 500 persons and groups coordinated by the National Women's History Project (no. 681). Publishes a newsletter *Women's History Network News*.

General bibliographies

BYRNE, Pamela R. and Suzanne R. ONTIVEROS, *Women in the Third World: A Historical Bibliography*. (no. 243)

683.   FREY, Linda, Marsha FREY and Joanne SCHNEIDER, *Women*

in Western European History: A Select Chronological, Geographical and Topical Bibliography, 831 p., Harvester, Brighton, 1982. (Also published by Greenwood, Westport, CT, 1982, in 2 vols. Volume 1: from antiquity to the French Revolution. Volume 2: nineteenth and twentieth centuries.)

This monumental work, with over 17,000 entries, is an essential beginning for research in this area – Britain, France, Italy, the Iberian peninsula, Germany and the Low Countries (and Greece for the antiquity section only). Arranged by time period, then country, then topic, it provides author and name indexes and a rudimentary subject index. There are no annotations and there are some quirks in the geographical classification (e.g. Greece is a heading only in Antiquity; eighteenth and nineteenth centuries use England as a heading, every other time period has British Isles or Britain. But these minor irregularities do not really detract from the value of a massive resource. Criterion for inclusion was easy availability in the United States, so rare and unpublished material is not included.

684.   FREY, Linda, Marsha FREY and Joanne SCHNEIDER, *Women in Western European History, First Supplement: A Select Chronological, Geographical and Topical Bibliography*, 764 p., Greenwood, Westport, CT, 1986.

Supplements and updates the earlier work, following the same format. Includes a guide to nearly 300 quotations by or about women which are used to introduce the subject areas.

685.   McFEELY, Mary Drake, *Women's Work in Britain and America: From the Nineties to World War I: An Annotated Bibliography*, 155 p., G.K. Hall, Boston, 1982.

Over 500 items thoroughly described in this interesting compilation. Unusual in that it gives equal weight to Britain and America, it provides an informative introduction and author, title and subject indexes. Invaluable for the study of this period.

686.   REESE, Lyn and Jean WILKINSON, *Women in the World: Annotated History Sources for the Secondary Student*, 220 p., Scarecrow, Metuchen, NJ, 1987.

This bibliography is designed for secondary schools. The term 'history' is interpreted widely, the priority being 'to select materials that will make visible the lives of women, that provide authenticity, and that tell an interesting story'. The scope is worldwide, and the references are divided by region, and under that by form. The book is attractively laid out with illustrations, and each item is annotated with Themes, Description, and sometimes Suggested uses. There are title and place indexes, and an appendix of publishers' addresses.

687.   WIESNER, Merry, *Women in the Sixteenth Century: A Bibliography*, 80 p., Center for Reformation Research, St Louis, MO, 1983. (From the Center, 6477 San Bonita Avenue, St Louis, MO 63105.)

A useful collection of very specific material including books and journals from several subject areas. Contains 753 unannotated entries, arranged in nineteen precise sections and within each section by country or group of countries in Europe. Of particular interest are the collections of original sources by and 'to or about' women. An author index, and a list of journal abbreviations is provided.

Diaries

CLINE, Cheryl, *Women's Diaries, Journals and Letters: A Historical Guide*. (no. 161)

DAVIS, Gwenn and Beverly A. JOYCE, *Personal Writings by Women to 1800: A Bibliography of American and British Writers*. (no. 162)

AMERICAN HISTORY

Resources

Archives and libraries are mentioned above in this chapter. The National Women's History Project is an important source for teaching and reference materials, listed in their Resource Service catalog. A published source is:

688. PEREGOY, Marjorie, Julia RHOLES and Sandra TUCKER, 'National Women's History Week: first week in March', *Reference Services Review*, vol. 14, pp. 16–30, Winter 1986.

A resource guide for librarians to help promote history week (soon to become history month). Covers resource groups, reference materials, periodicals, monographs and microforms. Emphasis is on US history rather than on current issues.

Dictionaries

689. ZOPHY, Angela Howard and Frances M. KAVENIK, *Dictionary of American Women's History*, *c*. 750 p., Garland, New York, 1989.

'Consists of short essays with bibliographies on fundamental terms and concepts, events and organizations and individuals important to an understanding of mainstream, minority and ethnic women's history in the US from 1607 to the present.' (From publisher's announcement.)

Bibliographies

See also the general bibliographies above.

690. BLAIR, Karen J., *The History of American Women's Voluntary*

Organizations, 1810–1960: A Guide to Sources, 363 p., G.K. Hall, Boston, 1989.

A specialized bibliography of nearly 700 articles and books about women's voluntary organizations in America, with long annotations. A coding system indicates the category of organization (philanthrophy, suffrage, race, etc.). The index is also coded to show which entries have illustrations, or consist of an illustration only.

691.   BUHLE, Mari Jo, *Women and the American Left: A Guide to Sources*, 281 p., G.K. Hall, Boston, 1983.

Nearly 600 annotated entries, arranged in broad chronological periods: 1871–1900, 1901–1919, 1920–1964, 1965–1981. Within these groups, material is arranged into general works and histories, material specifically addressing 'the woman question' (i.e. how could women advance both their own liberation and the welfare of the working class in general), periodicals, fiction, drama and poetry. Invaluable. Author, subject and title index provided, plus a short list of works useful for further study.

692.   BYRNE, Pamela R. and Susan K. KINNELL, *Women in North America: Summaries of Biographical Articles in History Journals*, 146 p., ABC-Clio, Santa Barbara, CA, 1988.

Identifies 241 articles, drawn from ABC-Clio's history database, with the abstracts arranged alphabetically by the name of the woman. Aimed at a pre-college readership.

693.   CONWAY, Jill K., *The Female Experience in Eighteenth-and Nineteenth-Century America: A Guide to the History of American Women*, 314 p., Princeton UP, Princeton, NJ, 1985. (Originally published by Garland in 1982 as *Society and the Sexes*. Due to be followed by a further work covering the twentieth century.)

Arranged in six main subjects: Culture and society 1750–1840, Industrialization, Roles of middle class women, Religion, Politics, Biology; within these in more specific subject areas. Each section is preceded by interpretative discussion of literature and explanations of the context of the times. Fundamental. Author index provided.

694.   CORDASCO, Francesco, *The Immigrant Woman in North America: An Annotated Bibliography of Selected References*, 231 p., Scarecrow, Metuchen, NJ, 1985.

This attempt to redress some of the biases of written American history includes over 1000 entries in five main groups: Bibliography and reference, Biographical, Work and politics, Reform, Family and education. Subject, author and title index provided. A broad multidisciplinary work.

695.   EVANS, Helen, *Index of References to American Women in Colonial Newspapers through 1800*, 2 vols, The Bibliographer, Bedford, NH, 1979, 1985.

Solid and abstruse. The author considers this a work in progress so more may be expected. At present vol. 1 covers 1756–1770 and vol. 2 1771–1785. Both include New Hampshire newspapers only.

FAIRBANKS, Carol and Sara Brooks SUNDBERG, *Farm Women on the Prairie Frontier: A Sourcebook for Canada and the United States*. (no. 499)

696. FARR, Sidney Saylor, *Appalachian Women: An Annotated Bibliography*, 187 p., University Press of Kentucky, Lexington, KT, 1981.

Over 1000 entries, dating from 1925 to 1979, of material about the women of the Southern Appalachians. Arranged in thirteen subject groups, including fiction and drama, poetry, oral history, coalmining. A combined author, title and subject index is provided. The compiler is herself a mountain woman and the annotations have a special value as commentary on the validity of texts.

697. HARRISON, Cynthia E., *Women in American History: A Bibliography*, 2 vols, ABC-Clio, Santa Barbara, CA, 1979–1985.

Volume 1 contains 3395 abstracts and annotations to articles and a few collections published between 1964 and 1975, and taken from the relevant volumes of *American History and Life*. Volume 2 updates this, adding material to 1984. Both volumes are arranged topically with author and subject indexes, and cover the history of the US and Canada. It is a pity the Canada part does not figure in the title.

HUDAK, Leona M., *Early American Women Printers and Publishers 1639–1820*. (no. 166)

698. KENNEDY, Susan Estabrook, *America's White Working-Class Women: A Historical Bibliography*, 253 p., Garland, New York, 1981.

An extended and readable introduction discusses the problems of definition encountered in compiling this annotated bibliography of over 1000 items. After an opening selection of general works, items are classified chronologically in four groups: seventeenth and eighteenth centuries, nineteenth century, 1900–1940, 1940 to the present. Within the sections there is further subdivision by subject, with an author/subject index.

699. KINNAIRD, Cynthia, *Antifeminism in American Thought: An Annotated Bibliography*, 321 p., G.K. Hall, Boston, 1986.

A collection of over 1000 antifeminist articles, books and pamphlets by both women and men from colonial times through women's suffrage (1920–1). Topics are Women's rights, Women's suffrage, Domesticity and motherhood, Education, Women's intellect and character, Work and creativity, Religion, Women's bodies. The annotations are not critical but seek to give the flavour of the original, with frequent quotations. The author says the compiling of this work gave her a 'colicky gallbladder' because of the strength of feeling against women.

700. KRICHMAR, Albert, *The Women's Rights Movement in the United States, 1848-1970: A Bibliography and Sourcebook*, 436 p., Scarecrow, Metuchen, NJ, 1972.

A large (5170 item) retrospective bibliography, covering the legal, political, economic, religious, educational and professional status of women since 1848, divided by broad subject. There is also a separate list of manuscript sources arranged by state, and a list of 'women's liberation serial publications' also arranged by state (curious, now, given the international status of some of the periodicals). There are indexes including separate indexes to manuscript sources and periodicals. The later volume, *The Women's Movement in the Seventies* (no. 25), is a broader-based work altogether.

701. LERNER, Gerda, *Women are History: A Bibliography in the History of American Women*, Dept of History, University of Wisconsin, Madison, WI, 1986. (Available from Dept of History, Publications, University of Wisconsin, Madison, WI 53706.)

702. MANNING, Beverly, *Index to American Women Speakers, 1828-1978*, 672 p., Scarecrow, Metuchen, NJ, 1980.

Compiled to help students locate women's speeches, this work indexes nearly 200 works by author/speaker, subject and title. Works include conference proceedings, symposia, edited collections of addresses and other forms.

703. MANNING, Beverly, *We Shall Be Heard: An Index to Speeches by American Women 1978-1985*, 620 p., Scarecrow, Metuchen, NJ, 1988.

Supplement to her *Index to American Women Speakers*, this indexes citations from a further 350 sources.

SIMS-WOOD, Janet L., 'The Afro-American woman: researching her history'. (no. 643)

704. SOLTOW, Martha Jane and Mary K. WERY, *American Women and the Labour Movement, 1825-1974: An Annotated Bibliography*, 247 p., Scarecrow, Metuchen, NJ, 1976. (2nd updated edition of *Women in American History, 1825-1935*.)

Arranged by subject – Employment, Trade unions, Working conditions, Strikes, Legislation, Worker education, Labor leaders, Supportive efforts. Detailed annotations; a cross-reference index, plus subject and author index. Also an invaluable appendix listing archival sources on women and labour.

705. STEINER-SCOTT, Elizabeth and Elizabeth Pearce WAGLE, *New Jersey Women, 1770-1979: A Bibliography*, 167 p., Farleigh Dickinson UP, Rutherford, NJ, 1978.

Occasional short annotations in this 100 item collection; arranged first chronologically, followed by sections on biographical material, and education, welfare, work and politics. Local organizations and magazines follow. Index provided. Of local interest.

706. TINGLEY, Elizabeth and Donald F. TINGLEY, *Women and Feminism in American History: A Guide to Information Sources*, 289 p., Gale, Detroit, MI, 1981.

Defining feminism as 'all efforts and sets of beliefs that have proposed bettering the condition of women in any way' this guide lists 'the primary and most important sources on women in history, women today, and the feminist struggle'. Lists of bibliographies, periodicals, MS material, etc., are followed by chronologically arranged historical material. Author, subject and title indexes are provided. Unfortunately, much relevant material has been published since this work, making it seem old-fashioned.

Diaries

See also the general works on diaries above in this chapter, and in Chapter 2.

ADDIS, Patricia K., *Through a Woman's I: An Annotated Bibliography of American Women's Autobiographical Writings, 1946–1976.* (no. 160)

GOODFRIEND, Joyce D., *The Published Diaries and Letters of American Women: An Annotated Bibliography.* (no. 163)

RHODES, Carolyn H., *First Person Female American: A Selected and Annotated Bibliography of the Autobiographies of American Women Living after 1950.* (no. 165)

Guidebooks

TINLING, Marion, *Women Remembered: A Guide to Landmarks of Women's History in the United States.* (no. 1029)

ANCIENT HISTORY

707. GOODWATER, Leanna, *Women in Antiquity: An Annotated Bibliography*, 171 p., Scarecrow, Metuchen, NJ, 1975.

Covers ancient Greece and Rome from earliest records to AD 476, and includes women of the Minoan, Etruscan and Hellenistic civilizations and some Roman provinces. Cleopatra is excluded but a couple of bibliographies on her are mentioned. Classical works are listed, together with their translations. Works published since 1972 are comprehensive in English, and selective in Greek, Latin, French, German and Italian. The material is limited to books and articles. There is a large list of sources, and an index to authors/translators/editors. There is also a name index to notable women with brief biographical information. Over 500 entries, most fully annotated. See also Frey (nos 683-684)

ASIAN HISTORY

SAKALA, Carol, *Women of South Asia: A Guide to Resources*. (no. 330)

AUSTRALIAN HISTORY

708. BETTISON, Margaret and Anne SUMMERS, *Her Story: Australian Women in Print, 1788-1975*, 181 p., Hale & Ironmonger, Sydney, 1980.

A bibliography of over 3000 items aiming to be 'a practical aide [sic] for anyone needing information about any facet of women's lives, past or present'. The range of material is correspondingly wide, many of the items being general works, not specific to women. The book is divided by broad subject, and there is a subject index, a list of periodicals and an additional list of books published between 1976 and 1978. Attractively produced, with photographs, this is a thorough and comprehensive work.

DANIELS, Kay, Mary MURNANE and Anne PICOT, *Women in Australia: An Annotated Guide to Records*. (no. 354)

REED, Janet and Kathleen OAKES, *Women in Australian Society, 1901-1945: A Guide to the Holdings of Australian Archives Relating to Women, 1901-1945*. (no. 355)

BRITISH HISTORY

Archives and libraries are mentioned in the general section above. See also guides to collections, especially Barrow (no. 671).

Bibliographies

709. BAILEY, Susan F., *Women and the British Empire: An Annotated Guide to Sources*, 185 p., Garland, New York, 1983.

An excellent and thoughtful work in four chapters: Wives of administrators, Settlers, Missionaries and Native women. Each chapter starts with a review essay followed by an annotated bibliography listing primary and secondary sources. The index covers author, title and subject. A substantial introduction to the book gives a 'state of the art' of women's history studies, with lists of sources and organizations used. (More detail for South Asia is given in Sakala (no. 330).)

710. EMERSON, Kathy Lynn, *Wives and Daughters: The Women of Sixteenth Century England*, 407 p., Whitston Pub. Co., Troy, NY, 1984.

Really a biographical dictionary of English sixteenth-century women, with an enormous bibliography including many very early works which the author used in her searches. Highly specialized, but invaluable for those studying the period.

711. KANNER, Barbara, *The Women of England: From Anglo-Saxon Times to the Present: Interpretive Bibliographical Essays*, 429 p., Archon Books, Hamden, CT, 1979.

The collection includes twelve chapters by varied authors surveying the research literature on aspects of women in English history. The final chapter describes sources and archives for the study of early twentieth-century women. Victorian women are described via demographic data and via novels. Earlier times are treated more broadly. The bibliographies of each chapter are substantial.

712. KANNER, Barbara, *Women in English Social History, 1800–1914*, 3 vols, Garland, New York, 1987–.

This work aims to be 'the largest and most comprehensive guide for study and research on women of nineteenth and early twentieth century England'. So far only Vol. 3: *Autobiographical Writings* has appeared, and is an annotated list of 776 autobiographies with an introduction consisting of a bibliography of works relevant to the study of autobiography.

713. PALMEGIANO, E.M., *Women and British Periodicals 1832–1967: A Bibliography*, 118 p., Garland, New York, 1976.

'The purpose of this bibliography is to demonstrate the volume and scope of ideas about women in the periodical press 1932–1876.' It includes a checklist of all journals addressed to women, and of more general publications with information on women.

Diaries

See also the works mentioned in the general section above, and in Chapter 1.

HUFF, Cynthia, *British Women's Diaries: A Selected Descriptive Bibliography of Selected Nineteenth-Century Women's Manuscript Diaries*. (no. 164)

Guidebooks

LEGGET, Jane, *Local Heroines: A Women's Gazetteer to England, Scotland and Wales*. (no. 1026)

CANADIAN HISTORY

Resources

714.   RIELLY, Heather and Marilyn HINDMARCH, *Some Sources for Women's History in the Public Archives of Canada* (National Museum of Man, History Division, paper no. 5), 93 p., National Museums of Canada, Ottawa, 1974.

Covers nineteenth- and twentieth-century English-language private papers in the Public Archives of Canada. Federal archives material is not included. Extensively annotated. No index.

Bibliographies

FAIRBANKS, Carol and Sara Brooks SUNDBERG, *Farm Women on the Prairie Frontier: A Sourcebook for Canada and the United States*. (no. 499)

715.   LIGHT, Beth and Veronica STRONG-BOAG, *True Daughters of the North: Canadian Women's History: An Annotated Bibliography*, 210 p., OISE Press, Toronto, 1980.

The arrangement here is in five groups: general references, New France, British North America, Canada 1867–1917, and post World War I Canada. Within each section divisions are made between primary and secondary sources, the latter being further subdivided into general histories, biographies and a section of thirteen specific topics. The first general section also contains a list of bibliographies and inventories, and a section headed historiography. The annotations are short but clear. There is an author index.

GERMAN HISTORY

716.   ARENDT, Ingrid and Hans-Jurgen ARENDT, *Bibliografie zur Geschichte des Kampfes der deutschen Arbeiterklasse für die Befreiung der Frau und zur Rolle der Frau in der deutschen Arbeiterbewegung: Von den Anfangen bis 1970*, 214 p., Pädagogische Hochschule Clara Zetkin, Leipzig, 1974.

Contains 2207 references, mainly to works published in the 1950s and 1960s, giving a full historical picture of women in the labour movement in Germany.

CHAPTER 16

Law and politics

This chapter covers women and the law, equal rights and political participation. The last few years have seen a growth in feminist study of the law, and a burgeoning of academic law reviews addressing this subject. The matter of equal rights for women in the political process is as old as feminism itself, and there are a number of interesting works which look at the matter from a comparative perspective. Politics being somewhat vague in its definition, we include here only those works which concern themselves explicitly with the political process. Many other works, in particular those in Part II, also include material on politics.

GENERAL WORKS

Reference works

717. INTER-PARLIAMENTARY UNION, *Participation of Women in Political Life and in the Decision-Making Process: A World Survey as at 1 April 1988*, 53 p., International Centre for Parliamentary Documentation (CIDP), Geneva 1988.

This useful work presents data on the political participation of women throughout the world under the following headings: Right to vote and to stand for election, Women's access to parliament, Posts held by women in national parliaments, Role of women in national parliaments, Women within political parties, and women's involvement in the activities of the Inter-Parliamentary Union. A poster map is included showing the percentage of women in parliaments worldwide.

Bibliographies

718. AUSMAN, Jon M., *Published Works on Women and Politics*, 15 p., Vance Bibliographies, Monticello, IL 1979.

719. FITCH, Nancy Elizabeth, *Women in Politics; the United States and*

Abroad: A Selected Annotated Bibliography, 33 p., Vance Bibliographies, Monticello, IL, 1982.

A bibliography with emphasis on individual women in politics, rather than women in general.

720. FLANZ, Gisbert, *Comparative Women's Rights and Political Participation in Europe*, 520 p., Transnational Pubs, Dobbs Ferry, NY, 1983.

Concerned with 'the contemporary status of women in all the 34 countries of Europe'. The first half of the book consists of essays comparing countries; they are divided into three sections, before 1918, 1918–1945, post 1945. Two chapters follow on international organizations. The second half of the book is composed of the legal documents (acts, treaties, agreements, etc.) of the individual countries and of the international bodies.

721. HEVENER, Natalie Kaufman, *International Law and the Status of Women*, 249 p., Westview, Boulder, CO, 1983.

A reproduction of twenty-three international legal documents, some treaties, some agreements, which relate to the status of women. A preliminary section discusses the background from 1945 through the 1980s and analyses the changing concepts and approaches. Each document is then briefly introduced and reproduced or summarized. A table showing ratifications by different countries is appended.

722. HUGHES, Marija Matich, *The Sexual Barrier: Legal, Medical, Economic and Social Aspects of Sex Discrimination*, 843 p., Hughes Press, Washington, DC, 3rd ed., 1977.

First published in 1970, this is the third and substantial update of this work, widening the scope to include medical and social aspects of discrimination. Covers sources published from 1960–75, including books, articles, pamphlets and government publications, not restricted to US publications. Includes a table of legal cases. Arranged in subject groups with index. Now rather out of date.

723. WEIS, Ina J., *Women in Politics: A Bibliography*, 56 p., Vance Bibliographies, Monticello, IL, 1979.

Periodicals

724. *Berkeley Women's Law Journal*, Annual, Boalt Hall School of Law, University of California, Berkeley, CA 94720, 1985–.

Student-edited law journal, 'a forum from which to give voice to the complex and varying perspectives affecting the legal concerns of women'.

725. *Canadian Journal of Women and the Law*, 2/yr, Suite 400, 1 Nicholas St, Ottawa, Ontario K1N 7B7, Canada, 1985–.

Bilingual journal. Aimed at a wider readership than lawyers, the purpose is to 'establish a feminist forum for publication of discussion and debate of issues that concern women and law'.

726. *Harvard Women's Law Journal*, Annual, Publications Center, Harvard Law School, Cambridge, MA 02138, 1978–.

'Devoted to the development of a feminist jurisprudence . . . political, economic and sociological perspectives combined with a legal one.'

727. *Wisconsin Women's Law Journal*, Annual, University of Wisconsin Law School, Madison, WI, 1985–.

Another women's law journal from an American law school, inter-disciplinary in approach.

728. *Women and Criminal Justice*, 4/yr, Haworth Press, New York, 1989–.

Covers sociology, criminology and law enforcement.

729. *Women and Politics*, 4/yr, Haworth Press, New York, 1980–.

Contains articles and book reviews. Special theme for each issue. Aimed at the academic market (with most sales probably to institutions).

730. *Women's Rights Law Reporter*, 4/yr, 15 Washington St, Newark, NJ 07012, 1970–.

The pioneer among women's law reviews. Contains scholarly articles and monitors legal developments involving women's rights and sex discrimination.

731. *Working Papers in Women's Law*, University of Oslo Dept of Women's Law, Oslo, Norway, 1983–.

BRITISH ISLES

Reference works

732. COOTE, Anna and Tess GILL, *Women's Rights: A Practical Guide*, 555 p., Penguin, Harmondsworth, 3rd ed., 1981.

Greatly expanded since its first edition, mainly in the light of the sex Discrimination Act 1975, this is the essential guide to women's rights in the UK. It is arranged in sections dealing with marriage, housing, money, etc. The contents list includes a breakdown of the sections of particular interest to special groups, such as single women, divorced women, those living in Scotland, Northern Ireland, etc. There is a useful subject index, and the work is a model of clarity.

733. HUNTER, Eveline, *Scottish Women's Handbook*, 400 p., Stramullion, Edinburgh, 1987.

A compendium of information on women's rights, the law, etc. A Scottish equivalent to Coote and Gill (no. 732).

Periodicals

734. *Rights of Women Bulletin*, 4/yr, Rights of Women, 52–54 Featherstone St, London EC1Y 8RT.

Articles and news on legal issues concerning women in Britain. Also has news from Europe.

735. *300 Group News*, 2/yr, 9 Poland St, London W1V 3DG, 1981.

Newsletter of the 300 Group (no. 737), containing articles and news on equal opportunities, status of women, women in public life.

Organizations

EQUAL OPPORTUNITIES COMMISSION. (no. 376)

736. RIGHTS OF WOMEN, 52–54 Featherstone St, London EC1Y 8RT.

Started in 1975 with a membership of women in the legal profession and others concerned about the law and women. Research, advice and information unit monitors law and legal practices and their impact on women's lives, and advises government bodies on legislation affecting women. Publishes *Rights of Women Bulletin* (no. 734).

737. 300 GROUP, 9 Poland St, London W1V 3DG.

An all-party organization which aims to work towards a minimum of 300 women members of Parliament, the encouragement of women in seeking and holding public office, and in participating in public decision-making processes at all levels. Carries out training in assertiveness and awareness skills. Publishes information packs, etc. and *300 Group News* (no. 735).

738. WOMEN'S LEGAL DEFENCE FUND, 29 Great James St, London WC1N 3ES.

Launched in 1989 to help women to take sex discrimination cases to court. Offers a free service to women by recruiting volunteer lawyers. Publishes a quarterly journal *Between Equals*.

CANADA

Reference works

739. ATCHESON, Elizabeth, Mary EBERTS and Beth SYMES, *Women and Legal Action: Precedents, Resources and Strategies for the Future*, 200 p., Canadian Advisory Council on the Status of Women, Ottawa, 1984.

Covers mainly Canadian law and experience but includes a section on the

United States. Appendices list addresses of relevant groups in both
countries.

Bibliographies

740. RANDALL, Melanie, *The State Bibliography: An Annotated
Bibliography on Women and the State in Canada*, RFR/DRF Resources for
Feminist Research, Toronto, 1988. (Special publication of *Resources for
Feminist Research*.)

'An up-to-date and annotated bibliography of selected analyses of women
and the state in Canada. Using a broad definition of the state and drawing
on work by academics, women's groups and activists, it includes annotations of interdisciplinary writers . . .' (From publisher's announcement.)

741. SHEEHY, Elizabeth and Susan BOYD, *Feminist Perspectives on
Canadian Law: An Annotated Bibliography of Interdisciplinary Writings*,
RFR/DRF Resources for Feminist Research, Toronto, 1989. (Supple-
ment to *RFR/DRF*, vol. 17, no. 4.)

'This bibliography is the most comprehensive and up-to-date collection of
interdisciplinary feminist analyses of law and legal thought in Canada.'
(From publisher's announcement.)

Organizations

742. NATIONAL ASSOCIATION OF WOMEN AND THE
LAW/ASSOCIATION NATIONALE DE LA FEMME ET LE
DROIT, Suite 400, 1 Nicholas St, Ottawa, Ontario K1N 7B7, Canada.

To promote equality of women in Canada by improvement in legal status.
Publishes *Jurisfemme* and *Canadian Journal of Women and the Law* (no. 725).
Founded in 1976.

INDIA

YAGIN, Anwarul, *Protection of Women under the Law: An Annotated
Bibliography*. (no. 345)

UNITED STATES

Reference works

ATCHESON, Elizabeth, Mary EBERTS and Beth SYMES, *Women and
Legal Action: Precedents, Resources and Strategies for the Future*. (no. 739)

743. CHEROW-O'LEARY, Renee, *The State-by-State Guide to Women's
Legal Rights*, 523 p., McGraw-Hill, New York, 1987.

Part 1 is an overview of legal rights in the US, covering home and family, education, employment and women in the community. Part 2, compiled by the National Organization of Women, is a state-by-state guide following the same broad categories. Appendices list factors taken into account in various cases, addresses of regional civil rights offices, and further reading.

744.   LEFCOURT, Carol, *Women and the Law*, Clark Boardman, New York, 1984.

This book aims to enhance the eradication of sex discrimination 'by offering analysis and practical advice in selected relevant areas of law not ordinarily addressed in the texts used by law practitioners and teachers . . . Each chapter describes the general state of the law in an area that directly affects women, analyses the area as it relates to furthering women's rights . . . and offers practical suggestions and practice aids, such as sample complaints or contracts.' Chapters cover work, family, interpersonal contracts, violence against women, childbirth and nurturing. Contributors discuss cases in US law and provide addresses and resources where possible.

745.   NILES, Gayle and Douglas SNIDER, *Woman's Counsel: A Legal Guide for Women*, 240 p., Arden Press, Denver, CO, 1984.

'This book was written to demystify the law as it relates to those problems most often encountered by women.' It is a comprehensive compilation on basic rights, obligations, legal procedures, etc., in America. The main sections are Dealing with attorneys. The courts, Dealing with the police, The family, Women as victims, Purely financial. The work is clearly laid out and written, with the subsections immediately identifiable in the contents list. There is a subject index to enable topics to be located.

746.   PAIZIS, Suzanne *Getting Her Elected: A Political Woman's Handbook*, 129 p., Creative Eds, Sacramento, CA, 1977.

A practical guide to running an election campaign. US oriented, but contains much information of general applicability. Includes sections on finance, campaign organization, advertising and media, personnel and research.

Biographical works

747.   CENTER FOR THE AMERICAN WOMAN AND POLITICS, Rutgers University, *Women in Public Office: A Biographical Directory and Statistical Analysis*, 510 p., Scarecrow, Metuchen, NJ, 2nd ed., 1978.

The main part of this work is a directory of women office-holders, brief biographical information being given where it was available. This is preceded by a statistical analysis.

748.   STINEMAN, Esther, *American Political Women: Contemporary and Historical Profiles*, 228 p., Libraries Unlimited, Littleton, CO, 1988.

Sixty portraits, with individual biographies, of congresswomen, ambassadors, mayors, governors and presidential assistants active in US politics in the late 1970s and early 1980s. The entries describe legislative and other achievements, views towards the women's movement, and the individual's own career development. Five appendices list other women in government, and a thirty-page bibliography provides additional resources, concentrating on the role of women in traditional American politics. It includes feminist critiques of political science literature, lists some dissertations, and has a resource list of libraries and organizations for women in politics. An excellently organized and well thought out guide.

See also the general biographical works in Chapter 2, and in particular:

LEAVITT, Judith A., *American Women Managers and Administrators: A Selective Biographical Dictionary of Twentieth-Century Leaders in Business, Education and Government*. (no. 171)

Bibliographies

749.   ARIEL, Joan, Ellen BROIDY and Susan SEARING, *Women's Legal Rights in the United States: A Selective Bibliography*, 55 p., American Library Association, Chicago, IL, 1985.

This brief and useful bibliography is preceded by a short article by Judith Lichtman on the need for the ERA. The main purpose of the book is 'to provide access to sources of practical information about women's legal rights and responsibilities'. There is a final section of further information and addresses.

750.   BENJAMIN N. CARDOZO SCHOOL OF LAW, Yeshiva University, *Women's Annotated Legal Bibliography*, 329 p., Clark Boardman Co., New York, 1984.

This is a 'comprehensive annotated bibliography of American legal commentary concerning women's issues'. It provides synopses of law review articles and student works from 1978 to 1983. In twelve sections: abortion, battered women, DES, employment discrimination, ERA, pornography, prostitution, rape, the draft, health, international law, taxation. A table of cases is appended.

BUHLE, Mari Jo, *Women and the American Left: A Guide to Sources*. (no. 691)

751.   ELLISON, Charles E., *Women and Citizen Participation: A Selected Bibliography*, 19 p., Vance Bibliographies, Monticello, IL, 1981.

752.   EQUAL RIGHTS AMENDMENT PROJECT, *The Equal Rights Amendment: A Bibliographic Study*. Anita Miller, project director, Hazel Greenberg, editor, 367 p., Greenwood, Westport, CT, 1976.

Taken together with Feinberg (no. 753) the two books provide a comprehensive bibliographic survey of the ERA to 1985. This volume, to 1975, lists congressional publications, other government publications, books, chapters of books, dissertations, pamphlets and brochures, and periodical and newspaper articles. There are no annotations. Author and organization indexes are provided.

753. FEINBERG, Renee, *The Equal Rights Amendment: An Annotated Bibliography of the Issues 1976–1985*, 151 p., Greenwood, Westport, CT, 1986.

This is a sequel to the Miller and Greenberg bibliography (see Equal Rights Amendment Project, no. 752), covering the literature on the ERA since then. It includes mainly newspaper and journal articles, government publications and television broadcasts. Articles shorter than three pages are not annotated. Arranged topically with indexes. Unusual in its summaries of TV coverage, which the compiler suggests is partly to blame for the failure of enough states to ratify the amendment by 1982.

754. NELSON, Barbara J., *American Women and Politics: A Selected Bibliography and Resource Guide*, 254 p., Garland, New York, 1984.

Contains 1611 items, including books, articles, government publications and research reports mainly published between 1970 and 1982. Arranged in chapters covering social movements, women's rights, nature and nurture, the family, political dependants, political leadership, social policy, feminist theory. The last chapter lists reference sources for women and politics. Author, title and subject indexes are provided. Material was selected with a particular aim of illustrating the diversity of women's experience. Thus minority women are slightly more 'present' than usual here.

755. SCHRAMM, Sarah Slavin, 'Women in the American political system: a selected bibliography', *Women and Politics*, vol. 1, no. 1, Spring 1980.

The eighty-eight items are not annotated, but divided into short sections and given context by the introduction to each section. The subjects are, for example, roles and expectations, access to the policy process. A useful work.

756. SELLEN, Betty-Carol and Patricia A. YOUNG, *Feminists, Pornography and the Law: An Annotated Bibliography of Conflict*, 204 p., Library Professional Pubs, Hamden, CT, 1987.

An annotated bibliography of materials representing all sides of the anti-pornography debate in the US, and explicitly neutral in its position. The bibliography is arranged by type of publication – books, magazine articles, newspapers, non-print media, unpublished material – and there is a list of organizations. There is an appendix of periodicals containing frequent references to the pornography debate, and a chronology of newspaper articles.

757. STANWICK, Kathy and Christine LI, *The Political Participation of Women in The United States: A Select Bibliography, 1950–1976*, 160 p., Scarecrow, Metuchen, NJ 1977. (Published for the Center for the American Woman and Politics, Rutgers University.)

A comprehensive, though unannotated, bibliography of material published between 1950 and 1976. Unusually arranged by form of material: reference material, periodicals, books, reports, dissertations, unpublished papers and research in progress. There is an author index and a bibliographical index.

Periodicals

Many organizations produce newsletters, which we have not listed.

758. *National NOW Times*, 8/yr, National Organization for Women, 1401 New York Ave. NW, Suite 800, Washington, DC 20005, 1977–.
Tabloid format, with news of NOW activities.

759. *Women's Times*, 26/yr, Washington News Services Inc., PO Box 39113, Washington, DC 20016, 1986–.

A fortnightly news-sheet on constitutional and other progress on women's rights in the US, including notes of pressure groups, cases, congressional news, etc.

Organizations

We have only been able to note some of the major national organizations in America. There are innumerable state-wide and local organizations as well as other national ones, all easily accessible via the standard reference works, and we offer the following as examples rather than as an authoritative list.

760. CENTER FOR THE AMERICAN WOMAN AND POLITICS, Eagleton Institute of Politics, Rutgers University, New Brunswick, NJ 08901.

Research and education centre to develop and disseminate information about women's participation in politics and public life.

761. CENTER FOR WOMEN POLICY STUDIES, 2000 P St NW, Suite 508, Washington, DC 20036.

Works for change in social, legal and political status of women. Conducts policy research. Publishes *Response to the Victimization of Women and Children* quarterly (no. 937)

762.   NATIONAL ORGANIZATION FOR WOMEN (NOW), 1401 New York Ave. NW, Suite 800, Washington, DC 20005.

Established in 1966 as one of the pioneers of the modern feminist movement. Lobbies on a wide range of social and political issues. Publishes *National NOW Times* (no. 758)

763.   WOMEN'S LAW PROJECT, 112 S 16th St, Suite 1012, Philadelphia, PA 19102.

Conducts test case litigation for women's rights.

CHAPTER 17

Lesbians

On the whole, material specifically about lesbian women is collected and described here. The main exceptions are books about literary works; in these cases the main entry is made in Chapter 18, with a cross-reference here.

In recent years the increased visibility of lesbians in the women's movement, and to a lesser extent outside it, has made it possible to recognize the pervasive and often implicit assumptions of heterosexuality in our culture. Some books on women's issues now attempt not to make these assumptions, and hopefully will be more useful to lesbian women as a result. However, there is a long way to go.

As usual there is a predominance of American material listed here which is partly due to the steady bibliographical efforts of Naiad Press during the last decade. It is good to have the Allen bibliography (no. 764) in time to be included, as an indication of works available in Britain.

GENERAL BIBLIOGRAPHIES

764. ALLEN, Jane *et al.*, *Out on the Shelves: Lesbian Books into Libraries*, 81 p., AAL Publishing, Newcastle-under-Lyme, 1989.

A well-annotated and nicely laid out bibliography of books for libraries and library users based on the idea that 'everybody should be able to read about their own lives in books supplied by libraries'. In the UK this has become a contentious issue with the passage of the 1988 Local Government Act, whose Clause 28 forbids the promotion of homosexuality by a local authority. An appendix reprints the Library Association's brief to librarians on this issue. There is a section on how to order lesbian books, and lists of periodicals and organizations.

765. ARNUP, Katherine and Amy GOTTLIEB, 'Annotated bibliography', *RFR/DRF Resources for Feminist Research*, vol. 12, no. 1, pp. 90–105, 1983.

'A review of lesbian sources, both historical and contemporary.'

Covers Canada, US and UK. Excludes biography and literature. Arranged in topics. Includes lists of special issues of periodicals devoted to lesbianism, of archives, and of special collection and history projects. An unusual and valuable feature is the list of lesbian articles in six Canadian periodicals: *The Other Woman, Broadside, Fireweed, Radical Reviewer, Kinesis* and *Uream.*

766. MAGGIORE, Dolores J., *Lesbianism: An Annotated Bibliography and Guide to the Literature 1976–1986*, 156 p., Scarecrow, Metuchen, NJ, 1988.

A good bibliography of some 350 publications and organizations, compiled primarily for social workers. A detailed introduction surveys the issues and the literature, but it is marred by a slightly distant and stilted tone.

RESOURCES

767. CRUIKSHANK, Margaret, *Lesbian Studies Present and Future*, 286 p., Feminist Press, Old Westbury, NY, 1982.

This book is a rich source of ideas and material. It contains numerous contributions from women active in lesbian culture, and covers academia, schools, research and documentation, including essays on using subject indexes to trace lesbian material (difficult), a bibliographical article on Black lesbians, one on biographical material, and a study of lesbianism in women's studies textbooks. It also has a useful resources list covering Canada (partially) and the US, a periodicals list (including a list of special issues), bibliographies, dissertations, publishers, grants, work in progress, and sample syllabi from courses on lesbianism. It closes with a substantial bibliography of books and articles.

768. RFR/DRF RESOURCES FOR FEMINIST RESEARCH, 'The lesbian issue/Etre lesbienne', *RFR/DRF Resources for Feminist Research*, vol. 12, no. 1, p. 109, 1983.

The whole of this issue of *RFR* is devoted to 'the lesbian experience in English Canada and Quebec'. In fact its relevance is international. It includes short articles on many topics, book reviews and a resource section with lists of organizations and groups in Canada, periodicals worldwide, a list of the lesbian periodical holdings of the Canadian Gay Archives, and a list of films, videos and slideshows that are about some aspect of lesbian experience. See also the separately listed bibliography by Arnup (no. 765).

LITERATURE

CRAMER, Patricia, 'Building a tradition for lesbian feminist literary criticism: an annotated bibliography'. (no. 839)

GARBER, Eric and Lyn PALEO, *Uranian Worlds: A Reader's Guide to Alternative Sexuality in Science Fiction and Fantasy*. (no. 843)

GRIER, Barbara J., *The Lesbian in Literature*. (no. 840)

KUDA, Marie J., *Women Loving Women: A Select and Annotated Bibliography of Women Loving Women in Literature*. (no. 841)

OTHER SPECIFIC WORKS

769.   DUGGAN, Lisa, 'Lesbianism and American history: a brief source review', *Frontiers*, vol. 4, pp. 80–85, 1976.

A review of the paucity of historical material describing 'the social arrangements which devalue me, and the lives and resistance of women before me', and a briefly annotated bibliography of available material. Also a list of archives, projects and resources in the USA.

770.   ROBERTS, J.R., *Black Lesbians: An Annotated Bibliography*, 93 p., Naiad Press, Tallahassee, FL, 1981.

Everything the author could find in this rather underdocumented field is listed here, grouped into Lives and lifestyles, Oppression, Resistance & liberation, Literature, Music, Periodicals, Research, Reference and Popular studies. There is a subject/author index and a directory of organizations.

GUIDES TO PERIODICALS

771.   MALINOWSKY, H. Robert, *International Directory of Gay and Lesbian Periodicals*, 226 p., Oryx Press, Phoenix, AZ, 1987.

This contains by far the most comprehensive and up-to-date listing of lesbian periodicals. Includes 1924 gay and lesbian periodicals, with considerable detail where available (including circulation, advertising and subscription rates, etc., as well as details of frequency, publisher, and a description of the content). There is a subject/geographic index enabling all lesbian journals to be easily identified, and also all feminist ones. 'Lesbian' here is applied to many feminist journals which are not specifically so (e.g. many of the scholarly women's studies journals). The coverage also includes erotic magazines and directories. There is a publisher/editor index.

772.   POTTER, Clare, *The Lesbian Periodicals Index*, 413 p., Naiad Press, Tallahassee, FL, 1986.

An author and subject index to forty-two lesbian periodicals, most now no longer published. These were basically 1970s publications; one comes from the 1940s, and only two were still current at the time of writing, but of course others have taken the place of discontinued ones. Includes a list of libraries and archives with holdings of lesbian periodicals.

See also:

CLARDY, Andrea Fleck, *Words to the Wise: A Writer's Guide to Feminist and Lesbian Periodicals and Publishers*. (no. 33)

Other useful sources are the list of Canadian periodicals in the *RFR/DRF* Lesbian issue (no. 768) and the list of periodicals in Cruikshank (no. 767). For special issues of periodicals see the lists in Arnup (no. 765) and in Cruikshank.

PERIODICALS

773. *Common Lives/Lesbian Lives*, 4/yr, PO Box 1553, Iowa City, IA 52244, 1981–.

'Seeks to document the lives of ordinary lesbians.'

774. *Gossip*: a journal of lesbian feminist ethics, 3/yr, Onlywoman Press, London, 1986–.

Lesbian journal of discussion.

775. *Lesbia: Revue Lesbienne d'Expressions, d'Information, d'Opinions*, 11/yr, BP 539, 75529 Paris, France, 1982–.

Magazine with articles, news, adverts, reviews.

776. *Lesbian Archive and Information Centre Newsletter*, 1/yr, BCM 7005, London WC1N 3XX, 1987–.

Annual journal of the Archive (no. 784) covers news, reviews and articles about the collection, and about events organized by the centre. Issue no. 2 lists periodical titles, but does not indicate exact holdings.

777. *Lesbian Ethics*, 3/yr, PO Box 4723, Albuquerque, NM 87106, 1986–.

Articles on lesbian themes, aimed very much at the lesbian community.

778. *Lesbian Herstory Archives Newsletter*, irreg., Lesbian Herstory Educational Foundation, PO Box 1258, New York, NY 10116, 1975–.

Reports of the work of the Archive in each issue, often including lists of holdings.

779. *Lesbian Information Service Newsletter*, 12/yr, Lesbian Feminist Press, PO Box 194, Leicester LE1 9HP, 1987–.

International and national news and listings, also letters, articles and book reviews. Starting November 1988 there are quarterly listings which are extensive for Britain, slightly sketchy but useful for other countries. Both sections include publications. The intervening issues carry listing updates.

780. *Matrices: A Lesbian–Feminist Research Newsletter*, 3/yr, Women's Studies Dept 492 Ford Hall, University of Minnesota, Minneapolis, MN 55455, 1977–.

'Matrices is an international network of lesbian-feminists, sharing information.' The newsletter includes notes on research, news, reviews, current awareness, bibliographies.

781.   *Sinister Wisdom: A Journal for the Lesbian Imagination in the Arts and Politics*, 4/yr, PO Box 3252, Berkeley, CA 94703, 1976–.

A mixture of creative writing – stories, poems – and articles with bibliographical and/or political content, often a special theme for each issue. A good read.

ORGANIZATIONS

782.   INTERNATIONAL LESBIAN INFORMATION SERVICE (ILIS), COC, Rosenstraat 8, 1016 NX Amsterdam, Netherlands.

Clearing-house and networking service. Publishes *ILIS Newsletter*.

783.   LESBIAN INFORMATION SERVICE, PO Box 194, Leicester LE1 9HP.

'To facilitate communication between Lesbians and promote understanding of Lesbian experience in order to combat discrimination.' Produces a newsletter (no. 779).

LIBRARIES AND ARCHIVES

784.   LESBIAN ARCHIVE, BCM Box 7005, London WC1N 3XX.

Started in 1984 to collect 'material from the past and present of specific interest to lesbians'. Includes much ephemera, as well as books, periodicals, badges, MSS, souvenirs, etc. Publishes an annual newsletter (no. 776).

785.   LESBIAN HERSTORY ARCHIVES, Lesbian Herstory Educational Foundation, PO Box 1258, New York, NY 10016.

Exists to gather and preserve records of lesbian lives and activities. Publishes *Lesbian Herstory Archives Newsletter* (no. 778).

786.   PARKINSON, Phil, 'Lesbian and gay archives in New Zealand: a minority gathers its history', *Archifacts*, vol. 4, pp. 7–14, 1984.

An account of one of the archives of gay and lesbian material in New Zealand.

CHAPTER 18

Literature and language

The bibliography of women writers is well developed, especially as far as American literature is concerned, and there are a number of important reference works and general bibliographies, with new ones coming off the press with great regularity. We have completely omitted here bibliographies on individual writers. There are a great many of these, and they are readily accessible for the most part.

GENERAL WORKS

Bio-bibliographical works

We have included here encyclopaedic and biographical reference works on women writers. Much biographical information can also be found in the general works in Chapter 2 (nos. 152–159).

787.   FAUST, Langdon Lynne, *American Women Writers: A Critical Reference Guide from Colonial Times to the Present*, 2 vols, Ungar, New York, 1983.

This is an abridged version of a four volume work originally published from 1979 to 1982, including over 1000 'biocritical' articles on women writers. Of these 400 are included in the abridged edition. Arranged alphabetically with index.

788.   MAINIERO, Linda, *American Women Writers: A Critical Reference Guide from Colonial Times to the Present*, 4 vols, Ungar, New York, 1979–.

This four-volume work includes about 1500 authors arranged A–Z by surname, with a short biographical essay of one to four pages with bibliographical notes appended to each entry. Children's authors are included, and so are some women writers whose *œuvre* is not primarily literary, e.g. Margaret Mead.

789.   MARSHALL, Alice, *Pen Names of Women Writers*, 181 p., Alice Kahler Marshall, Camp Hill, PA, 1985. (Available from: The Alice Marshall Collection, 211 North 17th Street, Camp Hill, PA 17011.)

Subtitled 'A compendium of the literary identities of 2650 women novelists, playwrights, poets, diarists, journalists and miscellaneous writers . . . fully cross-referenced'. The alphabetical lists of names and pseudonyms are illustrated with photographs and quotes, and there is a chilling section called 'Some views of the authoress, or why she chose anonymity' just in case we wondered. A really nice book.

790. ROBINSON, Doris, *Women Novelists, 1891–1920: An Index to Biographies and Autobiographical Sources*, 458 p., Garland, New York, 1984.

Intended as a companion to Grimes and Daims (no. 800) whose database was used in compiling the work, this index gives biographical sources for 1565 of the authors, including obituary notices, mainly in the *New York Times* and the London *Times*. Useful lists of biographical dictionaries and collected biography are included, as is an index to women by country.

791. SCHLUETER, Paul and June SCHLUETER, *Encyclopedia of British Women Writers*, 516 p., Garland, New York, 1988.

Originally designed as a companion volume to Mainiero (no. 788) and its abridgment Faust (no. 787), this work contains nearly 400 entries. Each writer is provided with a substantial biographical/critical essay, followed by bibliographies of works and works about her. The entries occupy between one and three pages each. The compilers claim that while they do not pretend that the work is definitive, 'within its limits of space and resources, it is reasonably so'. Perhaps the quibble is with the name 'encyclopedia', wherein one might expect a comprehensive coverage, but there are certainly some controversial omissions among living writers. The term 'writer' is taken literally, and includes Queens Elizabeth and Victoria as well as some literary critics.

792. TODD, Janet, *British Women Writers: A Critical Reference Guide*, 608 p., Crossroad/Continuum, New York, 1988.

Contains 400 entries on 'the life and work of all of the well-known as well as lesser-known women writers of the United Kingdom'. (From publisher's announcement.)

793. TODD, Janet, *A Dictionary of British and American Women Writers, 1660–1800*, 344 p., Methuen, London, 1984. (Published in US by Rowman & Allanheld, Totowa, NJ, 1985)

Exactly as in its title, this is an A–Z dictionary aimed to 'stimulate research into female literary history' and remedy the impression gained from the *DNB* and the *Dictionary of American Biography* that 'women did not become writers till the Victorian era'. About 600 women are included, each with a biographical and literary sketch of varying length, written by one of a number of contributors. A great resource.

794. WILSON, Katharina, *Encyclopedia of Continental Women Writers, c.* 2000 p., Garland, New York, 1989.

'The lives and works of over 1800 continental European women writers from antiquity to the present are recorded in this monumental reference work . . . A wide range of languages and literatures is included . . . Arrangement is alphabetical by writer, cross-referenced by pseudonyms, but several indexes by language, nationality, genre and chronology are included to give complete access.' (From publisher's announcement.)

Bibliographies

795. BACKSCHEIDER, Paula, Felicity NUSSBAUM and Philip B. ANDERSON, *An Annotated Bibliography of Twentieth-Century Critical Studies of Women and Literature 1660-1800*, 287 p., Garland, New York, 1977.

Includes material published between 1900 and 1975. Divided into three parts: 1 – General studies; 2 – Genre studies: biographies, memoirs, conduct books, drama, fiction, women's studies and major authors (Cleland, Defoe, Fielding, Richardson, Smollett, Sterne), periodicals and poetry; 3 – individual women. Name and author indexes. Well annotated.

796. BOOS, Florence and Lynn MILLER, *Bibliography of Women and Literature*, 2 vols, Holmes & Meier, New York, 1989. (volume 1: Articles and books [published] 1974-1978 by and about women from 600 to 1975. Volume 2: Supplement . . . 1979-1981)

This is a 'compilation of the three annual bibliographies issued by the journal *Women and Literature* in 1976-1978, augmented by an appendix of entries from the PMLA and MLR bibliographies for 1979-81'. Over 10,000 publications of literary criticism are indexed. The coverage is English-language literature. The main arrangement is chronological, and within that the entries are subdivided by genre. They are coded by a system which facilitates retrieval by genre, and enables comparisons to be made on that basis. This is a vast work covering a very short time span. The compilers express the hope that it will be followed up with further volumes.

CLINE, Cheryl, *Women's Diaries, Journals and Letters: A Historical Guide*. (no. 161)

797. DAIMS, Diva and Janet G. GRIMES, *Towards a Feminist Tradition: An Annotated Bibliography of Novels in English by Women, 1891-1920*, 885 p., Garland, New York, 1982.

An annotated list of English-language novels by women published between 1891-1920. It includes 3407 titles by 1723 authors, plus fifty-one anonymous novels and novels by another 136 authors who may not be women. The novels were selected from Grimes and Daims' *Novels in English by Women* (no. 800), using the criterion of unusual treatment of women characters, focusing on their efforts to control their lives and on the social mores and conditions which militate against that. Thus these are novels with unconventional heroines. The annotations are summaries of reviews of the novels. The arrangement is alphabetical with a title index.

DAVIS, Gwenn and Beverly A. JOYCE, *Personal Writings by Women to 1800: A Bibliography of American and British Writers*. (no. 162)

798. FAIRBANKS, Carol, *More Women in Literature: Criticism of the Seventies*, 457 p., Scarecrow, Metuchen, NJ, 1979.

An extension of the earlier *Women in Literature: Criticism of the Seventies* (1976 – under the name Carol Fairbanks Myers – see no. 802). Includes material published between 1970 and 1977. Included is literary criticism examining women characters in various ways, essays on feminist criticism, biographical studies of women writers (and some men relevant to their female characters), interviews and book reviews. Arranged alphabetically by subject author, plus a bibliography listing works that are relevant to the study of women in literature but general in approach. No index.

799. FROST, Wendy and Michele VALIQUETTE, *Feminist Literary Criticism: A Bibliography of Journal Articles, 1975–1981*, 892 p., Garland, New York, 1989.

'Records seven important and highly productive years in feminist critical activity . . . based on a search of approximately 450 English-language periodicals.' Contains 1900 entries. Narrower in scope than Boos and Miller (no. 796), although presumably competing for the same readership. (Information from publisher's announcement.)

800. GRIMES, Janet and Diva DAIMS, *Novels in English by Women, 1891–1920: A Preliminary Checklist*, 805 p., Garland, New York, 1981.

Lists 5267 authors and 15,174 novels published in England or the United States, together with place and date of birth where known. Three-quarters of the novels are annotated. The arrangement is in three series: the first lists authors and titles which the compilers had verified, the second lists anonymous works and authors of unclear sex, the third lists works which the compilers could not verify. There is a title index.

801. GUY, Patricia A., *Women's Poetry Index*, 174 p., Oryx Press, Phoenix, AZ, 1985.

An index to the poems in fifty-one anthologies, including 'multiethnic' and translated works, excluding anthologies already covered by Granger's *Index to Poetry*. The anthologies are listed at the beginning, followed by a poet index, with birth and death dates where known, a title index and an index to first lines. An example of essential hard work undertaken simply to make women's work accessible and to stop it disappearing without trace.

HUFF, Cynthia, *British Women's Diaries: A Selected Descriptive Bibliography of Selected Nineteenth-Century Women's Manuscript Diaries*. (no. 164)

802. MYERS, Carol Fairbanks, *Women in Literature: Criticism of the Seventies,*, 256 p., Scarecrow, Metuchen, NJ, 1976.

See entry under Carol Fairbanks (no. 798).

803. PALMER, Paulina, *An Annotated Bibliography of Women's Fiction and Feminist Theory*, 256 p., Harvester, London, 1988.

'The first work of reference to highlight the importance of relating contemporary women's fiction to developments in feminist theory . . . As well as providing annotated lists of women's fiction and feminist theory, it includes lists of feminist journals and periodicals which contain reviews and critical analyses of fiction by women'. (From publisher's announcement.)

804. RESNICK, Margery and Isabelle de COURTIVRON, *Women Writers in Translation: An Annotated Bibliography, 1945-1982*, 272 p., Garland, New York, 1984.

The dates 1954-1982 in the title of this work refer to the publication dates of the translations, not the originals, and therefore the coverage includes early writers as well as twentieth century (although not ancient – no Sappho). The entries are arranged by country of origin, some being grouped by language. The divisions are: Brazil and Portugal, France, Francophone Canada, Austria, Federal Republic of Germany, German Democratic Republic and Switzerland, Italy, Japan, Russia, Spain, Spanish America. Other areas (notably Asian and Middle Eastern) are not included. The areas covered were determined by the interest and availability of scholars on the original project, and in the introduction the authors complain about the lack of interest in and support given to this kind of work, and compare it to the obstacles faced by the women writers and translators whom they list. The entries are annotated with a description of the work, and the original title is given with bibliographic details. There is an author index.

805. SCHWARTZ, Narda Lacey, *Articles on Women Writers: A Bibliography*, 2 vols, ABC-Clio, Santa Barbara, CA, 1977, 1986. (Second volume entitled: *Articles on women writers, 1976-84.*)

The author describes these works as 'handlists' of articles published in English about women writers. Volume 1 covers articles published between 1960-75 about over 600 women. Volume 2 covers 1976-84, and includes over 1000 women writers. The women are from the United States, Great Britain, Ireland, Australia, Canada and New Zealand. Twenty-one abstracting and indexing services were checked to compile the list, with the addition, for vol. 2, of *Women Studies Abstracts* and *Women in Literature*. A feature of the work is its very detailed contents lists, which provide a useful overview.

Periodicals

We have listed here periodicals which are specifically concerned with literary criticism. There are many magazines publishing women's creative writing, but we have excluded these unless they also contain theoretical, critical or other material.

806.   *New Moon*, 4/yr, PO Box 2056, Madison, WI 53701, 1981–.

'To provide critical resources on the status of feminist theory and women's issues in science fiction and fantasy genres.'

807.   *Tulsa Studies in Women's Literature*, 2/yr, University of Tulsa, 600 S College Ave, Tulsa, OK 74104, 1982–.

A scholarly journal, concerned with the 'recovery and redefinition of writing by women'.

808.   *Women and Literature*, annual, Holmes and Meier, New York, 1981–.

Previously published as a quarterly journal (1972–79), this now appears as an annual series, each issue on a separate topic.

Organizations

Organizations of writers are listed under Media in Chapter 12 (nos 621–629).

AFRICAN AND CARIBBEAN LITERATURE

Bio-bibliographical works

809.   BERRIAN, Brenda, *Bibliography of African Women Writers and Journalists: Ancient Egypt–1984*, 279 p., Three Continents Press, Washington, DC, 1985.

The subtitle is misleading: this is overwhelmingly a work about contemporary African writers. It is a thorough bibliography, serving to open up the work of African women writers, and including 913 works in European languages, fifty-two in vernacular languages. The division is by form: Fiction, Drama, Poetry, Folklore, Miscellaneous prose, Journalistic literature, Broadcast literature, Bibliography and Interviews. The remainder of the work consists of criticism and bibliographical information. There are a number of appendices grouping authors by genre and by country, forthcoming works, sections on non-African women married to African men. There are two addenda of recent additions, and an index. Particularly valuable for its non-Anglocentric emphasis.

Bibliographies

810. BERRIAN, Brenda, *Bibliography of Women Writers from the Caribbean*, 250 p., Three Continents Press, Washington, DC, 1989.

This new work is likely to be the standard source on this subject.

811. CARR, Glynis, 'Caribbean women writers: a bibliography for teachers', *NWSA Perspectives*, vol. 5, pp. 16–18, Spring/Summer 1987.

AMERICAN LITERATURE

Several important works on literature by or about American women writers will be found in the general section in this chapter (nos 787–805). Works on Black American writers are in the section on Black literature (nos 832–838).

Bibliographies

ADDIS, Patricia K., *Through a Woman's I: An Annotated Bibliography of American Women's Autobiographical Writings, 1946–1976.* (no. 160)

812. BAKERMAN, Jane S. and Mary Jean DeMARR, *Adolescent Female Portraits in the American Novel 1961–1981*, 254 p., Garland, New York, 1983.

Sensitive and informative annotations for 579 novels by 477 authors. The main work is arranged alphabetically by author, with subject and title indexes. Works are also listed chronologically. Fourteen dominant types or images emerged in the novels, and these are grouped in a checklist at the beginning.

813. COVEN, Brenda, *American Women Dramatists of the Twentieth Century: A Bibliography*, 244 p., Scarecrow, Metuchen, NJ, 1982.

A bibliography of 133 American playwrights, preceded by a general list of articles, chapters and dissertations on US women dramatists. The bibliographical list includes play titles, production if known, publications giving biographical information, and bibliography of criticism and reviews. A play-title index is provided.

814. DUKE, Maurice, Jackson R. BRYER and M. Thomas INGE, *American Women Writers: Bibliographical Essays*, 434 p., Greenwood, Westport, CT, 1983.

A collection of literature reviews covering the following women: Anne Bradstreet, Mary Rowlandson, Sarah Kemble Knight, Sarah Orne Jewett, Mary Wilkins Freeman, Mary Murfree, Kate Chopin, Edith Wharton, Gertrude Stein, Djuna Barnes, Anais Nin, Ellen Glasgow,

Katherine Anne Porter, Eudora Welty, Flannery O'Connor, Carson McCullers, Zora Neale Hurston, Constance Rourke, Pearl Buck, Marjorie Rawlings, Margaret Mitchell, Marianne Moore, Anne Sexton, Sylvia Plath.

GOODFRIEND, Joyce D., *The Published Diaries and Letters of American Women: An Annotated Bibliography*. (no. 163)

815.   REARDON, Joan and Kristine A. THORSEN, *Poetry by American Women, 1900–1975: A Bibliography*, 674 p., Scarecrow, Metuchen, NJ, 1979.

Lists, alphabetically by author, about 5500 women poets, giving bibliographic details of their work. A title index to volumes of poetry is also provided.

RHODES, Carolyn H., *First Person Female American: A Selected and Annotated Bibliography of the Autobiographies of American Women Living after 1950*. (no. 165)

816.   SWEENEY, Patricia, *Women in Southern Literature: An Index*, 117 p., Greenwood, New York, 1986.

An index of some 1000 female characters in American Southern literature. The characters are listed alphabetically by name or title (e.g. 'Aunt Charlotte'). An appendix places them into fifteen categories, such as 'Black Mammies', 'Poor Whites'. There is an author and a title index. There are no cross-references – it is necessary to know the characters' surnames if they have them. Mark Twain is listed under Clemens with no cross-reference. A curious work.

817.   WHITE, Barbara Anne, *American Women Writers: An Annotated Bibliography of Criti..ism*, 126 p., Garland, New York, 1977.

This is a collection of material on women writers in general, i.e. criticism treating women writers as a distinct group. It is restricted to American writers of fiction, drama and poetry, up to 1975. Dissertations and newspaper articles are not included. It is arranged in four sections: Biography, Special groups, Special topics, Literary history. There is an index to editors and critics.

AUSTRALIAN LITERATURE

Bibliographies

818.   ADELAIDE, Debra, *Australian Women Writers: A Bibliographic Guide*, 209 p., Pandora, London, 1988.

'Primarily a guide to novelists, poets, dramatists' but includes other writers 'especially those who have contributed significantly to the history of women in Australia'. Each entry includes brief biographical details, followed by a list of publications.

BRITISH LITERATURE

Works on British literature by or about women are included in the general works in this chapter (nos 787–805).

FRENCH LITERATURE

Theses

819.   BENEDICT, Marjorie A., 'US doctoral research on women in French literature', *Women Studies Abstracts*, vol. 11, nos. 3 and 4, pp. 1–19 and 1–12, Fall 1982 and Winter 1982–3.

Lists doctoral dissertations from 1894 to 1980, covering US theses only. Part 1 lists theses about women writers and their works. Part 2 covers theses in which women are the focus of literary research. Each part is arranged chronologically by subject, and within that alphabetically by author. Both parts end with a short general section. The sources were *Comprehensive Dissertation Index, Dissertation Abstracts International, The French Review* and *American Doctoral Dissertations*. Could be an invaluable short cut for thesis tracing in this area.

Bibliographies

820.   GELFAND, Elissa D. and Virginia Thorndike HULES, *French Feminist Criticism: Women, Language and Literature: An Annotated Bibliography*, 318 p., Garland, New York, 1985.

'The subject of this bibliography is women, language, writing, and their interrelationship as they have been conceived and articulated by French feminist thinkers.' It lists not only French authors but 'all books, essays and articles from the period 1970–1982 that concentrate on women and language, including work by feminist scholars in the US'. It also includes Belgian and Quebecois writing. There are two introductory sections on the differences between French and American theory and practice and the general theory of feminist criticism. The main list is arranged by author, subdivided by type of publication. There is a list of special issues of periodicals.

GERMAN LITERATURE

Bio-bibliographical works

821. BRINKER-GABLER, Gisela, Karola LUDWIG and Angela WOFFEN, *Lexikon deutschsprachiger Schriftstellerinnen 1800–1945*, 363 p., DTV, Munich, 1986.

A biographical dictionary of German-speaking women writers, the entries consisting of a paragraph of biographical information followed by a bibliography of works by and about the writer. The entries vary from half to several pages in length, and many are illustrated with a portrait

822. FRIEDRICHS, Elisabeth, *Die deutschsprachigen Schriftstellerinnen des 18. und 19. Jahrhunderts: Ein Lexikon*, 388 p., Metzler, Stuttgart, 1981.

A list of women writers in German of the eighteenth and nineteenth centuries. It includes brief biographical details, and references to work about each writer in a number of standard sources.

823. PATAKY, Sophie, *Lexikon deutscher Frauen der Feder: Eine Zusammenstellung der seit dem Jahre 1840 erschienen Werke weiblicher Autoren nebt Biographien der Lebenden und einem Verzeichnis der Pseudonyme*, 2 vols, Herbert Lang, Bern, 1971. (Reprint of the ed. published by C. Pataky, 1889.)

Nineteenth-century biographical dictionary of German women writers.

824. SCHMID-BORTENSCHLAGER, Sigrid and Hanna SCHNEDL-BUBENIČEK, *Österreichische Schriftstellerinnen 1880–1938: Eine Bio-Bibliographie* (Stuttgarter Arbeiten zur Germanistik, Nr. 119. Salzburger Beiträge, Nr. 4), 209 p., Heinz, Stuttgart, 1982.

A dictionary of Austrian women writers, including writers of critical works as well as literature. A chronological list of publications is given under each. Biographical details are confined to dates and places of birth and death, and place of residence and pseudonym, where applicable.

ITALIAN LITERATURE

Bibliographies

825. GOLINI, Vera F., 'A bibliography of medieval and renaissance Italian women writers', *RFR/DRF Resources for Feminist Research*, vol. 14, no. 2, pp. 71–73, 1985.

This bibliography includes thirty critical studies and anthologies of women writers, eleven mediaeval and renaissance works which study women, and nineteen works by women writers.

SPANISH LITERATURE

This includes works on women writers writing in Spanish, from Spain and elsewhere.

Bio-bibliographical works

826. GALERSTEIN, Carolyn L., *Women Writers of Spain: An Annotated Bio-bibliographical Guide*, 389 p., Greenwood, Westport, CT, 1986.

A selected bibliography of the works of 300 Spanish women writers, with indexes to author by birth date, Catalan authors, Galician authors, translated titles, and all titles.

827. MARTING, Diane, *Women Writers of Spanish America: An Annotated Bio-bibliographical Guide*, 448 p., Greenwood, New York, 1987.

The compiler says of this mammoth work that it is designed 'in many ways . . . to serve as a manual for intelligent affirmative action . . . to compensate for past sexism in the study of Spanish-American literature, as well as to celebrate the wealth of existing works.' Arranged alphabetically it lists hundreds of women writing in Spanish, with bibliographical details where known, and a list of published works up to 1980, many of which are substantially annotated. Appendices include a list of anthologies, authors born before 1900, authors by country, dramatist, translations and bilingual editions. Some information given in Resnick and Courtivron (no. 804) and Knaster (no. 457) is not repeated in these appendices.

Bibliographies

828. ALARCON, Norma and Sylvia KOSSNAR, *Bibliography of Hispanic Women Writers*, 86 p., Chicano-Riqueno Studies, Bloomington, IN, 1983.

This is an extraction of entries appearing in the *MLA International Bibliography* from 1922–1978, and is arranged alphabetically by the name of the writer. There is an index 'by chronology' subdivided into Spanish and Spanish-American writers, of which the latter predominate.

829. CORTINA, Lynn Ellen Rice, *Spanish-American Women Writers: A Bibliographical Research Checklist*, 292 p., Garland, New York, 1983.

Nearly 2000 references to works by women writing in Spanish, from nineteen countries of Spanish America. Arranged by country and within that alphabetically by author, usually giving birth dates and listing publications. Name index provided.

830. CORVALAN, Graciela N.V., *Latin American Women Writers in English Translation: A Bibliography*, (Latin American Bibliography Series, no. 9), 109 p., Latin American Studies Center, California State University, Los Angeles, 1980.

This work developed from the need to gather materials for a course, and includes work published up to 1979. As well as individual writers, there is a bibliography of anthologies in which women writers appear in translation, a selective general bibliography on Latin American women writers, and a selection of other reference material.

831. SALSTAD, Louise M., *The Presentation of Women in Spanish Golden Age Literature: An Annotated Bibliography*, 129 p., G.K. Hall, Boston, 1980.

This is a well annotated collection of 372 items about women in sixteenth- and seventeenth-century Castilian literature. Most of the material dates from 1944–1977. Arranged alphabetically by author, with topic and author indexes.

BLACK LITERATURE

We include here works which have identified themselves as concerning Black literature specifically. See also the section on African and Caribbean literature (nos 809–811).

Theses

832. SIMS-WOOD, Janet, 'African-American women writers: a selected listing of master's theses and doctoral dissertations', *Sage*, vol. 2, no. 1, pp. 69–70, Spring 1985.

A brief listing of forty-nine theses on Black women writers, including ones on thirteen individual writers.

Bibliographies

833. CHAPMAN, Dorothy H., *Index to Poetry by Black American Women*, 424 p., Greenwood, Westport, CT, 1986.

The main body of this book is a title and first-line index to over 4000 poems by over 400 poets. Some anonymous poems, including folk songs and spirituals, are also listed. The index relates to 120 books by individual poets and eighty-three anthologies. There are also author and subject indexes.

834. CREQUE-HARRIS, Leah, 'Literature of the diaspora by women of color', *Sage*, vol. 3, no. 2, pp. 61–64, Fall 1986.

A 'sampling of creative writing by women of color throughout the diaspora' (i.e. the African diaspora created by the dispersal of Africans through the slave trade, excluding the US). This is a list of works by women writers of African origin, arranged by country. It includes African writers, since women slaves were transported throughout Africa.

835. DANDRIDGE, Rita B., 'On the novels written by selected Black American women: a bibliographical essay', in HULL, Gloria T. *et al.*, *But Some of Us Are Brave* (no. 634), pp. 261–279, Feminist Press, New York, 1982.

A guide to the sparse and scattered critical and bibliographical material, including sections on six individual writers: Brooks, Fauset, Hurston, Larsen, Marshall and Petry.

836. FERRIER, Carole, 'Black women's prose fiction in English: a selective bibliography', *Hecate*, vol. 14, no. 1, pp. 104–111, 1988.

This short bibliography includes social and political history and theory, literary criticism, reviews and interviews as well as works of fiction. It is mainly valuable for its coverage of non-American writers.

837. RUSHING, Andrea Benton, 'An annotated bibliography of images of Black women in Black literature', *CLA Journal*, vol. 21, pp. 435–42, March 78.

A bibliography of thirty-three items with useful detailed annotations, including chapters from books as well as articles and monographs, and extracting the subject matter from more general works (e.g. on Blacks in literature in general). A good starting point for the subject, which could usefully be updated.

838. SHERMAN, Joan R., 'Afro-American women poets of the nineteenth century: a guide to research and bio-bibliographies of the poets', In HULL, Gloria T. *et al.*, *But Some of Us Are Brave* (no. 634), pp. 245–260, Feminist Press, New York, 1982.

An article partly on how to find material, covering biography, criticism, periodicals, poetry anthologies, manuscripts; and partly providing bio-bibliographies for six poets and briefer details for several more.

LESBIAN LITERATURE

Bibliographies

839. CRAMER, Patricia, 'Building a tradition for lesbian feminist literary criticism: an annotated bibliography', *Feminist Teacher*, vol. 2, no. 3, pp. 20–22, 1987.

840. GRIER, Barbara J., *The Lesbian in Literature*, 168 p., Naiad Press, Talahassee, FL, 3rd ed., 1981. (The first ed., published in 1967, contained hundreds of 'trash' novels which are omitted from this edition.)

This famous book lists books alphabetically by author. The third edition includes material published up to 1980, both fiction and non-fiction, in one sequence with a coding system to indicate quality and the centrality of lesbian themes in the work. Alas there is no index. There are photos of eighty-nine women authors.

841. KUDA, Marie J., *Women Loving Women: A Select and Annotated Bibliography of Women Loving Women in Literature*, 28 p., Womanpress, Chicago, IL, 1975.

The author calls this 'a bibliography in the loosest sense of the word'. It is actually a list of some hundred or so works of fiction, poetry, biography and autobiography with a fairly positive lesbian theme. It was prepared in a hurry for a conference in 1974, so makes no claim to be comprehensive. Nevertheless it is of considerable interest.

SPECIAL GENRES

842. BETSKO, Kathleen and Rachel KOENIG, *Interviews with Contemporary Women Playwrights*, 480 p., Beech Tree Books, New York, 1987.

Interviews with: Liliane Atlan, Bai Fengxi, Kathleen Betsko, Alice Childress, Caryl Churchill, Anne Commire, Gretchen Cryer, Donna de Matteo, Rosalyn Drexler, Laura Farabough, Maria Irene Fornes, Mary Gallagher, Griselda Gambaro, Pam Gems, Beth Henley, Tina Howe, Corinne Jacker, Adrienne Kennedy, Karen Malpede, Emily Mann, Eve Merriam, Janet Neipris, Marsha Norman, Rochelle Owens, Louise Page, Ntozake Shange, Megan Terry, Michelene Wandor, Wendy Wasserstein, Susan Yankowitz.

843. GARBER, Eric and Lyn PALEO, *Uranian Worlds: A Reader's Guide to Alternative Sexuality in Science Fiction and Fantasy*, 177 p., G.K. Hall, Boston, 1983.

Although this work is not limited to material related to women we have included it because it provides an unusual access to otherwise quite lost literature. It is an annotated list to more than 500 novels with homosexual, lesbian or bisexual imagery. Works are listed A–Z by author. Following the usual bibliographic details comes an indication of the sexual content – male or female, overt, latent, androgynous, etc. There is a summary of the plot and an evaluation. Chronological and title indexes are provided. There are interesting introductions by Samuel Delaney and Joanna Russ.

844. MUSSELL, Kay, *Women's Gothic and Romantic Fiction: A Reference Guide*, 157 p., Greenwood, Westport, CT, 1981.

A series of review chapters with appended bibliographies covering the history of the genre, reference sources, related writing (e.g. mystery, melodrama), and various literary and sociological approaches to the study of the material. An appendix lists research collections. There is an index and a chronology.

845. SCHLOBIN, Roger C., *Urania's Daughters: A Checklist of Women Science Fiction Writers, 1692–1982*, 79 p., Starmont House, Mercer Island, WA, 1983.

An A–Z list of 375 authors covering over 800 titles, giving brief information (publisher, place and date) on each. Authors are listed by their 'real' name: a directory of pseudonyms and other variant names is given, and there is an index to titles.

846. YNTEMA, Sharon, *More Than 100 Women Science-Fiction Writers: An Annotated Bibliography*, Crossing Press, Freedom, CA, 1988.

After being announced in 1988 this work has been slow to appear. We await its arrival with interest.

LANGUAGE

Bibliographies

847. ANDERSEN, Marguerite, 'Bibliography [on women and language],' *RFR/DRF Resources for Feminist Research*, vol. 13, no. 3, pp. 72–78, 1984.

Contains 227 references on women and language designed as a supplementary bibliography to Kramarae, Thorne and Henley (no. 850). Unannotated.

848. HENLEY, Nancy and Barrie THORNE, *She Said/He Said: An Annotated Bibliography of Sex Differences in Language, Speech and Non-verbal Communication*, 311 p., Know Inc., Pittsburgh, PA, 1975.

See Kramarae (no. 850).

849. JARRARD, Mary W. and Phyllis R. RANDALL, *Women Speaking: An Annotated Bibliography of Verbal and Non-verbal Communication, 1970–1980*, 478 p., Garland, New York, 1982.

This book surveys the work done on women's communications during the 1970s and includes aspects of many disciplines – psychology, linguistics, anthropology, sociology, speech and hearing sciences, education and so on. It covers a very wide range, starting with settings for communication, characteristics of communication, means of communication, including verbal and non-verbal, and closing with a short section of comprehensive references. There is a subject index. Entries are well annotated and number over 1200. Much more emphasis on non-verbal communication than Kramarae (no. 850).

850. KRAMARAE, Cheris, Barrie THORNE and Nancy HENLEY, 'Sex similarities in language, speech and nonverbal communication', in THORNE, Barrie *et al.*, *Language, Gender and Society* (no. 854), pp. 153–342, Newbury House, Rowley, MA, 1983.

This is an updated version of the bibliography originally published in Thorne and Henley's *Language and Sex: Difference and Dominance* (1975) (also published separately as Henley and Thorne (no. 848) and contains much more recent material, including some early 1980s publications not covered by Jarrard (no. 849). Subject headings are Comprehensive sources, Gender marking & sex bias in language structure & content, Stereotypes and perceptions, Sex differences and similarities, Conversational interaction, Genre & style, Children & language, Language varieties in American English, Nonverbal aspects of communication. Useful aspects of this compilation are the section on children's language and the subdivisions in most sections on languages other than English. The section on nonverbal aspects is very small. Consult Jarrard for more detail.

851. LUNDBERG, Norma, 'De l'autre côté', *RFR/DRF Resources for Feminist Research*, vol. 13, no. 3, pp. 69–72, 1984.

This introductory bibliography on European feminist linguistic theory gives forty-nine references, mostly from French, German, Dutch and Scandinavian sources.

852. SHIMANOFF, Susan B., 'Sex as a variable in communication research 1970–76', *Bulletin: Women's Studies in Communication*, vol. 1, no. 1, pp. 8–20, 1977.

Included for its coverage of earlier research.

853. SILBERSTEIN, Sandra, 'Bibliography: women and language', *Michigan Occasional Papers in Women's Studies*, no. 12, p. 67, Ann Arbor, MI, 1979.

This bibliography reflects work mainly written through the 1970s. Around 200 books and articles are listed, divided by subject: Gender differences in language acquisition, Linguistic behavior, Bibliographies, Case studies, Cross-cultural examples, Language of feminism, Gay community, Gossip, Guidelines for non-sexist language use. The entries are not annotated and there is no index.

854. THORNE, Barrie, Cheris KRAMARAE and Nancy HENLEY, *Language, Gender and Society*, 342 p., Newbury House, Rowley, MA, 1983.

See Kramarae (no. 850) for entry.

Thesauri and dictionaries

The following works will be found listed in detail in Part I, and are mentioned here because of their importance in the study of women's language.

CAPEK, Mary Ellen S., *A Women's Thesaurus: An Index of Language Used to Describe and Locate Information by and about Women*. (no. 117)

DICKSTEIN, Ruth, Victoria A. MILLS and Ellen J. WAITE, *Women in LC's Terms: A Thesaurus of Library of Congress Subject Headings Relating to Women.* (no. 118)

KRAMARAE, Cheris and Paula TREICHLER, *A Feminist Dictionary.* (no. 85)

MAGGIO, Rosalie, *The Nonsexist Wordfinder: A Dictionary of Gender-Free Usage.* (no. 119)

MARSHALL, Joan K. *On Equal Terms: A Thesaurus for Nonsexist Indexing and Cataloging.* (no. 120)

Periodicals

855. *Women's Studies in Communication*, 4/yr, ORWAC, Dept of Communication, University of Oklahoma, Norman, OK 74104, 1978–.

Journal of the Organization for Research on Women and Communication (ORWAC) (no. 857). Articles, long and short, and reviews on 'gender and communication, deriving from any perspective, including those of interpersonal communication, small group communication, organizational communication, the mass media and rhetoric'. ORWAC also produces a *Newsletter*, a separate sheet included in the journal, with news and announcements.

856. *Women and Language*, 2/yr, Dept of Communication, 4400 University Drive, George Mason University, Fairfax, VA 22030, 1975–.

Articles, research in progress, reviews. Includes scholarship from communication, journalism, linguistics, sociology, etc

Organizations

857. ORGANIZATION FOR RESEARCH ON WOMEN AND COMMUNICATION (ORWAC), c/o Dept of Speech Communication, Humboldt State University, Arcata, CA 95521.

Network for women researching on gender and communication. Publishes *Women's Studies in Communication* (no. 855) and a newsletter with information about the activities of the organization.

CHAPTER 19

Mind and body.

The issues in this chapter are among those of most central concern to women, and include areas, such as healing and midwifery, where women have traditionally taken a major role. In the last two centuries in the West this role has been eroded, and one of the results of the feminism of the late twentieth century has been an enormous effort to reinstate some of the practices and benefits that were abandoned.

Looking at the reference literature collected for this chapter though, there are clearly large gaps, so it does not give a true picture of feminist activity. There is inevitably a time lag between grassroots work being reported in primary literature and monographic studies, and again between the proliferation of such literature and its appearance in bibliographies. We seem to be in the second gap at present, as far as this chapter goes. There are general bibliographies on women's health, though little on alternative medicine, but in specific areas the coverage is patchy. For instance, we found little reference material on childbirth and childcare from a feminist perspective. Needless to say, we have not included orthodox medical and gynaecological reference books. These are numerous, riddled with sexist assumptions, and easily traceable elsewhere.

Other topics in this chapter contain only sparse entries; there is a dearth of woman-oriented bibliographical work on disability, eating problems, body image and drug dependency, for instance, though there is now a growing number of primary sources, and lots of women work in these areas.

To trace this work, short of going through the shelves of your nearest women's bookstore (never a bad idea), it is necessary to use general bibliographies or tools such as *Women Studies Abstracts* (no. 4), or the subject-based general medical and psychological secondary services described in Searing (no. 14). Alternatively, if you are lucky enough to live near an active women's health group or information centre (like the WHRRIC in London (no. 879) or the Boston Women's Health Collective (no. 878) then up-to-date resources will be available.

General women's movement magazines and newspapers, e.g.

Spare Rib (no. 81), *Off Our Backs* (no. 78) and *Sojourner* (no. 80), are vital for contact numbers and news of local groups, rape crisis and refuge phone numbers, and news of events and activities.

GENERAL HEALTH

Resources

858. BOSTON WOMEN'S HEALTH BOOK COLLECTIVE, *The New Our Bodies Ourselves*, 647 p., Simon & Schuster, New York, 1984. (The British edition of the earlier version is edited by Angela Phillips and Jill Rakusen and published by Penguin Books. They are preparing a new edition for late 1989.)

The first edition of this ground-breaking and now famous book came out in 1973. This version, twice as big and largely rewritten, maintains its reputation as a *sine qua non* for women's health information. Chapter 5, on aging, has now been expanded into a book in itself – see *Ourselves, Growing Older* (no. 938). There is a strong emphasis on self-help and access to information. Extensive bibliographies and resource lists follow each chapter.

859. *Health Education Resources on Women's Health*, 105 p., Paddington and North Kensington Health Authority and Victoria Health Authority, London, 1984.

A list of resources and materials available from the above health authorities for use by individuals and organizations (although this is not made explicit) in making presentations on women's health. The catalogue was produced as a result of a continuing demand for materials on women's health. The materials include leaflets, posters, etc., audiovisuals, resource packs, books, and there is a list of contact addresses. The division is by subject, such as Work, Sexuality, Disability, etc.

860. ISIS-WICCE, 'Well being/being well: a dossier on women and health', *Women's World*, no. 6, p. 55, June 1985.

A moving collection of articles, together with bibliographies, resource lists and book reviews.

861. ISIS-WICCE/BOSTON WOMEN'S HEALTH COLLECTIVE, *International Women & Health Resource Guide*, 177 p., Boston Women's Health Collective and ISIS International, West Somerville, MA and Carouge, Switzerland, 1980.

An annotated guide to material and resources. Many non-English language items are included. The introductory articles and headings are in five languages (Spanish, French, German, Italian and English) but the annotations are in English.

862. NATIONAL WOMEN'S HEALTH NETWORK, *Resource Guide*, 9 vols, National Women's Health Network, Washington, DC, 1980.

A series of nine resource guides of around fifty pages each, covering breast cancer, hysterectomy, menopause, maternal health and childbirth, birth control, DES, abortion and sterilization. The guides follow a similar format with articles, discussion of controversy, resource lists of various media and organizations and a section listing general resources on women and health, with addresses listed state by state. The resources are American only but the issues are global.

863. WEISS, Kay, *Women's Health Care: A Guide to Alternatives*, 426 p., Reston Pub. Co., Reston, VA, 1984.

A collection of thirty-one essays falling roughly into two sections – medicine's treatment of women's health problems, and alternative approaches. The latter is the most interesting and largest part of the book, with many individual contributors discussing many different therapies, with resources and further readings.

Bibliographies

864. PAN AMERICAN HEALTH ORGANIZATION, *Women, Health and Development in the Americas: An Annotated Bibliography*, 106 p., Pan American Health Organization, 1984.

Contains 286 items, 164 on women and health, 126 on women and development. Many items are not specific to the Americas.' (From Townsend (no. 254.)

865. RUZEK, Sheryl K., *Women and Health Care: A Bibliography* (Program on Women Occasional Papers, no 1), 76 p., North Western University, Evanston, Illinois, 1975.

This is one of the first results, bibliographically speaking, of the women's health movement, and lists some mainstream and some hard to come by early 1970s feminist material. Something of a classic, but for practical use needs supplementing.

See also:

GIORGIS, Belkis Wolde, *A Selected and Annotated Bibliography on Women and Health in Africa.* (no. 262)

Periodicals

866. *Health Care for Women International*, 4/yr, Hemisphere Pub. Co., New York, 1980–.

'International, interdisciplinary approach to health care for women.' Medical in approach. Formerly *Issues in the Health Care of Women* (1979–).

867. *Healthsharing*, 4/yr, 14 Skey Lane, Toronto, Ontario M6J 3C4, Canada, 1979–.

A critical analysis of women's health issues from a feminist perspective.

868. *Sisterlinks*, 4/yr, FORWARD, 38 King St, London WC2E 8JT, 1985–.

Magazine of the Foundation for Women's Health Research and Development (FORWARD). Concentrates on women's health issues, mainly in the Third World.

869. *Women and Health*, 4/yr, Haworth Press, New York, 1976–.

Contains feature articles, research, bibliographies, book reviews, news and notes.

870. *Women's Health and Reproductive Rights Information Centre Newsletter*, 4/yr, WHRRIC, 52 Featherstone St, London EC1 8RT, 1988–.

Formerly *Women's Health Information Centre: The Newsletter*. Contains news of women's health activities and developments, etc.; mainly British.

871. *Womenwise*, 4/yr, Concord Feminist Health Center, 38 S. Main St, Concord, NH 03301, 1978–.

Women's health quarterly with a feminist perspective.

Organizations

872. FOUNDATION FOR WOMEN'S HEALTH RESEARCH AND DEVELOPMENT (FORWARD), Africa Centre, 38 King St, London WC2E 8JT.

An organization set up by African and British women as a focal point in the UK for African women's health issues. Organizes meetings, workshops, etc., publishes health promotion materials and a quarterly magazine *Sister Links* (no. 868). Campaigns against female circumcision.

873. INTERNATIONAL COUNCIL ON WOMEN'S HEALTH ISSUES, c/o College of Nursing, University of S. Florida, Box 22, 12901 Bruce B. Downs Blvd, Tampa, FL 33612.

Founded in 1983 by a group of professionals interested in health care for women worldwide. Information exchange network for health care professionals.

874. WOMEN AND FOOD INFORMATION NETWORK, 24 Peabody Terrace #1403, Cambridge, MA 02138.

Primarily made up of practitioners and researchers interested in women's roles in world food systems. Publishes a newsletter.

875. WOMEN'S HEALTH INTERACTION, 58 Arthur St, Ottawa, Ontario K1R 7B9, Canada.

'A network of women from across Canada who are concerned about health.'

876. WOMEN'S INTERNATIONAL PUBLIC HEALTH NET-WORK (WIPHN), 7100 Oak Forest Lane, Bethesda, MD 20817.

Formed in 1987 as a grassroots movement, to provide a network for women working in public health worldwide. Publishes a newsletter.

Libraries and information centres

877. ARCHIVES AND SPECIAL COLLECTIONS ON WOMEN IN MEDICINE, Medical College of Pennsylvania, 3300 Henry Ave., Philadelphia, PA 19129.

Founded in 1850 as the Female Medical College of Pennsylvania, the Medical College as it is now called was 'the first and is the only extant medical school founded exclusively for the education of women physicians'. The archives include college and hospital records and the personal papers of many alumnae and women physicians from all over the US. Special collections include a nineteenth-century textbook collection and the Black Women Physicians Project. There is a twice-yearly newsletter called *Collections*.

878. BOSTON WOMEN'S HEALTH COLLECTIVE, 47 Nichols Ave, Watertown, MA 02172.

Notable for its pioneering publication *Our Bodies Ourselves*. Maintains a public reference library and information service.

879. WOMEN'S HEALTH AND REPRODUCTIVE RIGHTS INFORMATION CENTRE (WHRRIC), 52 Featherstone St, London EC1Y 8RT.

Formed in 1988 from the amalgamation of the Women's Health Information Centre and the Women's Reproductive Rights Information Centre. Maintains an information centre and a library. Publishes broadsheets on many aspects of women's health, and *Women's Health and Reproductive Rights Newsletter* (no. 870).

HEALTH-RELATED OCCUPATIONS

General

880. PENNELL, Maryland and Shirlene SHOWELL, *Women in Health Careers*, 147 p., US Dept of Health Education and Welfare, Washington, DC, 1975.

Described as a 'chartbook', prepared for an international conference on women and health in 1975, this book is made up of tables, graphs and figures illustrating the statistics of women in the health professions. About half the data relate to the United States and the rest to other countries. Useful and unusual, though an update would be welcome.

Doctors

881. AMERICAN ACADEMY OF FAMILY PHYSICIANS, Committee on Women in Family Medicine, *Reference Guide on Women in Medicine*, 18 p., American Academy of Family Physicians, Kansas City, MO, 1985. (Available from publisher, 1740 W 92nd St, Kansas City, MO 64114.)

A briefly annotated bibliography of recent American publications on women doctors. Arranged by subject in fifteen sections. No index.

882. CHAFF, Sandra, *Women in Medicine: A Bibliography of the Literature on Women Physicians*, 1124 p., Scarecrow, Metuchen, NJ, 1977.

A monumental work covering world literature from the eighteenth century to 1975. Foreign language entries (9 per cent of total) have titles translated and annotations in English. Broad subject headings are History, Biographies, Recruitment, Medical education, Graduate education, Medical activity, Specialties, Missionary and wartime activity, Psychosocial factors, Medical institutions. Within sections material is subdivided by country. Author, subject and name indexes are provided.

Nurses

883. BULLOUGH, Vern L., Olga CHURCH and Alice P. STEIN, *American Nursing: A Biographical Dictionary*, 358 p., Garland, New York, 1988.

This work includes substantial biographies of nursing leaders, with bibliographies. The criterion for inclusion was that the biographee should be deceased or born before 1890 (one was still alive at the time of writing). Two of the nurses are men. Bullough makes the point that in nursing, unlike most other female-dominated professions, women were not only numerically dominant but held the key leadership roles. Few of these leaders have appeared in standard biographical works. The book is illustrated with fifty-six portraits, and indexed.

884. KAUFMAN, Martin *et al.*, *Dictionary of American Nursing Biography*, 472 p., Greenwood, Westport, CT, 1988.

'The first work to provide a detailed account of the lives and contributions of those who have had the most significant impact on the development of nursing as a profession . . . Comprising a total of 196 biographical sketches . . . Each entry describes major professional contributions and supplies data on the nurse's background, education and career. Important or representative writings are listed, together with bibliographies and other source materials.' (From publisher's announcement.)

Dentists

885.   BOQUIST, Constance and Jeanette V. HAASE, *An Historical Review of Women in Dentistry: An Annotated Bibliography*, 107 p., US Dept of Health Education and Welfare, Rockville, MD, 1977.

Contains 263 references, mainly from the professional literature.

886.   TILLMAN, Randi, 'Women in dentistry; a review of the literature', *Journal of the American Dental Association*, vol. 91, pp. 1214–1215, 1975.

Contains 25 books and articles, mainly from the early 1970s.

Periodicals and organizations

887.   ASSOCIATION FOR WOMEN IN PSYCHOLOGY, CUNY Graduate Center Rm 609, 33 W 42nd St, New York 10036.

Feminist academic organization, aiming to attack assumptions about the nature of women in psychology, to achieve equal opportunity.

888.   *Journal of the American Medical Women's Association*, 6/yr, AMWA, 465 Grand St, New York, NY 10003, 1915–.

Primarily a membership journal but available to non-members. Contains news, letters, review notices and occasional articles.

889.   *Medical Woman*, 3/yr, Medical Women's Federation, Tavistock House North, Tavistock Square, London WC1H 9HX, 1982–.

Bulletin of the MWF. Formerly entitled *Women in Medicine*.

890.   MEDICAL WOMEN'S FEDERATION, Tavistock House North, Tavistock Square, London WC1H 9HX.

Founded in 1917 to promote the education, study and practice of medicine among women. Concerned with equality of opportunity and the fulfilment of career potential among women. Publishes *Medical Woman* (no. 889).

891.   MEDICAL WOMEN'S INTERNATIONAL ASSOCIATION, Herbert-Lewin-Strasse 5, 5600 Cologne 41, W. Germany.

Affiliation of national women's medical associations and individual members.

892.   WFMH WOMEN'S NETWORK, c/o Social Work Dept, St George's Hospital, Morpeth, Northumberland NE61 2NU.

A network started in 1987 by women members of the World Federation of Mental Health, it aims to address the issues of women's inequality and disadvantage and lack of recognition and response to women's mental health needs worldwide. Publishes a newsletter and directory of members.

ARCHIVES AND SPECIAL COLLECTIONS ON WOMEN IN MEDICINE. (no. 877)

HEALTH AND THE WORKPLACE

DENNING, John V. *Women's Work and Health Hazards: A Selected Bibliography*. (no. 1061).

For items on sexual harassment at work see nos 932–935 later in this chapter.

DISABILITY

893. RFR/DRF RESOURCES FOR FEMINIST RESEARCH, 'Women and disability/Les femmes handicapées', *RFR/DRF Resources for Feminist Research*, vol. 14, no. 1, March 1985.

Special issue including many short experiential and factual articles, reports of work in progress, lists of periodicals and groups, filmography and bibliography.

894. *Disabled Women's International Newsletter*, Annual, PO Box 323, Stuyvesant Station, New York, NY 10009, 1986–.

Rotates to different national groups every two years. Due to change in 1990.

FERTILITY AND REPRODUCTIVE RIGHTS

Bibliographies

BREWER, Joan Scherer, *Sex and the Modern Jewish Woman: An Annotated Bibliography*. (no. 1008).

CHUNG, Betty Jamie, *The Status of Women and Fertility in Southeast and East Asia: A Bibliography*. (no. 332).

FAN Kok-sim, *Women in Southeast Asia: A Bibliography*. (no. 334)

895. MULDOON, Maureen, *Abortion: An Annotated Indexed Bibliography*, 150 p., E. Mellen Press, New York, 1980.

Nearly 3000 mainly unannotated entries arranged alphabetically, with an indigestible subject index making the book difficult to use.

896.   NORDQUIST, Joan, *Reproductive Rights*, 68 p., Reference and Research Services, Santa Cruz, CA, 1988.

A bibliographic overview of materials on abortion, foetal rights, paternal rights, reproductive technology and sterilization, drawn from academic journals, law reports, magazines and alternative periodicals as well as books.

897.   PAIGE, Karen *et al.*, *The Female Reproductive Cycle: An Annotated Bibliography*, 615 p., G.K. Hall, Boston, 1985.

Arranged in six sections: Menarche, Menstruation, Pregnancy, Childbirth, Postpartum and Menopause, with each subject subdivided by topics, and with explanatory introductions. Major references (gauged by accessibility, currency and frequency of citation) are annotated and arranged chronologically, followed by an alphabetical sequence of unannotated additional references. The material is mostly post-1965, and in English. A mix of psychological, sociological and medical material. Excludes literature on abortion, contraception and hysterectomy.

898.   'Perceptions of menstruation: a literature review [and] Annotated bibliography', in WORLD HEALTH ORGANIZATION, *Patterns and Perceptions of Menstruation: A World Health Organization International Collaborative Study*, WHO/Croom Helm/St Martin's Press, 1983, pp. 148–242, 1983.

This work arises out of a large cross-cultural study of women's attitudes to menstruation, conducted in ten countries in the late 1970s. The bibliography is very detailed, listing mainly journal articles up to 1981.

899.   WINTER, Eugenia, *Psychological and Medical Aspects of Induced Abortion: A Selective Annotated Bibliography*, 162 p., Greenwood, Westport, CT, 1988.

Includes 500 selected titles, either classics, or representative of writing in this area, and including some audiovisual works. Mainly English language, but includes a handful of works originating elsewhere and translated into English. The selection aims to be neither pro- nor anti-abortion, and the compiler avoids 'emotion-laden' words in the annotations. Separate author, title and subject indexes provide detailed access to the material which is arranged in broad subject groups.

Resources

NATIONAL WOMEN'S HEALTH NETWORK, *Resource Guide*. (no. 862) Many of these nine guides are directly concerned with aspects of reproduction.

Legal resources

BENJAMIN N. CARDOZO SCHOOL OF LAW, Yeshiva University, *Women's Annotated Legal Bibliography.* (no. 750)

LEFCOURT, Carol, *Women and the Law.* (no. 744)

Statistics

UNITED NATIONS, Statistical Office, *Women's Indicators and Statistics Database (WISTAT).* (no. 145).

Women of the World. (no. 146)

Both the above contain statistics on fertility and childbirth.

Periodicals

900.   *Reproductive and Genetic Engineering: Journal of International Feminist Analysis*, 3/yr, Pergamon Press, New York, 1988–.

Scholarly articles on this topic produced by the Feminist International Network FINRRAGE (no. 901).

Women's Health and Reproductive Rights Information Centre Newsletter. (no. 870)

Organizations

901.   FEMINIST INTERNATIONAL NETWORK OF RESISTANCE TO REPRODUCTIVE AND GENETIC ENGINEERING (FINRRAGE), Box 38 LOP, 52 Call Lane, Leeds LS1 6DT.

A network of over 1000 women in 35 countries, with headquarters and library in Germany. Aims to monitor developments in reproductive technology, to assess their implications for women, and to pool information. Publishes the journal *Reproductive and Genetic Engineering* (no. 900)

902.   WOMEN'S GLOBAL NETWORK ON REPRODUCTIVE RIGHTS, Nieuwe Zijds, Voorburgwal 32, 1012 RZ Amsterdam, Netherlands.

Network of groups and individuals who support and who are working for reproductive rights for women. Monitors research, organizes campaigns, collects and disseminates information, organizes practical support (e.g. the supply of contraceptives). Publishes a quarterly newsletter.

WOMEN'S HEALTH AND REPRODUCTIVE RIGHTS INFORMATION CENTRE (WHRRIC). (no. 879)

PROSTITUTION

Bibliographies

903.   BULLOUGH, Vern *et al.*, *A Bibliography of Prostitution*, 419 p., Garland, New York, 1977.

The standard resource on this subject, with a worldwide scope, and including fiction with prostitution as a theme. Nearly 6500 entries provide a comprehensive overview, although it is now limited by its date. The entries are unannotated, and arranged in subject order, with an extensive section on area studies subdivided by region and country. There is an author index.

Organizations

904.   ENGLISH COLLECTIVE OF PROSTITUTES, PO Box 287, London NW6 5QU.

Organization for prostitute women. Publishes *Network*, a news bulletin three times per year for each other and for the public.

905.   INTERNATIONAL COMMITTEE FOR PROSTITUTES' RIGHTS, Postbus 725, 1000 AS Amsterdam, Netherlands.

906.   JOSEPHINE BUTLER SOCIETY, c/o Candida, 49 Hawkshead Lane, North Mymms, Hatfield, Herts.

Old-established organizations whose objects are to abolish the state regulation of prostitution, and to promote a single moral standard for men and women. Its papers are deposited in the Fawcett Library, and the main interest in it for women's studies is as a historical resource.

PSYCHOLOGY

Bibliographies

907.   ASTIN, Helen, Allison PARELMAN and Anne FISHER, *Sex Roles: A Research Bibliography*, 362 p., National Institute of Mental Health, US Dept of Health, Education and Welfare, Rockville, MD, 1975.

An annotated compilation of research in sex roles published between 1960 and 1972, mainly from journals in social science subjects, but also including some books and conference papers, and some medical literature. Arranged by subject with lengthy annotations and author and further subject indexes. Now rather old.

908.   DILLING, Carole and Barbara CLASTER, *Female Psychology: A Partially Annotated Bibliography*, 328 p., New York City Coalition for Women's Mental Health, New York, 1985.

A bibliography 'designed to integrate new perspectives on female development into the previously generalized and largely masculine perspective of
the existing literature'. The references are arranged by topic in six broad
sections: The historical perspective, Gender differences in the life cycle and
current research on female development, Special issues, Mental health
issues, Sex role issues in psychotherapy and supervision, and Female
psychology in a biological, political and sociological context. There is an
appendix of sources and other bibliographies.

See also:

FAUNCE, Patricia Spencer, *Women and Ambition: A Bibliography*.
(no. 1041).

Curriculum studies

909.   GOLUB, Sharon and Rita Jackway FREEDMAN, *The Psychology
of Women: Resources for a Core Curriculum*, 160 p., Garland, New York, 1987.

'A curriculum guide for teachers wishing to update their courses to include
new research on gender issues. It includes material on all aspects of the
psychology of women.' (From publisher's announcement.)

910.   PALUDI, Michele A., *Exploring/Teaching the Psychology of Women: A
Manual of Resources*, 384 p., State University of New York Press, Albany,
NY, 1988.

Resources

911.   BEERE, Carole A., *Women and Women's Issues: A Handbook of Tests
and Measures*, 550 p., Jossey-Bass, San Francisco, 1979.

A compendious and scholarly book describing psychological measuring
instruments used for gathering data about women. The methodology for
identifying these is described in the introductory chapters, as is the
organization of the book. The 235 tests are presented divided by subject,
such as sex roles, marital and parental roles, attitudes towards women's
issues, etc. Each test is carefully described in a standard format, enabling it
to be directly compared with the others. There are indexes to instrument
titles, names, and variables measured.

See also:

PARKS, Beverly J. *et al.*, *Sourcebook of Measures of Women's Educational
Equity*. (no. 660)

912. RFR/DRF RESOURCES FOR FEMINIST RESEARCH,
'Research on the psychology of woman/Recherches sur la psychologie de la
femme', *RFR/DRF Resources for Feminist Research*, vol. 9, no. 2, 1980.

A special issue including short article-style accounts of research and theory, book reviews, and a bibliography of publications of 1979 and 1980. Also includes notes on research in progress, theses and resources.

Periodicals

913. *Psychology of Women Quarterly*, 4/yr, Cambridge University Press, London, 1976–. (Published for Division 35 of the American Psychological Association.)

Contains scholarly articles. Aims to 'encourage and develop a body of feminist research'. As well as book reviews it publishes media reviews (of films and videos).

Organizations

ASSOCIATION FOR WOMEN IN PSYCHOLOGY. (no. 887)

WFMH WOMEN'S NETWORK. (no. 892)

PSYCHOTHERAPY

Resources

914. AVIS, Judith Myers, 'Reference guide to feminism and family therapy', *Journal of Feminist Family Therapy*, vol. 1, no. 1, pp. 94–100, 1989.

An unannotated list of 'all the existing family therapy literature' related specifically to feminist, gender and political issues. Contains about 150 recent references, most from the late 1980s.

915. ROSEWATER, Lynne Bravo and Lenore WALKER, *Handbook of Feminist Therapy: Women's Issues in Psychotherapy*, 352 p., Springer, New York, 1985.

A collection of review essays with bibliographies which grew out of a conference of feminist therapists in the US in 1982. It seeks to present the 'cutting edge' of feminist therapy, contrasting approaches with more traditional methods. Essays are grouped into seven sections covering philosophy, techniques and practice, women's issues, violence, power and advocacy, ethics and training. Excellent.

916. ZUCKERMAN, Eyse, *Changing Directions in the Treatment of Women: A Mental Health Bibliography*, 494 p., National Institute of Mental Health, Rockville, MD, 1979.

Compiled out of the momentum generated by the criticism during the 1970s of traditional psychiatric approach to women. This work covers material published from 1960 to 1977. First a section on theoretical literature on psychology and biology of women, then criticism of treatment; research response to such criticism, modifications of theory; specific problems and specific groups of women; alternative approaches. The annotations are long and intentionally descriptive rather than critical. This is a valuable book; only the last section on alternatives now seems out of date.

Periodicals

917.   *Affilia: Journal of Women and Social Work*, 4/yr, Sage, Newbury Park, CA, 1986–.

'Committed to the discussion and development of feminist values, theories and knowledge as they relate to social work research, education and practice.' It contains articles and reviews, and also creative writing, and has a feature called 'On the lookout' of news and announcements. Strictly American.

918.   *Journal of Feminist Family Therapy*, 4/yr, Haworth Press, New York, 1989.

'Provides a multidisciplinary forum to further explore the relationship between feminist theory and family therapy practice and theory.'

919.   *Women and Therapy*, 4/yr, Haworth Press, New York, 1982–.

'To facilitate dialogue about therapy, experiences among therapists, consumers, and researchers. The journal is feminist in orientation and views therapy as an educational, expanding process for personal growth.'

· Organizations

920.   WOMEN'S THERAPY CENTRE, 6 Manor Gdns, London N7 6LA.

A pioneering organization for therapy for women in the UK. Also runs courses and workshops.

SEXUALITY

BREWER, Joan Scherer, *Sex and the Modern Jewish Woman: An Annotated Bibliography*. (no. 1008)

921.   SAHLI, Nancy, *Women and Sexuality in America: A Bibliography*, 404 p., G.K. Hall, Boston, 1984.

A selected bibliography of 1684 items, about half of which are annotated. Material was chosen that directly relates to the definition and behaviour of (American) women as sexual beings, and covers nineteenth- and twentieth-century publications in English. Arranged in broad subjects, with two chapters for pre-1920 publications. Author and title indexes are provided.

VIOLENCE AND ABUSE

General bibliographies

922. BAR ON, Bat-Ami, 'Violence against women: philosophical literature overview' [and] 'Violence against women: a bibliography', *APA Newsletter on Feminism and Philosophy*, no. 88:1, pp. 8–13, Nov. 1988.

These two articles consist of a literature review and bibliography, together listing about 100 references. Useful for the recent material.

DAVIS, Nanette J. and Jane M. KEITH, *Women and Deviance: Issues in Social Conflict and Change: An Annotated Bibliography*. (no. 976).

Contains a section on crimes against women.

923. ENGELDINGER, Eugene A., *Spouse Abuse: An Annotated Bibliography of Violence between Mates*, 317 p., Scarecrow, Metuchen, NJ, 1986.

Noting in the introduction that the *Journal of Marriage and the Family* included not a single article with 'violence' in its title from 1939 to 1969, the author has attempted a comprehensive listing of material on spouse abuse, the vast majority of which has appeared since the early 1970s. He has excluded material from ephemeral publications which can no longer be found, and audiovisual materials. Coverage is both British and American (with the impetus for the current attention, as the author points out, largely deriving from Erin Pizzey's pioneering work in Britain). The 1783 annotated entries are arranged in a single sequence, with subject and name indexes.

924. KEMMER, Elizabeth Jane, *Violence in the Family: An Annotated Bibliography*, 204 p., Garland, New York, 1984.

Contains publications in English issued from 1960 to 1982 with descriptive annotations. Its use is limited by its alphabetical arrangement and the rather unwieldy subject index, which does, however, include titles of organizations sponsoring work. Most of the entries are from American medical or social science sources. There is little sign of a feminist perspective.

925. STARK, Evan, *Woman Battering: Survivors and Assailants: A Source Book, c.* 350 p., Garland, New York, 1989.

'Organizes the vast literature in the field of battering into short topical chapters and selective bibliographies . . . The more than 300 selective annotations direct students, researchers and practitioners to the primary data, theory and case material from which conclusions and questions arise.' (From publisher's announcement.)

926. WILSON, Carolyn F., *Violence against Women: An Annotated Bibliography*, 111 p., G.K. Hall, Boston, 1981.

A selective bibliography of articles and books from 1975 to 1980, with a few earlier works which were too important to omit, covering 213 thoroughly annotated items, and an author/title index. After an introductory chapter of more general works, there follow four chapters on battered women, rape, sexual abuse of children and pornography. Entries are further subdivided by subject within each chapter as appropriate, and each has a short introductory essay. There is also a list of journals consulted, mainly, but not exclusively, American. There is an excellent introduction.

Legal aspects of violence

BENJAMIN N. CARDOZO SCHOOL OF LAW, Yeshiva University, *Women's Annotated Legal Bibliography*. (no. 750)

LEFCOURT, Carol, *Women and the Law*. (no. 744)

Rape

927. BARNES, Dorothy L., *Rape: A Bibliography, 1965–1975*, 175 p., Whitston Pub. Co., Troy, NY, 1977.

A comprehensive unannotated compilation of material published in the ten years 1965–75, with the majority being from the 1970s. In three sequences: Books alphabetically by author, periodical articles alphabetically by title, and periodical articles by subject. There is a detailed list of subject headings and an author index.

928. KEMMER, Elizabeth Jane, *Rape and Rape-Related Issues: An Annotated Bibliography*, 187 p., Garland, New York, 1977.

Includes 348 items published between 1965 and 1976, almost all American. There is a subject index and a list of periodicals represented. Cf. Barnes (no. 927) which has more than twice the number of entries covering the same period.

Also see the chapter on rape in Wilson (no. 926).

Incest and child sexual abuse

929. BASS, Ellen and Laura DAVIS, *The Courage to Heal: A Guide for Women Survivors of Child Sexual Abuse*, 493 p., Harper & Row, New York, 1988.

An excellent workbook and guide to resources which does not assume . heterosexuality.

930. COMPENDIUM WOMEN'S SECTION, *Incest and Sexual Violence: A Booklist*, 14 p., Compendium Bookshop, 234 Camden High St, London NW1, 1988.

Briefly annotated list of over 100 titles, including many 1988 publications.

931. DE YOUNG, Mary, *Incest: An Annotated Bibliography*, 161 p., McFarland, Jefferson, NY, 1985.

Contains 410 items arranged according to 'type' of incest, with father–daughter by far the largest section. Also covers intervention and treatment, statistical studies and literature reviews. Author and subject index provided.

Also see the chapter on sexual abuse of children in Wilson (no. 926).

Sexual harassment

932. CROCKER, Phyllis L., 'Annotated bibliography on sexual harassment in education', *Women's Rights Law Reporter*, vol. 7, pp. 91–106, Winter 1982.

The bibliography was prepared as part of the Sexual Harassment in Education Project of the NOW Legal Defense and Education Fund, and consists of an annotated listing arranged by form (papers and reports, books, cases, organizational publications, etc.). US oriented.

933. McCAGHY, M. Dawn, *Sexual Harassment: A Guide to Resources*, 181 p., G.K. Hall, Boston, 1985.

Covers a wide variety of material from the period 1974–1984, reflecting, as the author says, the currency of concern with the issue of sexual harassment. General works are followed by a chapter on sexual harassment in higher education; other chapters are Coping strategies, The legal perspective and Management response, including policies and training materials. Useful and thorough account of the US situation.

934. MILLER, Alan V., *Sexual Harassment of Women in the Workplace: A Bibliography with Emphasis on Canadian Publications*, 22 p., Vance Bibliographies, Monticello, IL, 1981.

Alphabetical list of 340 references, including articles from newspapers and popular magazines as well as the usual books and periodical articles.

935. STORRIE, Kathleen and Pearl DYKSTRA, 'Bibliography on sexual harassment', *RFR/DRF Resources for Feminist Research*, vol. 10, no. 4, pp. 25–32, 1981/2.

Preceded by a lengthy introduction, the bibliography contains newspaper articles as well as a list of legal cases and of books and articles (mainly American and Canadian).

Substance abuse

936.   CHALFANT, Paul and Brent S. ROPER, *Social and Behavioral Aspects of Female Alcoholism: An Annotated Bibliography*, 161 p., Greenwood, Westport, CT, 1980.

A solid bibliography of 488 articles, mainly dating from 1970–1980, but with some essential earlier items. The entries have brief but informative abstracts, and are divided into broad subjects such as social and cultural aspects, medical and physical concomitants, etc. There is an author index, and an introduction giving a review of the subject. A useful work.

DAVIS, Nanette J. and Jane M. KEITH, *Women and Deviance: Issues in Social Conflict and Change: An Annotated Bibliography.* (no. 976).

MAZUR, Carol and Sharon PEPPER, *Women in Canada: A Bibliography 1965–1982.* (no. 502).

Contains a section on alcoholism.

Periodicals

937.   *Response to the Victimization of Women and Children*, Center for Women Policy Studies, 2000 P St NW, Suite 508, Washington, DC 20036.

International feminist publication containing information on violence against and exploitation of women and children.

WIN News (no. 202)

Notable for its campaign against genital mutilation.

WOMEN AND AGEING

Resources

938.   DORESS, Paula Brown and Diana Laskin SIEGAL, *Ourselves, Growing Older: Women Aging with Knowledge and Power*, 511 p., Simon & Schuster, New York, 1987.

In the style and format of *Our Bodies Ourselves*, this is an affirmative and informing book about health and lifestyles as women age. The substantial resources list is mainly North American but the content of the text is universal.

939.   RFR/DRF RESOURCES IN FEMINIST RESEARCH, 'Women as elders/Nos ainées', *RFR/DRF Resources for Feminist Research*, vol. 11, no. 2, 1982.

This special issue on older women includes (as well as the bibliography by Jaffee and Nett (no. 944), articles, bibliographies on the social history of women in old age and Canadian plays about older women. There are also four outline syllabi of courses on old age, with bibliographies. Resources and organizations are listed in the Jaffee and Nett bibliography.

Bibliographies

940.   BORENSTEIN, Audrey, *Older Women in 20th Century America: A Selected Annotated Bibliography*, 351 p., Garland, New York, 1982.

Lengthy annotations characterize this bibliography. It is arranged by subject and is wide-ranging in scope, including art works, literature, biographical material, oral history, ageism and so on.

941.   COYLE, Jean M., *Women and Aging: A Selected Annotated Bibliography*, Greenwood, Westport, CT, 1989.

'The primary objective of this work is to provide the reader with extensive references to useful and appropriate materials on women and ageing. The major subject areas covered include roles and relationships, economics, employment, retirement, health, sexuality, religion, housing, racial and ethnic groups, policy issues, international concerns, and middle age.' (From publisher's announcement.)

942.   DOLAN, Eleanor F. and Dorothy M. Group, *The Mature Woman in America: A Selected Annotated Bibliography 1979-1982*, 122 p., National Council on the Aging, Washington, DC, 1984.

Contains 420 items from 1979 to 1982, with emphasis on statistics and research. All items are found in the library of the National Council on the Aging. Arranged alphabetically with a detailed subject index.

943.   EISLER, Terri A., 'Older women, policy and politics: an annotated bibliography', *Women and Politics*, vol. 6, pp. 71-82, Summer 1986.

944.   JAFFEE, Georgina and Emily M. NETT, 'Annotated bibliography on women as elders', *RFR/DRF Resources for Feminist Research*, vol. 11, no. 2, pp. 253-288, 1982.

The entries have detailed annotations, and are divided into ten broad subjects. There are also lists of (Canadian) theses, bibliographies, and the final section on sources and resources includes lists of periodicals, organizations, film and audiovisual materials, etc.

945.   SYNGE, Jane, 'Some selected materials on women in old age in the nineteenth and early twentieth century', *RFR/DRF Resources for Feminist Research*, vol. 11, no. 2, pp. 241-243, 1982.

A listing of books and articles that deal with the social position of women in old age, mostly relating to working-class women.

Periodicals

946.   *Broomstick: By, for and about Women over Forty*, 6/yr, 3543 18th St#3, San Francisco, CA 94110, 1978–.

A lively magazine of writing by older women, includes poems, stories and articles as well as news and announcements.

947.   *Journal of Women and Aging*, 4/yr, Haworth Press, New York, 1989–.

'Designed to enhance the knowledge of a wide variety of professionals who are concerned with the health and well-being of women as they age.'

CHAPTER 20

Science, mathematics and technology

Women's participation in the traditionally male preserves of science and technology is poorly documented, mainly because of the lack of material. There is a growing interest, however, in the areas of scientific education for girls, and new technology networks are being established all the time. Paradoxically some of the oldest established organizations are in the scientific professions where women have had to struggle for admittance - see the Engineering section below.

GENERAL WORKS

Bio-bibliographical works

HERZENBERG, Caroline L., *Women Scientists from Antiquity to the Present: An Index; An International Reference Listing and Biographical Directory of Some Notable Women from Ancient to Modern Times.* (no. 167)

948. OGILVIE, Marilyn Bailey, *Women in Science: Antiquity through the Nineteenth Century: A Biographical Dictionary with Annotated Bibliography*, 254 p., MIT Press, Cambridge, MA, 1986.

Biographical entries for nearly 200 Western women are followed by a good bibliography, subdivided into reference material, general histories and collective bibliographies and five chronological sections covering the range of the book. The annotations are brief but informative. Some of the biographical entries are quite substantial, especially the American ones for which information was more easily available.

SIEGEL, Patricia Joan, *Women in the Scientific Search: An American Bio-bibliography 1724-1979.* (no. 168)

Bibliographies

949. 'Bibliography - women in science', *Hypatia*, vol. 3, pp. 145-155, Spring 1988. (Update of bibliography published in *Frontiers*, vol. 8, no. 3, 1985.)

An unannotated list of nearly 200 books and articles, divided into three sections: Women in science, Feminist critiques of sexism in the practice of science, and Science and feminist epistemology. Some items are starred to indicate their suitability as an introduction to the subject.

950. CHINN, Phyllis Zweig, *Women in Science and Mathematics: Bibliography*, 38 p., American Association for the Advancement of Science, Washington, DC, 1979.

This is an unannotated list of works on women in science and mathematics. It also lists some bibliographies of the 1970s, and some special issues of periodicals.

951. HOYRUP, Else, *Women and Mathematics, Science and Engineering: A Partially Annotated Bibliography with Emphasis on Mathematics and with References on Related Topics*, 62 p., Roskilde University Library, Roskilde, Denmark, 1978.

A listing of books, chapters, articles and reports, most from the 1960s and 1970s, but some dating from the early 1900s.

952. KELLY, Alison, 'Women in science: a bibliographic review', *Durham Research Review*, vol. 36, pp. 1092–1108, 1976.

A review article, with 131 references, covering such topics as intellectual ability, occupational choice, school subjects, etc.

953. RFR/DRF RESOURCES FOR FEMINIST RESEARCH, 'Femmes et/Women and sciences', *RFR/DRF Resources for Feminist Research*, vol. 15, no. 3, 1986.

This special issue is useful in this particularly sparsely documented area. Many of the articles have short bibliographies.

954. SEARING, Susan, 'Further readings on feminism and science', in BLEIER, Ruth, *Feminist Approaches to Science*, Pergamon, 1988, pp. 191–195.

A list of references up to 1985 which 'highlights recent feminist critiques of scientific theory and practice'.

Organizations

955. ASSOCIATION OF WOMEN IN SCIENCE, Suite 303, 3401 Virginia Ave. NW, Washington, DC 20037.

Founded in 1971 to improve the educational and employment opportunities for women in all science fields. Publishes resource materials, a newsletter and legislative update.

956. CANADIAN ASSOCIATION FOR WOMEN IN SCIENCE (CAWIS), 1087 Meyerside Drive, Suite 5, Mississauga, Ontario L5T 1M5, Canada.

Aims to promote equal opportunities for women in scientific professions. Publishes *CAWIS News* two to three times a year, a newsletter with information on the activities of the association.

Periodicals

957. *Women for Science for Women: A Radically Different Newsletter*, Stockgrove Farm, nr Leighton Buzzard, Beds., LU7 0DB, 1988-.

'Newsletter by and for women with an interest in science, medicine and technology.'

See also:

FEMINIST FUTURES INTERNATIONAL NETWORK/INSTITUTE FOR WOMEN AND THE FUTURE (FFIN). (No. 983)

WOMEN'S ENVIRONMENTAL NETWORK (WEN). (no. 984)

COMPUTING AND NEW TECHNOLOGY

Handbooks

958.   BRECHER, Deborah L., *The Women's Computer Literacy Handbook*, 254 p., New American Library, New York, 1985.

The co-founder of the Women's Computer Literacy Project and the National Women's Mailing List has written this book out of her experience as a teacher. She explains that the title emphasizes 'that the explanations of computer technology reflect my own very personal frame of reference . . . the analogies and examples are drawn from female experience . . . because almost all books on technological subjects do the reverse – they base themselves on a male environment.' Describes how computers work, what they do, types of software, how to buy one, how to set up a system, word processing, etc.

Periodicals

959.   *Women and Computing Newsletter*, 4/yr, Microsyster, Wild Court, Wesley House, off Kingsway, London WC2B 5AU, 1981-.

Contains 'articles on women's technology initiatives worldwide', news, conferences, reviews, special sections of technical information, contributions from women working with computers. The newsletter was originally started by the National Women and Computing Network, and carries news of network meetings and developments.

Organizations

GENDER AND NEW INFORMATION TECHNOLOGIES (GRANITE). (no. 621)

960.   MICROSYSTER, c/o London Women's Centre, Wesley House, 4 Wild Court, off Kingsway, London WC2B 5AU.

A collective set up in 1982 'to develop ways to use microcomputers for women'. Now provides computing services to women's groups, supports feminists working in computing, and has an educational function so that women can 'benefit from and critically assess' computer-based technology. Also publishes a quarterly *Women and Computing Newsletter* and administers the National Women and Computing Network.

961.   NATIONAL WOMEN AND COMPUTING NETWORK, c/o London Women's Centre, Wesley House, 4 Wild Court, off Kingsway, London WC2B 5AU.

Set up in 1981, this is a register of women interested in computer-based technology. It has several meetings a year and is active in various areas.

ENGINEERING

This traditionally male bastion has produced organizations for women which date back to the early twentieth century.

Periodicals

962.   *US Woman Engineer*, 6/yr, Society of Women Engineers, 345 E 47th St, New York, NY 10017, 1980–.

House magazine of the Society.

963.   *Woman Engineer (The)*, 4/yr, Women's Engineering Society, Imperial College of Science and Technology, Dept of Civil Engineering, Imperial College Rd, London SW7 2BU, 1919–.

Old-fashioned magazine with articles of technical and career interest, Official organ of the Women's Engineering Society.

Organizations

964.   ASSOCIATION FRANÇAISE DES FEMMES INGENIEURS, 10 rue Vauquelin, 75005 Paris, France.

Formed in 1982 to encourage girls into the engineering profession, to promote the employment of women engineers and to represent French women engineers nationally and internationally. Publishes a newsletter called *Graffiti*.

965. SOCIETY OF WOMEN ENGINEERS, 345 E. 47th St, New York, NY 10017.

Professional organization for women in engineering, publishes *US Woman Engineer* (no. 962).

966. WOMEN'S ENGINEERING SOCIETY, c/o Imperial College of Science and Technology, Dept of Civil Engineering, Imperial College Rd, London SW7 2BU.

Formed in 1919 in order to help girls and women to become engineers. Still active as 'the authoritative voice of women engineers in the UK'. Publishes *The Woman Engineer* (no. 963), a quarterly journal.

MATHEMATICS

Bio-bibliographical works

967. GRINSTEIN, Louise and Paul CAMPBELL, *Women of Mathematics: A Bibliographic Sourcebook*, 292 p., Greenwood, New York, 1987.

An edited collection of essays on forty-three mathematicians from all ages and countries, but excluding anyone born after 1925. The entries are arranged alphabetically but a chronological index is provided, as are lists by place of origin, place of work and field of work. Subject and name indexes, and an appendix of references in biographical dictionaries and other works is also given. Each entry in the main work follows a standard format, namely a biographical section, a description of her work, and a bibliography listing first works by the subject, followed by works about her.

Bibliographies

968. GENDER AND MATHEMATICS ASSOCIATION (GAMMA), *Bibliography*, 27 p., GAMMA, Dept of Mathematical Sciences, Goldsmith's College, London SE14 6NW, 1984.

About 200 references on gender and mathematics, arranged in the following sections: Ability/attainment, Adult education, Assessment of performance, Attitudes to maths, Careers, Choosing maths at school/college, Cross cultural, Female mathematicians, Government reports, etc., Initiatives, Resources, Reviews of research, Social factors, Teachers' attitudes, Texts.

HOYRUP, Else, *Women and Mathematics, Science and Engineering: A Partially Annotated Bibliography with Emphasis on Mathematics and with References on Related Topics*. (no. 951)

Organizations

969. ASSOCIATION FOR WOMEN IN MATHEMATICS, Women's Research Centre, Box 178, Wellesley College, Wellesley, MA 02181.

Concerned with education, employment, legal issues, history, etc., of women and mathematics. Publishes a bi-monthly newsletter.

970. EUROPEAN WOMEN IN MATHEMATICS, General Coordinator: Dr Marion Kimberley, National Heart & Lung Institute, Dovehouse St, London SW3 6LY.

Affiliation of women in Europe bound by a common interest in the position of women in mathematics. Cooperation with groups in European countries.

971. GENDER AND MATHEMATICS ASSOCIATION (GAMMA), c/o Dept of Mathematical Sciences, Goldsmiths' College, London SE14 6NW.

A national association concerned with gender bias in mathematics and which aims to evolve strategies and create resources aimed at improving the situation and maintaining and extending a national network for the exchange and sharing of ideas. Produces a newsletter for members.

972. INTERNATIONAL ORGANIZATION FOR WOMEN IN MATHEMATICS EDUCATION (IOWME), Ontario Institute for Studies in Education, 252 Bloor St W, Toronto, Ontario M5S 1V6, Canada.

Founded in 1976 with worldwide membership. Goals are to further research into gender and mathematics, and activities that enhance the participation of girls in mathematics. Publishes a twice-yearly newsletter.

CHAPTER 21

Society and the environment

Since most works deal with society in one aspect or another, this section contains only those works which explicitly do so, the rest being elsewhere in this book.

SOCIOLOGY

Bibliographies

973. BRITISH SOCIOLOGICAL ASSOCIATION, *Society without Sexism: A Sourcebook*, 77 p., British Sociological Association, London, 1978.

Now mainly of historical interest, this short bibliography was produced as a result of pressure engendered at the BSA Annual Conference 1974 on Sexual Divisions in Society for the Association to address itself to sexism within academic sociology itself.

974. DINER, Hasia R., *Women and Urban Society: A Guide to Information Sources*, 150 p., Gale, Detroit, MI, 1979.

Arranged in six main sections: Women and urbanization, Women in urban families, Urban fertility, Employment, Women's roles, Views of urban women. Well annotated. Entries of post-1940 works mainly on currently urbanizing societies. The introduction points to gaps in current literature, especially work on nineteenth-century urbanization and its implications for women. Appendices include a personal bibliography, lists of abstracts and indexes, and relevant periodicals. Worldwide coverage.

Organizations

975. SOCIOLOGISTS FOR WOMEN IN SOCIETY, 830 Sprowl Rd, Bryn Mawr, PA 19010.

Organization of academic and student sociologists, aiming to pursue anti-discrimination policies.

SOCIAL CONFLICT

See also Chapter 16 on law and politics.

Bibliographies

976.   DAVIS, Nanette J. and Jane M. KEITH, *Women and Deviance: Issues in Social Conflict and Change: An Annotated Bibliography*, 236 p., Garland, New York, 1984.

Over 500 substantially annotated items covering abortion, alcohol and drugs, bisexuality, corrections and punishment, crimes against women, crimes of women, divorce, lesbianism (*sic*), mental illness, poverty, singles, suicide, teenage pregnancy, older women and general works. Predominantly American. A lengthy introduction explains the definition of deviance and the philosophical background of social control of women, but does not justify the questionable categorization of what constitutes 'deviance'.

977.   DOERKSON, Linda, 'Women and crime: a bibliography', *RFR/DRF Resources for Feminist Research*, vol. 14, no. 4, pp. 60–61, 1985/6.

Contains 58 unannotated references to the main books and articles on the subject up to 1983.

MARTIN, Carol Ann, *Capable Cops – Women behind the Shield: A Selected Bibliography on Women Police Officers*. (no. 1071)

MARTIN, Carol Ann and Alice PHILBIN, *Women as Probation, Parole and Correctional Officers in the Criminal Justice Field: A Selected Bibliography*. (no. 1072)

Periodicals

Affilia: Journal of Women and Social Work. (no. 917)

Women and Criminal Justice. (no. 728)

PLANNING AND THE ENVIRONMENT

Bibliographies

978.   COATSWORTH, Patricia, *Women and Urban Planning: A Bibliography*, 21 p., Council of Planning Librarians, Chicago, IL, 1981.

This annotated bibliography covers literature on planning for and with women, and also on women as planners, their status and perspectives. It is in two parts, historical (1840–1965) and contemporary (1965–1980), with an appendix on how to locate material in the US.

979.   NOVAK, Sylvia, *Women and Housing: An Annotated Bibliography*, 26 p., Council of Planning Librarians, Monticello, IL, 1986.

A selection of references chosen from a feminist perspective, dealing with western industrialized countries, and covering the years 1980–1986 with an occasional earlier publication. Arranged by subject. No index. Small but useful section on reference sources, and another listing special periodical issues.

980.   WILSON, Hugh and Sally RIDGEWAY, *Women in Suburbia: A Bibliography*, 22 p., CPL Bibliographies, Chicago, IL, 1982.

An unannotated collection of otherwise very scattered material, arranged in ten subject sections with introductory paragraphs.

Periodicals

981.   *Web: Women and the Built Environment*, irreg., Women's Design Service, 62 Beechwood Rd, London E8 3DY, 1984–.

A planning and urban environment interest newsletter.

982.   *Women and Environments*, 4/yr, Centre for Urban and Community Studies, 455 Spadina Ave, Toronto, Ontario M5S 2G8, 1979–.

A lively magazine with illustrated articles on planning and housing issues. Also aims to provide a network of women of similar interests.

Organizations

983.   FEMINIST FUTURES INTERNATIONAL NETWORK/ INSTITUTE FOR WOMEN AND THE FUTURE (FFIN), PO Box 1081, Northampton, MA 01061.

Founded in 1980 to bring together women of diverse interests such as 'nuclear decision-making, world-scale economics, alternative "development" . . . ' Publishes *FFIN News* quarterly subscription lists.

984.   WOMEN'S ENVIRONMENTAL NETWORK (WEN), 287 City Rd, London EC1V 1LA.

Founded in 1988, a forum for 'women to link environment, health, ecology and aid'. Particularly concerned with environmental problems which affect women specifically. Produces a quarterly newsletter.

GEOGRAPHY

985.   LOYD, Bonnie, *Women and Geography: An Annotated Bibliography and Guide to Sources of Information*, 18 p., Council of Planning Librarians, Monticello, IL, 1976.

The introduction bemoans the paucity of material and the absence of women in geography. The works are listed in two sections: Women in the discipline of geography, and Geographic studies of women in society. Sadly, now out of date.

CHAPTER 22

Spirituality, mythology and religion

Feminist energies in this area take two main paths. One has strong roots in the women's movement, and involves developing and reclaiming knowledge and experience of matriarchies, witchcraft, goddess religions, mythology and the occult, with links to shamanism and healing. The term 'womanspirit' has come to be associated with this area of study and living, after the American journal of that name (no. 1022). The other path is based in traditional religions, where feminists work to rethink the patriarchal beliefs and structures from within, and fight for a recognition of the equal value of women as priests and participants. Much work is being done in both Christianity and Judaism and the literature reflects this, with bibliographies, biographical works, archive documentation and periodicals. Non-western religions are poorly represented in comparison, and relevant references have to be sought in the more general publications listed in Part II, particularly Chapters 6 and 10.

GENERAL WORKS

986. BASS, Dorothy and Sandra Hughes BOYD, *Women in American Religious History: An Annotated Bibliography and Guide to Sources*, 169 p., G.K. Hall, Boston 1986.

Over 500 well-annotated entries, in broad subject groups: General works, Protestantism, Roman Catholicism, Judaism, Afro-American religion, Native American religion, Alternative religious movements. Each section is further subdivided by subject, and the general section also lists bibliographies and indexes in periodicals. There are subsections for individual women and for feminist studies, and each subsection ends with guides for further information. There is an index to authors. Well thought out and a pleasure to use.

987. DE-CARO, Francis A., *Women and Folklore: A Bibliographic Survey*, 184 p., Greenwood, Westport, CT, 1983.

This is a rather indigestible list of 1664 references, arranged alphabetically by author, but there is nothing else yet. The author does provide a long introductory essay where he makes some sense of the material, and there is a subject index.

988. SINCLAIR, Karen, 'Women and religion', Chapter 5 of Duley and Edwards, *Cross Cultural Study of Women* (no. 191), pp. 107–124.

An excellent set of course outlines and reading lists for the feminist study of religions, ideology and women's roles.

See also:

RICHARDSON, Marilyn, *Black Women and Religion: A Bibliography.* (no. 640)

PERIODICALS

989. *Anima: An Experiential Journal*, 2/yr, Conococheague Associates, 1053 Wilson Ave, Chambersburg, PA 17201, 1975–.

Articles, poetry and artwork are included in this well-produced journal. The religious content is eclectic, ranging from west to east, and frequently including material on native American spirituality. Feminism and women's religious experiences are a central theme of the journal, together with an interest in 'thoughtful, imaginative encounters with the differences between woman and man, East and West, yin and yang, anima and animus'.

990. *Journal of Feminist Studies in Religion*, 2/yr, Scholars Press, Ithaca, NY, 1985–.

A solid academic journal containing articles, letters, reports and comment.

ORGANIZATIONS

991. CENTER FOR WOMEN AND RELIGION, Graduate Theological Union, 2400 Ridge Rd, Berkeley, CA 94709.

'The oldest center for women in theological education' (founded in 1970). It 'seeks to end sexism and promote justice in and through religion, focusing effort on the transformation of theological education'. Publishes a student newsletter and an annual *Journal of Women and Religion* (no. 1020).

992. HOUSE OF SARAH BOOKS: Women and religion, 79 Arvine Heights, Rochester, NY 14611.

'House of Sarah retrieves printed material which testifies to women's contributions, especially in the field of religion.'

'WOMANSPIRIT' AND GODDESS RELIGION

Bibliographies

993.   CARSON, Anne, *Feminist Spirituality and the Feminine Divine: An Annotated Bibliography*, 139 p., Crossing Press, Truemansbury, NY, 1986.

The introduction to this work defines feminist spirituality as a polytheistic, holistic religious approach that insists on the power, value and dignity of women, emphasizing the immanent qualities of the goddess, and the 'divine within'. It aims to provide access to the large explosion of writing in this area since the mid 1970s, also including earlier works on aspects of the goddess even if not explicitly feminist; works on witchcraft that stress the role of women, occult books with a feminist slant, some works on prehistoric matriarchies; works examining the concept of female deity, even coming out of traditional religions; works on the Amazons, and material to do with the creating of a female-centred religious environment be it traditional or not. The substance of the book is over 700 entries with informative and sometimes lengthy annotations, including quite a few non-English texts. A carefully compiled index does not quite compensate for the scattering of material in the alphabetical arrangement, but fundamentally this is a collection without compare, a marvellous gathering together of like-minded writings.

Encyclopaedias and dictionaries

994.   MONAGHAN, Patricia, *Women in Myth and Legend*, 318 p., Junction Books, London, 1981. (Published in the US as *The Book of Goddesses and Heroines*, by Elsevier-Dutton.)

A dictionary of over 1000 'goddesses and heroines', retold 'as though the goddess were my own goddess . . . I made her the focus of her own story, told it from her point of view' to redress the male bias the author found in the many sources she used. An introductory table groups the entries in geographical areas.

995.   WALKER, Barbara, *The Woman's Encyclopedia of Myths and Secrets*, 1124 p., Harper & Row, New York, 1983.

'Thousands of popular fantasies and hidden facts are expounded in this encyclopedia, where the complex subject of sexism is approached from both the historical and the mythic viewpoints' says the author's introduction to this awe-inspiring accumulation of information about the masculinization of religion and worship, and about goddesses and earlier woman-oriented rituals and beliefs.

996.   WALKER, Barbara, *The Woman's Dictionary of Symbols and Sacred Objects*, 563 p., Harper & Row, San Francisco, 1988.

Nicely produced and illustrated guide, organized in twenty-one sections within which the entries are dictionary style. Sections cover such things as the type and shape of motifs and objects, rituals, animals, birds, plants, stones and many other categories. The author aims to provide women with 'time-honored female symbols', 'to increase awareness of symbols generally', and to reclaim many symbols 'which evolved from very different contexts in the pre-patriarchal past'.

Resources

997.　WYNNE, Patrice, *The Womanspirit Sourcebook*, 277 p., Harper & Row, San Francisco, 1988.

This is an excellent collection of resources, mainly American. The compiler runs a business called the Gaia Catalogue Company (formerly the Womanspirit Catalogue) (no. 1005), supplying books, tapes and other resources for people interested in women's spirituality. She is thus well placed to cull the much broader information provided here, which she describes as 'the resources emerging from the contemporary women's spirituality movement that are finding and inspiring the spiritual empowerment of women and the feminine principle'. Chapters cover books, periodicals, organizations, music and teaching and meditation tapes, films, videos and tarot and I Ching cards, books and calendars. Full addresses are given for all items, and there is a list of US bookstores. Interspersed with the entries are articles, interviews and poems by various women, often well-known. There is a name and title index.

Periodicals

998.　*Arachne: A Journal of Matriarchal Studies*, irreg, Arachne Collective, c/o 14 Hill Crest, Sevenoaks TN13 3HN, 1984–.

A magazine 'focusing on female aspects of divinity'. Includes articles on aspects of the Goddess, often including archaeological and mythological information.

999.　*Of a Like Mind*, 4/yr, PO Box 6021, Madison, WI 53716, 1983–.

A newspaper with articles, resource lists and announcements 'designed to share spiritual information and ideas among women of a like mind'. Includes material on occult topics and witchcraft.

1000.　*Panakaeia: Woman, Myth and Magic*, irreg, 1 Ravenstone Rd, Turnpike Lane, London N8.

Used to be subtitled 'A journal of feminist psychics and alternative healing', but has expanded to 'look more deeply at symbol, myth and magic as it is practised today'.

1001.　*Sagewoman*, 4/yr, PO Box 1478, Hillsboro, OR 97123, 1986–.

'A feminist, grassroots quarterly centered on women's spirituality and earth-based spiritual practices.' Includes articles, artwork, poetry, letters and reviews. Aims to fill the gap left by the demise of *Womanspirit* (no. 1004).

1002.   *Snakepower: A Journal of Female Shamanism*, PO Box 5544, Berkeley, CA 94705, 1989–.

1003.   *Woman of Power: A Magazine of Feminism, Spirituality and Politics*, 4/yr, PO Box 827, Cambridge, MA 02238, 1984–.

An important journal committed to a holistic view of women's 'inter-connectedness; with all people, all forms of life, the earth, and the cycles and seasons of nature and our lives'. From this comes the political and environmental content of the journal, however, its predominant theme is feminist spirituality. Although describing itself as a quarterly only ten issues had been published by summer 1988. Future plans clearly expect a more regular schedule.

1004.   *Womanspirit*, 4/yr, Wolf Creek, OR 97897–9799, 1974–1984.

This magazine came to represent, in the ten years of its publication, a particular aspect of the feminist movement in religion. It includes articles, poetry, drawing, music, as well as much current awareness information. Back issues are still available.

These are perhaps the major periodicals; there are many others, often advertised in each other. See also Carson (no. 993) and Wynne (no. 997) for more information.

Organizations

1005.   GAIA CATALOGUE COMPANY, 1400 Shattuck Ave., 10, Shattuck Commons, North Berkeley, CA 94709.

Mail-order store specializing in 'women's spiritual resources, with an emphasis on Goddess spirituality'. Many items are described in the *Womanspirit Sourcebook* (no. 997).

JEWISH WOMEN AND JUDAISM

Some of the results of the activity of Jewish feminists in examining and rethinking the effects of their beliefs and heritage, both religious and social, are collected here.

General bibliographies

1006.   CANTOR, Aviva and Ora HAMELSDORF, *The Jewish Woman 1900–1985: A Bibliography*, 193 p., Biblio Press, Fresh Meadows, NY, 2nd ed., 1987.

This is the second edition of a 1979 bibliography, and more than doubles the original size. The two parts are not merged, though they follow the same subject headings. Part 2 includes works published from 1980–1986, and there is an extra supplement for further 1986 material. Most entries are briefly annotated. Topics covered include history, religious life and laws, Jewish women in the United States, Canada, Israel and other countries, holocaust, resistance, poetry, special journal issues, unpublished papers, conference proceedings, bibliographies. There is an index to authors, and a very informative introduction describing the current work and publications of Jewish feminists.

1007. RUUD, Inger Marie, *Women and Judaism: A Selected Annotated Bibliography*, 256 p., Garland, New York, 1989.

'The main purpose is to provide access to all sorts of works dealing with women's life from ancient to modern times: women in religion, education and employment, marriage and family, politics, and society'. The 842 items are not limited to a definite span of years, but most of the references are to works published this century. The items are arranged in a single alphabetical sequence by author, with topographical, subject and author indexes.

See also the relevant entries in Carson (no. 993).

Special bibliographies

1008. BREWER, Joan Scherer, *Sex and the Modern Jewish Woman: An Annotated Bibliography*, 125 p., Biblio Press, Fresh Meadows, NY, 1986. (Contains essays by Lynn Davidman and Evelyn Avery.)

Part 1 contains essays on Sex and the Jewish woman – an overview, and Sex and the Jewish women in twentieth-century fiction. Part 2 is a bibliography covering Stereotypes of the sexuality of the Jewish woman, Halakhic views on women and sexuality, Niddah and Mikveh, Contraception and reproduction, Orthodoxy and sexuality, Non-marital sexual behaviour, Judaism and homosexuality, Premarital sexuality, Marital sexuality, Extramarital sex behaviour, Sexual dysfunction, Aging and Adolescents, Sections of sources of information and resource centres.

1009. HAMELSDORF, Ora and Sandra ADELSBERG, *Jewish Women and Jewish Law Bibliography* 57 p., Biblio Press, Fresh Meadows, NY, 1980.

An introduction to the historical background and modern discussion about changes in Jewish practices relating to women, based on traditional Jewish law (Halacha). The bibliography reflects opinions from all branches of Judaism, but includes only works in English. Grouped into Bibliographies and guides, Background reading, Books, Periodical articles, Unpublished papers, Dissertations, Glossary and List of sources. No index, some annotations.

Resources

1010.   ELWELL, Ellen Sue Levi and Edward R. LEVENSON, *The Jewish Women's Studies Guide*, 142 p., University Press of America, Lanham, MD, 2nd ed., 1987.

A compilation of course outlines and bibliographies, covering mainly religion, history and literature. Covers university courses explicitly on Jewish women's studies and those integrating Jewish women's studies into the curriculum, also continuing education and adult education courses. Each section has reading lists. There is no central bibliography or list of resources, and no index, so this really limits its usefulness to a curriculum guide only.

1011.   SCHNEIDER, Susan Weidman, *Jewish and Female: Choices and Changes in Our Lives Today*, 640 p., Simon & Schuster, New York, 1984.

'This book is a guide to the choices and changes Jewish women have been making in our relationship to family and friends, our participation in the Jewish community, and our identification of ourselves as Jews in the wake of the women's movement . . . These pages map the issues we face and the resources available to us.' Each chapter concludes with addresses and resources; however, our main reason for including it here is the 'Networking Directory' which occupies the last ninety pages, and is a compendium of organizations and publications covering a whole range of topics, including lists of libraries and archives, educational institutions, periodicals, publishers, and vast numbers of groups and societies of one sort or another. Almost entirely limited to the United States (exceptions Women in Israel, Jewish Feminist Organizations).

Much Jewish symbolism and information about historical and mythic figures is contained in Walker (nos 995 and 996) and in Monaghan (no. 994). Further material on Jewish women in the United States is included in Bass and Boyd (no. 986).

Periodicals

1012.   *Lilith*, 4/yr, 250 W. 57th St, New York, NY 10107, 1976–.
Jewish women's magazine with articles, reviews, poetry, fiction.

1013.   *Shifra: A Jewish Feminist Magazine*, irreg., Leeds, 1984–7. (Ceased publication.)
Magazine of British Jewish women.

See also the following references on Israel in Chapter 10:

CONANT, Barbara, 'Women in Israel: a bibliography'. (no. 493)

LYTLE, Elizabeth Edith, *Women in Israel: A Selected Bibliography*. (no. 494)

Noga. (no. 495)

ISRAEL FEMINIST MOVEMENT. (no. 496)

CHRISTIANITY

Bio-bibliographical works

1014.   HAMMACK, Mary, *A Dictionary of Women in Church History*, Moody Press, The Moody Bible Institute, Chicago, IL, 1984.

Covers deceased women worldwide from AD 1 to the present, who have had an impact on the Christian church, positive or negative, and about whom there is sufficient reliable information. The entries are alphabetical. There is a chronological index and a bibliography. Includes over 900 women.

Bibliographies

1015.   KENDALL, Patricia A., *Women and the Priesthood: A Selected and Annotated Bibliography*, 57 p., Committee to Promote the Cause of and to Plan for the Ordination of Women to the Priesthood, Episcopal Diocese of Pennsylvania, Philadelphia, PA, 1976.

A list of short references in support of the ordination of women. Divided into books, articles, study reports and cassettes.

1016.   KOLMER, Elizabeth, *Religious Women in the United States since 1950: Survey of Literature*, 111 p., Michael Glazier Inc., Wilmington, DE, 1984.

This book is designed to cover a time of great change in the Catholic Church and its institutions, change both from within the church itself and change reflecting the response of Catholic women to the women's movement and the growth of feminist awareness in the church. There are five chapters reviewing literature: the first three chronological – pre- and post-Vatican II, and roughly 1975–1983, and the last two reflecting the process of change in religious orders – and a bibliography specifically on the topic of change and renewal is provided. This is an interesting and useful book to read, but it is not so easy to look up individual items as there is no index at all.

See also:

HUFF, Cynthia, *British Women's Diaries: A Descriptive Bibliography of Selected Nineteenth-Century Women's Manuscript Diaries* (no. 164)

for a list of diaries kept by religious women, and:

CONWAY, Jill K., *The Female Experience in Eighteenth-and Nineteenth-Century America: A Guide to the History of American Women*. (no. 693)

for a section listing works about women and religion.

Archives

1017.   THOMAS, Evangeline, *Women's Religious History Sources: A Guide to Repositories in the United States*, 329 p., Bowker, New York, 1983.

This is a list of the archives of American communities of 'vowed women religious'. Arranged by state, and within that by city and congregation name, entries give denomination, size and address, followed by a description of the community's history and its archival holdings. After the main list of sources there is a a bibliography, arranged by denomination, giving details of biographies and histories of the orders and their members. Then comes a table of US founding dates and locations of orders, which is followed by a biographical register of 'foundresses and major superiors' and an index to source list entries.

Church music

See:

CLAGHORN, Gene, *Women Composers and Hymnists: A Concise Biographical Dictionary* (no. 551)

ROGAL, Samuel, *Sisters of Sacred Song: A Selected Listing of Women Hymnodists in Great Britain and America*. (no. 554)

Periodicals

1018.   *Chrysalis: Women and Religion*, 3/yr, Movement for the Ordination of Women, Napier Hall, Hide Place, Vincent St, London SW1P 4NJ.

News and articles on the Movement for the Ordination of Women.

1019.   *Daughters of Sarah: The Magazine for Christian Feminists*, 6/yr, 3801 N. Keeler, Dept 1114, Chicago, IL 60641, 1974-.

Contains 'biblical, historical, socio-political and practical articles, addressing issues such as ageing, work, marriage, peace, abortion, the church'.

1020.   *Journal of Women and Religion*, annual, Center for Women and Religion, 2400 Ridge Rd, Berkeley, CA 94709, 1981-.

Articles, poems, news aimed at Christian readership.

1021.   *Vox Benedictina*, 4/yr, Peregrina Publishing Co., 409 Garrison Crescent, Saskatoon, Saskatchewan S7H 2Z9, Canada.

Aims 'to make available through translations and articles the rich heritage of feminine monastic spirituality from the period of the early church to the present'.

1022.   *Womanspirit: A Resource for Those Interested in Feminist Spirituality*, 3/yr, 52 Rosemount Court, Booterstown, Co. Dublin, Ireland, 1986–.

'Christian in its origins and primary orientation, *Womanspirit* wishes to promote and nurture a . . . dialogue between women of all traditions and spiritual journeys.' A useful resource for Irish events, groups and courses. Also contains articles and book reviews.

OTHER RELIGIONS

Bibliographies

We have not found any reference works solely concerned with women and religion other than those in the sections above. The following general works on women in Muslim countries contain many references to religion.

AL-QAZZAZ, Ayad, *Women in the Middle East and North Africa: An Annotated Bibliography*. (no. 483)

RUUD, Inger Marie, *Women's Status in the Muslim World: A Bibliographical Survey*. (no. 487)

Substantial sections on Buddhism and Hinduism can be found in:

SAKALA, Carol, *Women of South Asia: A Guide to Resources*. (no. 330)

There is a growing interest in Buddhism among Western women, and there are now several books about and by Buddhist women, but as yet no bibliographic work that we know of. Carson (no. 993) contains some entries for all three major eastern religions.

Periodicals

1023.   *Kahawai: Journal of Women and Zen*, 2/yr, 2119 Kaloa Way, Honolulu, HI 96822, 1979–88.

At first quarterly, and since 1985 twice-yearly, the newsletter was designed 'to serve as a forum for the discussion of crucial issues affecting men and women engaged in Buddhist practice in contemporary society . . . to examine the confluence of feminism and Buddhism, and to encourage and support the equal participation of women in Buddhism'. Back issues are still available.

CHAPTER 23

Travel, leisure, sport

TRAVEL

Bio-bibliographical works

TINLING, Marion, *Women into the Unknown: A Sourcebook on Women Explorers and Travelers*. (no. 173)

Guidebooks

1024. CLARKE, Jennifer, *In Our Grandmother's Footsteps: A Walking Tour of London*, 168 p., Virago, London, 1984. (Published in the USA by Atheneum, New York, 1986.)

A list of women who are commemorated in London with monuments, plaques, etc., and also with whom particular places are associated. Each entry has a concise biographical description enlivened with quotations. The work is a collaborative effort between writer and photographer, and the many photos are excellent. There is an area-by-area guide at the back. Complements Legget (no. 1026) and is also as good a read.

1025. LASKY, Jane and Brenda FINE, *The Women's Travel Guide: 25 American Cities*, 534 p., G.K. Hall, Boston, 1986.

Basically oriented towards American businesswomen, this describes cities in terms of hotels, restaurants, formality of attire, transport, shopping and climate. Interesting but very conventional and not especially woman-oriented despite the title.

1026. LEGGET, Jane, *Local Heroines: A Women's Gazetteer to England, Scotland and Wales*, 382 p., Pandora, London, 1988.

'This book is a reaction to all those guidebooks featuring too many men and few, if any, women.' Nearly 600 women are featured in this work which is arranged in usual gazetteer format, by place, with maps to indicate the places mentioned. There is a separate section on London. The women associated with the place are described and put in their historical context. Their published works are usually mentioned, but not where it would be inappropriate, so that the book is never cluttered with too much information. The work is followed by a biographical index, making it a source of biographical information in its own right. A really good book.

1027. MURPHY, Kate and LBC NEWS RADIO, *Women's London*, 176 p., Hamlyn, London, 1987.

A pocket-sized guidebook covering all the obvious information (women's centres, cafés, bookshops, public toilets, publishers), plus useful stuff on galleries that often put on exhibitions of women's art, theatres, and loads of addresses of groups of various interests. A lot of these change rapidly, particularly in the present harsh funding climate in the UK.

1028. SHERR, Lynn and Jurate KAZICKAS, *The American Women's Gazetteer*, 283 p., Bantam Books, New York, 1976.

An enjoyable 'feminist travel guide' arranged by state, listing places of particular relevance to women. Index and bibliography.

1029. TINLING, Marion, *Women Remembered: A Guide to Landmarks of Women's History in the United States*, 796 p., Greenwood, Westport, CT, 1986.

Arranged by state but in regional groups, e.g. New England, The South; entries are then alphabetically arranged by place, with a name index and a brief bibliographic essay on further sources. The author has tried to include only sites that can be visited.

Handbooks

1030. DAVIES, Miranda *et al.*, *Half the Earth: Women's Experiences of Travel Worldwide*, 453 p., Pandora, London, 1986.

A guide to travel, country by country, which includes lists of contacts, accommodation and other travel notes under each country, as well as much fascinating and useful information on the experience of travelling for women.

1031. MOSS, Maggie and Gemma MOSS, *Handbook for Women Travellers*, 259 p., Piatkus, London, 1987.

This compendious handbook by two experienced travellers gives information on all aspects of travelling, and is particularly useful for the Third World. Much of the advice it gives would be valuable for any travellers, not just women. An irresistible read.

1032. OWINGS, Alison, *The Wander Woman's Phrasebook: How to Meet or Avoid People in Three Romance Languages*, 112 p., Shameless Hussy Press, Berkeley, CA, 1987.

A phrasebook in French, Italian and Spanish giving invaluable conversational guidance on how to cope with tricky situations abroad – turn-ons and turn-offs – as well as basic phrases for shopping, etc.

1033. PIET-PELON, Nancy J. and Barbara HORNBY, *Women Overseas: A Practical Guide*,164 p., Institute of Personnel Management, London, 1986. (Originally published in the USA as *In Another Dimension: A Guide for Women Who Live Overseas*, by Intercultural Press, Yarmouth, ME.)

A guide for women living overseas, with information on preparation for departure, settling in, culture shock, children, health, stress, etc. Concentrates most on emotional and psychological adjustment, and contains much practical advice. There is a short bibliography.

SPORT AND LEISURE

No doubt this is an area which will become better documented over the next decade or so. In particular one might expect some feminist magazines to emerge.

Bibliographies and reference works

1034. MARKEL, Robert, Nancy BROOKS and Susan MARKEL, *For the Record: Women in Sports*, 195 p., World Almanac Publications; distributed by Ballantine Books, New York, 1985.

Discusses athletes sport by sport, with tables of records achieved for each sport

O'NEILL, Lois Decker, *The Women's Book of World Records and Achievements*. (no. 172)

1035. REMLEY, Mary L., *Women in Sport: A Guide to Information Sources*, 139 p., Gale Research Co., Detroit, MI, 1980.

Mary Remley has collected a wide range of material about women in sport, covering general reference and historical works which include useful sections of women, many biographical collections and biographies of specific sportswomen, books on techniques and instruction, descriptions of periodicals, films, sports halls of fame, and US sports organizations. Entries are annotated and indexed.

1036. SHOEBRIDGE, Michele, *Women in Sport: A Select Bibliography*, 248 p., Mansell, London, 1987.

This is a thorough and carefully arranged bibliography which updates Remley (no. 1035) and also includes more UK and other European material as well as much from North America and other English-speaking countries. Lists of bibliographies and conference proceedings are followed by material grouped into seventeen subject areas. After this selection, material is listed under individual sports and then there is a list of biographies, both collected and individual. Entries for monographs and conference proceedings are annotated. There are unannotated entries for chapters of books, articles and theses. There is an author and subject index, and a short list of serials, including special issues, and of organizations. Monographs and conference proceedings are included from 1900 onwards, and articles from 1970.

Organizations

1037.　WOMEN'S SPORTS FOUNDATION, c/o London Women's Centre, Wesley House, 4 Wild Court, off Kingsway, London WC2B 5AU.

Aims to promote the interests of all women in and through sport and to gain equal opportunities and options for women. Publishes a lively newsletter.

Periodicals

1038.　*Sistership*, 6/yr, PO Box 1027, Crow's Nest, NSW 2065, Australia, 1988–.

A new magazine for women involved in maritime issues, sharing experiences and developing further skills.

1039.　*Sportswoman*, Womansports Ltd, BCM Womansports, London WC1N 3XX, 1985–6.

A distinct 'equal opportunities' tendency was creeping into this standard-format sports magazine when it ceased publication. It was connected to the Women's Sports Foundation.

CHAPTER 24

Women in the labour force

The modern women's movement has been built substantially on the recognition of the exploitation of women in the workplace and in the home, and of their exclusion from positions of power and authority. These different strands have combined to put concerns about work at the very centre of feminism. Struggles of women for better pay and conditions in the workplace have become part of the mythology of the movement, from the matchgirls of the early twentieth century to the night cleaners of the 1970s.

We have been surprised to discover how little there is by way of sources of information in this area. Much of the organizing, and consequently the literature, has been at grassroots level, and often around specific campaigns. Clearly there is scope for bibliographic work to be done in this field. On the other hand, material on women in business and management is relatively well documented, a product of greater financial resources, one imagines.

GENERAL WORKS

Bibliographies

1040. CATALYST, *Two-Career Families: An Annotated Bibliography of Relevant Readings*, 2 vols, Catalyst Information Center, New York, 1982.

An annotated bibliography of nearly 1000 items, with the second volume updating the material to 1981.

1041. FAUNCE, Patricia Spencer, *Women and Ambition: A Bibliography*, 695 p., Scarecrow, Metuchen, NJ, 1980.

A large work (about 9000 entries) covering ambition in terms of education, careers, success, failure, personality, occupation, business. Includes mainly American books, articles and chapters, largely from the 1970s up to 1978. Arranged alphabetically by author under broad headings (e.g. Societal forces and women's ambition) and subheadings (e.g. Sex roles). No annotations. It is difficult see who would want to use this work.

1042.   FERBER, Marianne A., *Women and Work, Paid and Unpaid: A Selected, Annotated Bibliography*, 408 p., Garland, New York, 1987.

Over 1000 publications are listed in this authoritative bibliography. They are divided into General works, The family, Labor force participation, Occupational distribution, Earnings and the male–female pay gap, Discrimination, Unemployment, Women in individual occupations, Women throughout the world. The bulk of the work relates to the United States, with some comparative material, and the final chapter dealing with other countries. The works are coded to indicate whether the emphasis is on theory, methodology, empirical evidence or policy issues, and there is a further code to identify those works which are difficult to read without a considerable background in econometrics or mathematics.

1043.   GUILBERT, Madeleine, Nicole LOWIT and Marie-Hélène ZYLBERBERG-HOCQUART, *Travail et Condition Féminine: Bibliographie Commentée*, 247 p., Editions de la Courtille, Paris, 1977.

Very brief annotations grace the entries of this chronologically arranged bibliography. Section 1 contains works published before 1914; section 2 covers 1914–1945 (the authors complain of a paucity of material here, and include a few works written in the 1970s relating to the war years). In the much larger final section, 1945–1977, the material is subdivided by subject and arranged chronologically within that. There is an author index. The work is in French.

1044.   INTERNATIONAL LABOUR OFFICE, *Bibliography on Women Workers/Bibliographie sur le Travail des Femmes (1861–1965)*, 252 p., International Labour Office, Geneva, 1970.

A useful work for retrospective research, this contains 1800 unannotated references to publications and organizations. There are indexes to personal and corporate authors, and subject and geographical indexes.

1045.   WINSHIP, Janice, *Women at Work Bibliography*, 81 p., Centre for Contemporary Cultural Studies, University of Birmingham, Birmingham, 1978.

Over 200 entries, most of them annotated with fairly detailed description of contents, divided into eight broad subjects.

See also:

ANANT, Suchitra, Ramani RAO and Kabita KAPOOR, *Women at Work in India: A Bibliography*. (no. 340)

CATALUCCI, Emanuela and Rita SARINELLI, *Donna e Lavoro: Bibliografia 1970–1981*. (no. 430)

McFEELY, Mary Drake, *Women's Work in Britain and America: From the Nineties to World War I: An Annotated Bibliography*. (no.685)

PETERS, Anke and Maria GAWOREK-BEHRINGER, *Frauenerwerb-statigkeit: Literatur und Forschungsprojekte*. (no.413)

SOLTOW, Martha Jane and Mary K. WERY, *American Women and the Labour Movement, 1825–1974: An Annotated Bibliography*. (no. 704)

Databases

1046. CATALYST, *Catalyst Resources for Women (CRFW)*, Catalyst Information Center, New York, 1985.

A database available through BRS, the first to focus specifically on women. It is based on the holdings of the Catalyst (no. 1049) library, and covers the area of employment and careers. A thesaurus, available from Catalyst, gives the list of descriptors it uses.

Periodicals

Many general journals and magazines contain material on women and work of course. Most of these are among the periodicals listed in Chapter 1.

1047 *Women and Work*, annual, Sage, Beverly Hills, CA, 1985–.

Each issue, running to some 250–350 pages, contains articles covering all aspects of women and work, with the emphasis on multidisciplinary perspectives, critical analysis and proposals for change in public policy.

1048. *Women at Work*, 2/yr, International Labour Office, Geneva, 1977–. (Published in English and French editions. A Spanish edition is published by the Instituto de la Mujer, Ministeria de Cultura, Madrid.)

Describing itself as a 'news bulletin', its purpose is to 'disseminate information on trends and developments concerning women workers'. Much of the information presented is statistical, and it is therefore a major source for data on women and work in UN member countries.

Organizations

Much of the organization of working women is within the trade unions, most of which have women's committees. The Equal Opportunities Commission (no. 376) is concerned with anti-discrimination policies in the workplace.

1049. CATALYST, 250 Park Avenue S., New York, NY 10003.

Works to improve the status and condition of women in the workforce and provides career advice. Documents and disseminates information on women and work, especially in the context of management and leadership roles.

CENTRE FOR RESEARCH ON EUROPEAN WOMEN (CREW).
(no. 366)

Provides regular information on women and employment in European countries, as do the European Commission publications listed in Chapter 8.

WOMEN IN BUSINESS AND MANAGEMENT

Biographical works

LEAVITT, Judith A., *American Women Managers and Administrators: A Selective Biographical Dictionary of Twentieth-Century Leaders in Business, Education and Government*. (no. 171)

1050. *Women Directors: Who's Who in the World of Women directors, Compiled by Vivienne Kendall*, 176 p., Eurofi (UK) Ltd, Newbury, Berks., 1987.

A directory of some 1500 women company directors, of whom 200 are given biographical details based on answers to a questionnaire. An introductory section analyses the questionnaires and gives a brief summary of the results: statistics on the nature of the companies, and socio-economic data on the respondents. The compiler says in the introduction that the 1500 women were identified from 'a number of sources', but one wonders how some well-known women directors and companies came to be omitted (many publishers are notably absent). However, since who's whos are a haphazard source, this one can only be a useful addition, and it is to be hoped that it improves its coverage in the promised updates.

Bibliographies

1051. LEAVITT, Judith A., *Women in Management: An Annotated Bibliography and Sourcelist*, 197 p., Oryx Press, Phoenix, AZ, 1982. (Updated ed. of *Women in Management*, 1970–1979 (CPL Bibliographies no. 35).)

Over 700 entries from literature published between 1970 and 1980 arranged by subject with an author index, and appendices listing organizations, periodicals, bibliographies and other relevant resources. Mainly American; includes a section of women managers in other countries. The annotations are brief but pertinent.

Periodicals

Many of the women's business organizations produce newsletters and journals, not listed here.

1052. *Equal Opportunities International*, 4/yr, Barmarick Pubs, Hull, 1982-.

A management journal with articles and information on women and work.

1053. *Women in Management Review & Abstracts*, 4/yr, MCB University Press Ltd, 62 Toller Lane, Bradford, W. Yorks BD8 9BY, 1985-.

Published in association with the Equal Opportunities Commission. Contains articles and information on women and work in general, not just in management. Abstracts articles from journals to provide an overview of worldwide publication on women in management.

Organizations

There are innumerable organizations of business and professional women, many of them old-established. We have not listed them here, as they can easily be found in any of the standard guides to organizations. Very few of them have any feminist perspective.

EDUCATION, TRAINING, NEW TECHNOLOGY

Reference works

1054. DOSS, Martha Merrill, *The Directory of Special Opportunities for Women: A National Guide of Educational Opportunities, Career Information, Networks, and Peer Counseling Assistance for Entry or Reentry into the Work Force*, 293 p., Garrett Park Press, Garrett Park, MD, 1981.

Section 1 is an A–Z list of national (US) organizations, associations, programmes and government agencies. Section 2, which is by far the largest, lists similar statewide groups by state, including women's centres, state commissions, courses and individual counsellors. Section 3 lists women's colleges and universities in the United States. Section 4 is a resource collection of books, pamphlets, newsletters, periodicals, foundations, publishing companies and networks. Almost inevitably this is not complete, nor now up to date, but is nevertheless a very valuable compilation for Americans.

Bibliographies

1055. FEINBERG, Renee, *Women Education and Employment: A Bibliography of Periodical Citations, Pamphlets, Newspapers, and Government Documents, 1970–1980*, 274 p., Library Professional Publications (Shoestring Press), Hamden, CT, 1982.

Lists over 2500 items in English about the education and work of US women. Monographs and dissertations are not included. Arranged in two parts – education and training, and employment, and within them divided by subject. There is also a good subject index and an author index. Not annotated.

1056.   GUSSEFELD, Delia, *Women and Vocational Training: Publications in the EC Member States: Selected Bibliography*, 204 p., European Centre for the Development of Vocational Training (CEDEFOP), Berlin, 2nd ed., 1980. (Text in German, English and French.)

Contains 581 entries, arranged in a single alphabetical sequence, with indexes to subjects, institutions and countries. Useful for its comparative perspective (mainly EC countries, but also includes material on non-EC countries).

1057.   PARAMORE, Katherine, *Nontraditional Job Training for Women: A Bibliography and a Resource Directory for Employment and Training Planners*, Council of Planning Librarians, Chicago, IL, 1981.

1058.   PHELPS, Ann T., Helen S. FARMER and Thomas E. BACKER, *New Career Options for Women: A Selected Annotated Bibliography*, 144 p., Human Sciences Press, New York, 1977.

Covers 240 reports, papers, articles and a few books largely published since 1970. Subjects covered are both general – sex-free roles, career counselling for women, theories and techniques, legal issues – and specific – women at work in the 1970s, women's opportunities in training and education, topics of particular relevance to working women, e.g. child care, motivation. Needs updating.

1059.   SANCHEZ, James, *The New Telecommunications Technologies and Women in the Work Force: A Selective, Annotated Bibliography*, 7 p., Vance Bibliographies, Monticello, IL, 1987.

Periodicals

1060.   *Women and Training News*, 4/yr, The Women & Training Group, GLOSCAT, Oxstalls Lane, Gloucester GL2 9HW, 1980–.

Newsletter, covering news, reports, events, publications. Sponsored by the Training Commission, Moorfoot, Sheffield S1 4PQ.

OCCUPATIONAL HEALTH AND SEXUAL HARASSMENT

1061.   DENNING, John V., *Women's Work and Health Hazards: A Selected Bibliography*, 345 p., Dept of Occupational Health, London School of Hygiene and Tropical Medicine, London, 1984?.

Deliberately restricted to biomedical aspects of women's work, with no attempt to cover general literature of occupational medicine and hygiene, nor 'feminist political and legal documents . . . presented . . . by the women's movement or the unions'. Rather visually awkward (in typescript). The bibliography is divided into broad subjects: Health hazards of female-dominated jobs, Hazards of women's work, Work difficulties unique to women, Women's work and the menstrual cycle, Pregnancy and women's work, Women's work and stress. The material covered gives rather more logic to this arrangement than a listing of the subjects would suggest. A subject index gives more detailed access. Now somewhat out of date, particularly for material on new technology (no subject index entry under 'computers'!). Approximately 3000 entries, some annotated.

MILLER, Alan V., *Sexual Harassment of Women in the Workplace: A Bibliography with Emphasis on Canadian Publications*. (no. 934)

SPECIAL OCCUPATIONS

Women in the professions have traditionally organized themselves into women's caucuses or separate organizations, mainly to combat discrimination and to further equal opportunity. Most of these organizations produce their own newsletters. We have identified certain areas of interest here, but particular professions or occupations will also be found in other chapters, in the appropriate subject area (e.g. engineers and mathematicians are in Chapter 20, health-related professions in Chapter 19).

Academic professions

Most of the academic associations (American Sociological Association, etc.) have their own women's committees. In America these became prominent with the affirmative action programmes in the 1970s. Other sections of this book list works on organizations in particular subjects where relevant.

BIBLIOGRAPHIES

1062. FARLEY, Jennie, *Academic Women and Employment Discrimination: A Critical Annotated Bibliography* (Cornell Industrial and Labor Relations Series, no. 16), 103 p., New York State School of Industrial and Labor Relations, Cornell University, Ithaca, NY, 1982.

Detailed annotations to nearly 200 items, most published since 1970; mostly articles, some books, reports and conference proceedings, a few miscellaneous sources. Two interesting tables give statistics on women in Ivy League and seven sister colleges in the United States, and list fifty court cases relating to women in higher education in the United States. Well indexed – a fascinating book.

Librarianship

It is perhaps not surprising that this profession should have produced some excellent studies.

BIBLIOGRAPHIES

1063. HEIM, Kathleen and Katharine PHENIX, *On Account of Sex: An Annotated Bibliography on the Status of Women in Librarianship, 1977–1981*, 188 p., American Library Association, Chicago, IL, 1984.

Produced for the ALA Committee on the Status of Women in Librarianship, this is a continuation of Weibel and Heim (no. 1065). It is organized by year of publication. Entries are briefly annotated. There is a lengthy introduction and a separate index to these preliminary pages, as well as author, title and subject indexes.

1064. McKENNA, Colette, *Women in Librarianship 1970–1980: A Select Bibliography*, 32 p., School of Library and Information Studies, Ealing College of Higher Education, London, 1981.

Contains 88 entries, mainly from librarianship periodicals, on the role and status of women in librarianship since the re-emergence of the women's movement. Mainly British and American in coverage.

1065. WEIBEL, Kathleen and Kathleen M. HEIM, *The Role of Women in Librarianship 1876–1976: The Entry, Advancement and Struggle for Equalization in One Profession*, 510 p., Oryx Press, Phoenix, AZ, 1979. (Published in the UK by Mansell.)

Part VI of this work is a substantial bibliography, organized by year of publication. The annotated entries include correspondence in journals, and provide a comprehensive overview of the profession. The bibliography, which takes up pp. 298–503 of the book, has separate subject, author and title indexes.

PERIODICALS

1066. *WLW Journal*, 4/yr, c/o Women's Resource Center, Building T-9, University of California, Berkeley, CA 94720, 1976–.

Journal of Women Library Workers (no. 1069), containing feature articles, conference reports, reviews, news and notes.

1067. *Women in Libraries*, 4/yr, ALA Social Responsibilities Round Table Feminist Task Force, 1970–

Newsletter of the American Libraries Association task force.

ORGANIZATIONS

1068. WOMEN IN LIBRARIES, c/o London Women's Centre, Wesley House, 4 Wild Court, off Kingsway, London WC2B 5AU.

Association for women library workers, aims to counter discrimination in the profession and to address issues of feminist collection development. Publishes *WILpower*, a newsletter of activities.

1069.   WOMEN LIBRARY WORKERS, c/o Women's Resource Center, Rm 100 T-9, University of California, Berkeley, CA 94720.

Organization of American women library workers. Publishes *WLW Journal* (no. 1066).

Military and police

BIBLIOGRAPHIES

1070.   HARRELL, Karen Fair, *Women in the Armed Forces: A Bibliography, 1970-1980*, 11 p., Vance Bibliographies, Monticello, IL, 1980.

1071.   MARTIN, Carol Ann, *Capable Cops – Women behind the Shield: A Selected Bibliography on Women Police Officers*, 26 p., Vance Bibliographies, Monticello, IL, 1979.

1072.   MARTIN, Carol Ann and Alice PHILBIN, *Women as Probation, Parole and Correctional Officers in the Criminal Justice Field: A Selected Bibliography*, 22 p., Vance Bibliographies, Monticello, IL, 1980.

PERIODICALS

1073.   *Minerva's Bulletin Board: The News Magazine on Women and the Military*, 4/yr, The Minerva Center, 1101 S. Arlington Ridge Rd, 210, Arlington, VA 22202, 1988–.

A companion to *Minerva* (below), this contains news and correspondence.

·1074.   *Minerva Quarterly Report on Women and the Military*, 4/yr, The Minerva Center, 1101 S. Arlington Ridge Rd, #210, Arlington, VA 22202, 1983–.

A journal aimed at women in the military services, containing articles, commentary, stories, poems, etc., with a feminist slant.

Men's studies

One of the results of women's studies has been to lead some men to look at their own lives in the light of the feminist movement. This means taking themselves out of the centre of the stage, looking at the social constructs of their roles, and dealing, as best they can, with their excess of power. Two bibliographies have been published recently collating writings on men.

1075. AUGUST, Eugene R., *Men's Studies: A Selected and Annotated Interdisciplinary Bibliography*, 215 p., Libraries Unlimited, Littleton, CO, 1985.

Aims to provide an overview of recent English-language writing about men, from the standpoint of an awareness of gender roles and of work in women's studies. The compiler looked for material about men as men, and works that attempt to transcend stereotypes. Arranged by subject, including men's consciousness-raising, men's rights, war and peace, men's issues (including health, crime, prisons), masculinity, homosexuality, humour. There is an author and title index. Nearly 600 entries with detailed annotations.

1076. FORD, David and Jeff HEARN, *Studying Men and Masculinity: A Sourcebook of Literature and Materials*, 39 p., Dept of Applied Social Studies, University of Bradford, Bradford, 1988.

An attempt to cover British material. While American material is not excluded, the authors recognize its coverage by other works (e.g. August (no. 1075)). The material is 'primarily academic, but also more broadly cultural', arranged in ten subject sections. This is a work which has involved careful selection – as the authors point out, the study of men has frequently been taken for granted in the social sciences, though relatively few works deal explicitly with the social construction of men and masculinity. This will be an admirable introduction to the literature but unfortunately has no annotations.

Index

Numbers in square brackets refer to bibliographic entries, not pages.